Euripides: *Andromache*

COMPANIONS TO GREEK AND ROMAN TRAGEDY

Series Editor: Thomas Harrison

Aeschylus: Agamemnon, Barbara Goward

Aeschylus: Eumenides, Robin Mitchell-Boyask

Aeschylus: Libation Bearers, C. W. Marshall

Aeschylus: Persians, David Rosenbloom

Aeschylus: Prometheus Bound, I. A. Ruffell

Aeschylus: Seven Against Thebes, Isabelle Torrance

Aeschylus: Suppliants, Thalia Papadopoulou

Euripides: Alcestis, Niall W. Slater

Euripides: Bacchae, Sophie Mills

Euripides: Children of Heracles, Florence Yoon

Euripides: Cyclops, Carl A. Shaw

Euripides: Electra, Rush Rehm

Euripides: Hecuba, Helene P. Foley

Euripides: Heracles, Emma Griffiths

Euripides: Hippolytus, Sophie Mills

Euripides: Ion, Lorna Swift

Euripides: Iphigenia at Aulis, Pantelis Michelakis

Euripides: Medea, William Allan

Euripides: Orestes, Matthew Wright

Euripides: Phoenician Women, Thalia Papadopoulou

Euripides: Suppliant Women, Ian Storey

Euripides: Trojan Women, Barbara Goff

Seneca: Hercules Furens, Neil W. Bernstein

Seneca: Medea, Helena Slaney

Seneca: Oedipus, Susanna Braund

Seneca: Phaedra, Roland Mayer

Seneca: Thyestes, Peter Davis

Sophocles: Antigone, Douglas Cairns

Sophocles: Ajax, Jon Hesk

Sophocles: Electra, Michael Lloyd

Sophocles: Oedipus at Colonus, Adrian Kelly

Sophocles: Philoctetes, Hanna Roisman

Sophocles: Women of Trachis, Brad Levett

Euripides: *Andromache*

Hanna M. Roisman

BLOOMSBURY ACADEMIC
LONDON • NEW YORK • OXFORD • NEW DELHI • SYDNEY

BLOOMSBURY ACADEMIC
Bloomsbury Publishing Plc
50 Bedford Square, London, WC1B 3DP, UK
1385 Broadway, New York, NY 10018, USA
29 Earlsfort Terrace, Dublin 2, Ireland

BLOOMSBURY, BLOOMSBURY ACADEMIC and the Diana logo are
trademarks of Bloomsbury Publishing Plc

First published in Great Britain 2023
Paperback edition published 2024

Cover image © *Andromache and Astyanax* by Pierre-Paul Prud'hon, 1758–1823.
The Metropolitan Museum of Art. Bequest of Collis P. Huntington, 1900

Library of Congress Cataloging-in-Publication Data
Names: Roisman, Hanna, author.
Title: Euripides' Andromache / by Hanna M. Roisman. Description: [New York] :
[Bloomsbury Academic], [2022] | Series: Companions to Greek and Roman
tragedy | Includes bibliographical references and index.
Identifiers: LCCN 2022016032 | ISBN 9781350256262 (hardback) |
ISBN 9781350256309 (paperback) | ISBN 9781350256279 (ebook) |
ISBN 9781350256286 (epub) | ISBN 9781350256293
Subjects: LCSH: Euripides. Andromache. | LCGFT: Literary criticism.
Classification: LCC PA3973.A63 R65 2022 | DDC 882/.01—dc23/eng/20220601
LC record available at https://lccn.loc.gov/2022016032.

ISBN: HB: 978-1-3502-5626-2
        PB: 978-1-3502-5630-9
        ePDF: 978-1-3502-5627-9
        eBook: 978-1-3502-5628-6

Series: Companions to Greek and Roman Tragedy

Typeset by RefineCatch Limited, Bungay, Suffolk

To find out more about our authors and books visit www.bloomsbury.com
and sign up for our newsletters.

For
Yossi, Elad and Helaina
and my granddaughters Talia and Yael
and for
Shalev and Diana
and my granddaughters Noa and Esti

Contents

Preface

It is my hope that readers will discover that Euripides' *Andromache*, like many other ancient Greek tragedies, is a fascinating, poignant, action-packed play. Set in the distant mythic past, its timeless themes touch the hearts of all those who meet Andromache, the Trojan princess turned concubine, who has lost everything in the Trojan War. On the one hand, the play dramatizes Andromache's efforts to save her own life and that of the son she bore to her master, Neoptolemus, from the machinations of Hermione, her master's wife, and Menelaus, Hermione's father. On the other hand, the play also traces the emotional upheavals of the childless Hermione, who feels threatened by Andromache, because she fears that the concubine might supplant her in Neoptolemus' heart and in their home. In short, the play is an ancient version of the 'love triangle', although the notion of love as we understand it never comes up in the play, and Neoptolemus, the man at the apex of the triangle, only appears on stage at the end of the play as a corpse.

The aim of this book, written mainly for students and non-professionals, is to help readers with limited familiarity with the classical world and its literature better appreciate and enjoy the play. It discusses multiple aspects of the play, including the practices of ancient performance, the play's mythic background, and its themes and their unifying principle. In-depth analyses of the main characters are provided, while the play's complexities and ambiguities are highlighted as well. The intention was to combine substantial analysis with clarity and accessibility. Hopefully some points will also be of interest to scholars. Each chapter is written in a way that allows it to be read as a standalone chapter, while also conveying the distinctive plot structure and diverse themes Euripides introduced into this particular play. For this reason, some topics including the conflict between Andromache and Hermione, the suffering of both Greeks and Trojans after the War, and the centrality of the characters' legacy to the plot unity re-occur in various chapters. It is my hope that this adds to the quality of the book, rather than detracting from it.

Among the many people to whom I am grateful, my first thanks go to the generations of students who have studied Greek tragedy with me, whether in translations or in ancient Greek, at Tel Aviv University, Colby College, Cornell University, and American University. Their probing questions inspired me to consider not only this play but Greek tragedy as a whole from fresh points of view.

I owe special gratitude to a group of people whose encouragement and support during the writing of this book never wavered. Special thanks are owed to my good friend Dr. Jill Yonassi, who gave me the generous gifts of her patience, encouragement, insights, comments and inspiration over the years, as well as making this book more readable. She has been a constant source of strength and support. To Karen Gillum I owe thanks for her meticulous checking of references and insightful comments, and to Julie Brown for reading and commenting on early drafts. Alice Wright and Lily Mac Mahon helped me every step of the way in the development of this book and have my profound gratitude.

My beloved family was always there for me, even though the last part of this manuscript was written at a very challenging time for me. Thank you Yossi, Elad, Shalev, Helaina and Diana, and my most beautiful granddaughters Talia, Noa, Yael and Esti.

Hanna Roisman
March 2022
Washington, DC

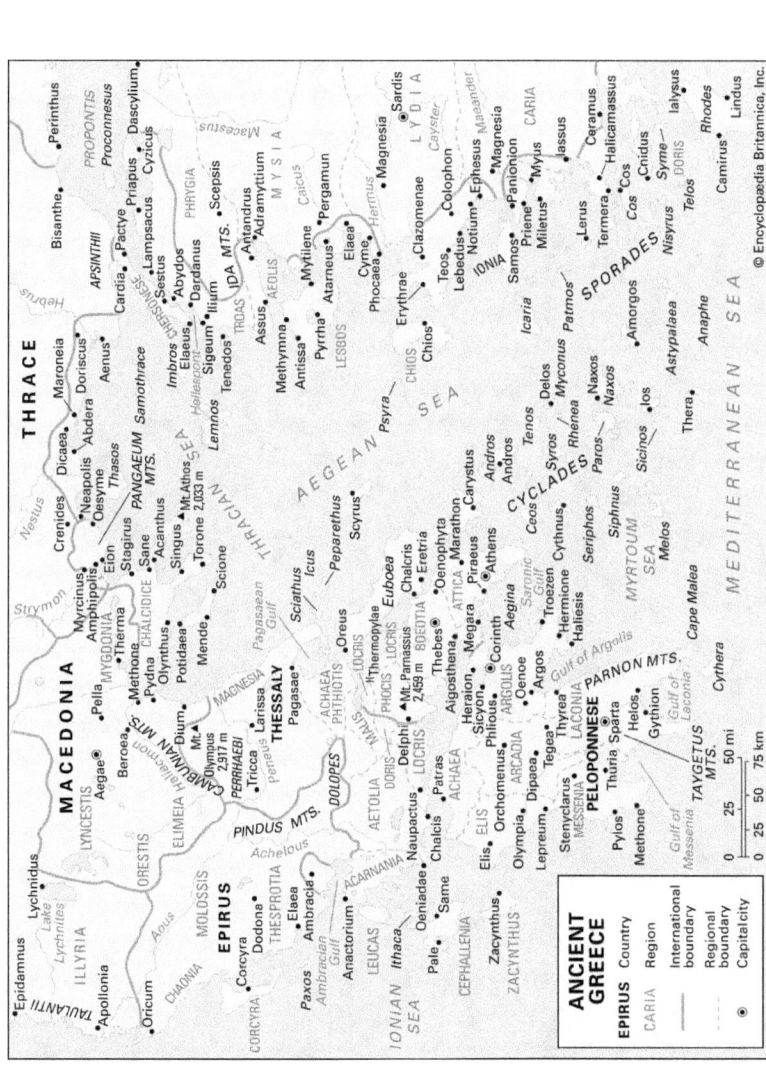

Map Ancient Greece. Copyright: Encyclopædia Britannica, Inc.

1

The Play

Plot Structure

Andromache presents a 'love' triangle; however, it is not 'love' in the modern, romantic sense of the word but rather a connection of two women to one man through their social roles. One is a slave, given to the man as a war-prize, who serves as his concubine; the other is his legitimate wife. Although there is no element of romance, the relationships serve as the basis on which future treatments of the play will introduce romantic love and obsession as dominant themes.

The unique structure that Euripides gave the drama, together with the rapid pace and high levels of tension maintained throughout, give it some aspects more in common with a modern-day thriller than with a classical tragedy. At first the audience is kept in suspense as to the fate of Andromache and then of Hermione, although both ultimately survive. Given the cruelty Neoptolemus has displayed in the past, there is perhaps some pleasure in his being overcome by Orestes. The oddest but most dramatically effective feature of the play is that the man over whom the two women fight never appears in the drama until his corpse is brought in at the end.

The uncertainty of the outcomes and the possibility of the characters being wrong-footed, wittingly or unwittingly, by each other increase the sense of tension throughout the play. The Chorus in *Andromache* also play an important role in maintaining the tension as the plot proceeds. As pointed out by Skouroumouni Stavrinou,[1] there is an element of inversion in the play, including role reversals, which will be discussed further below; for example, Andromache, who is now Neoptolemus' slave, is also the mother of his son, while Hermione, his lawfully wedded wife, is barren. However, it is not only with regard to motherhood that the roles of the two women appear to be inverted. Andromache is prepared to defend Neoptolemus' son with her life, while Hermione appears to be determined to kill him; furthermore, as we will see at the end of the play, it is the slave, Andromache, who remains loyal to Neoptolemus, while Hermione betrays him in every way possible.[2]

The play is set in Phthia, the Kingdom of Peleus, Neoptolemus' grandfather. It opens at the shrine of Thetis in the town of Thetideion near the city of

Pharsalus, where Peleus resides. Alongside the shrine is Neoptolemus' palace. Andromache enters from the palace and takes her place as a suppliant at the altar in the *orchēstra*. In a prologue of 116 lines she laments that she beheld her husband Hector being killed and then later saw their son Astyanax being thrown from the ramparts of Troy. After the Greeks took Troy, Andromache was brought to Phthia as the war-prize of Neoptolemus, and bore him a son, whose name is not mentioned in the play, but who is usually referred to as Molossus. After marrying Hermione, Neoptolemus shuns Andromache's bed, but Hermione, who is unable to give him children, blames Andromache for her sterility, saying that Andromache has poisoned her womb and is scheming to cast her out as Neoptolemus' wife. Andromache's declarations that she shared Neoptolemus' bed unwillingly, and now not at all, make no difference to the angry young woman. Hermione wants her dead, and has summoned her father Menelaus from Sparta to help with dispatching Andromache while Neoptolemus is absent. Meanwhile, Neoptolemus has travelled to Delphi to beg forgiveness from Apollo, whom he had angered by demanding satisfaction for the god's role in the death of Achilles.[3]

To save herself, Andromache has taken refuge as a suppliant at the altar in the shrine of Thetis, and fearing that Hermione and her father will also attempt to kill her son, she has hidden Molossus in another house. Andromache's Maidservant, who followed her from Troy, enters and tells Andromache that Menelaus and Hermione have discovered Molossus' hiding place. Andromache has already sent several messengers to Peleus, to inform him of the danger she and her son (i.e. Peleus' great-grandson) are facing, but to no avail. In her despair she tells the Maidservant to rush and bring Peleus at all cost. The prologue ends with Andromache's sung lament (103–16), the only lament in surviving Greek tragedy in the elegiac meter.

The first indication that Euripides is crafting a plot where the audience cannot be certain of anything comes with the brief *parodos* (117–46) by the Chorus of Women of Phthia, addressed to Andromache. Their words almost defy understanding. At this point, Andromache is certain that Hermione and Menelaus are intent on killing her and her son. While admitting that they pity Andromache, in the space of under thirty lines the Chorus instruct Andromache to reconcile herself to her fate: since she is a slave, she has no power over her situation. Then they indicate she shares a husband with Hermione, while technically she is nothing more than a concubine; and then suddenly they suggest that there may be a way of resolving the argument between Andromache and Hermione! In fact, there is no argument, but rather a clear intention of one person to kill another, with the one bent on murder having all the power needed to carry out that threat. After all of that, the Chorus inform the audience that they fear harm to themselves for wishing Andromache well!

If the audience were not already somewhat confused by the inconsistencies within the Chorus' *parados*, they must have been totally thrown when Hermione appears in the first episode (147–273) gorgeously attired, highlighting the distinction of rank between herself and Andromache. Her speeches reveal her own alternative reality, which has almost no shared ground with the situation Andromache has described. According to Hermione, Andromache has been plotting to throw her out of her own home, poisoning her womb and making her husband hate her. The Chorus, once again, seem to completely misunderstand, or disregard, the danger Andromache is faced with, commenting that women may be jealous of their rivals in love (181–82), making it sound as if two women of equal status, with equal means to defend themselves, were competing for one man's heart. The inner contradictions not only remain unresolved, but are later given a further spin by Menelaus, when he lures Andromache out of the shrine by promising that if she yields, she will indeed be killed but her son will be spared. When Andromache finally does leave the altar, he reveals that the fate of her son will be decided by Hermione (431–32).

Andromache and Hermione engage in a furious battle of wits, in which emotions are intensified due to the high stakes: the life of Andromache and of her son. In what is constructed as a formal debate (*agōn*), a pair of set speeches followed by an angry dialogue mostly in stichomythia, the women exchange their interpretations of their shared situation. In her thirty-three lines (147–80), Hermione replicates the previous bewildering thematic contradictions. She expounds her concocted theory that Andromache has poisoned her womb with drugs, a skill 'Asian woman excel in' (159–60). In Hermione's somewhat deranged universe, Andromache will die for crimes Hermione herself has invented, and furthermore, she will die despite her position as a suppliant at the altar of Thetis.

There is no firm ground for the internal or external audience to stand on in attempting to assess Hermione's true intentions. Hermione's threats to kill her alleged rival (161–62, 245, 254–55) have not only been countered by the Chorus, who advised Andromache to submit, implying that there is room for a more conciliatory approach, but also by Hermione's hint that she might be satisfied with something other than Andromache's death (163–68), when she tells her to cower in humility at her feet and sweep the house, scattering Achelous' water by hand from her gold-wrought vessels.

Despite the apparent confusion, Andromache appears to understand that there are no grounds for conciliation between the two women, and that in order to defend herself, she must attack Hermione, who is clearly her enemy, despite any confusing smokescreens. In her reply of forty-nine lines (183–231), which shows her predominance in the *agōn* (formal debate), Andromache rejects Hermione's accusations, pointing out that Hermione's barrenness and Neoptolemus' rejection of her bed have nothing to do with her womb being poisoned, but rather due to her being an impossibly difficult wife to live with. Andromache gives examples: Hermione chafes Neoptolemus by claiming that Scyros (Neoptolemus' birthplace) is of no account compared to Sparta (Hermione's birthplace); she claims that Menelaus is a greater man than Achilles, and is unreasonably jealous to boot. In the following stichomythic exchange (234–60), Andromache once again focuses on Hermione's youthful rashness and lack of propriety in discussing her sexual life. Hermione then repeats the threat of death to Andromache.

After Hermione exits the stage, re-entering Neoptolemus' house, the Chorus seem suddenly to wake up to the gravity of the situation. They narrate the background of the Trojan War, starting with the beauty contest between the three goddesses and the judgement of Paris (274–308). As in the *parodos*, they address themselves to Andromache while describing the suffering which would have been avoided if Paris had been killed as an infant.

In the second episode (309–463) Menelaus appears, bizarrely equipped in hoplite armour, ready to face the helpless Andromache. He is leading a young child, the son of Andromache and Neoptolemus. Menelaus boasts that he found the hidden child due to his sharp wit, and claims that he is going to kill him unless Andromache leaves the altar to be killed in place of the boy. Andromache replies with a defiant speech aiming to deter Menelaus from his threat by pointing out the repercussions this would have for Hermione from Neoptolemus. Menelaus' reply fails to justify his actions, but he is unyielding in his intention to kill either Andromache or her son. Andromache's second speech is heart-wrenching. Through a series of simple questions asking what wrong she has done to Menelaus to justify his killing her, she strips Menelaus of any reason to commit this act. She bemoans her lot and leaves the altar. In four lines (421–24) the Chorus again imply that there is still a place for reconciliation between the two women and calls on Menelaus to bring it about. Instead, Menelaus tells his slaves to bind Andromache's hands and announces that he is going to kill her, but says the fate of her son depends upon Hermione's decision, as if the boy has a hope of living. In her third speech in this episode, Andromache tears apart Spartan treachery, greed, and villainy.

In their second stasimon (464–93), in yet another series of *non sequiturs*, the Chorus argue that a man should be content with one wife, giving examples of problems caused by two tyrants in a city, two poets collaborating on a hymn, and two steersmen in a ship. They again ignore Andromache's complete lack of power over her situation. It would only be fair to note that

Hermione also has had no say in whom she married, or whom her husband takes as a concubine, but she does have the freedom to choose to blame Andromache for her situation and to send for her father, the king of another city-state, to come to her husband's home, and to murder not only her husband's concubine, but also her husband's son. By the end of their second stasimon (486–93), the Chorus not only take Hermione's threatened murder of Andromache and the boy as a *fait accompli*, but also warn Hermione that retribution will follow. This latter idea is of utmost importance in the second part of the play, in which Hermione rages in despair and fear that Neoptolemus will punish her, which of course will raise the off-stage audience's anxiety as the plot evolves. The goal of these misleading insinuations is unclear, unless Euripides intends to create tension in the minds of the spectators as to the fate of Andromache and her son as well as to the homicidal intentions of Hermione and her father.

The third episode (494–765) is split in two. A brief anapestic description of the bound Andromache and her son awaiting their deaths (494–500) is followed by Andromache's and her son's lyric laments, which are heartlessly rejected by Menelaus (501–44). The second half opens with Peleus' arrival (545–765). The two men face each other in the second formal debate of the play; each gets two speeches. At the end Peleus actually drives Menelaus off. Peleus serves as a vehicle for criticism not only of the way Spartan women are educated, dress, and behave, the chief example of which is Helen, but also for emphasizing the cowardice of Menelaus.

Unable to control the conduct of his wife and his daughter, Menelaus is even willing to kill because of them. He is responsible for the expedition against Troy that brought about the death of many young men and grief for their parents, and now is preparing to kill Peleus' great-grandson and the boy's mother. He is devoid of any morals. In addition, he proved himself a coward during the Trojan War. Menelaus defends his current decision to act against Andromache by claiming that he is expected to defend his daughter, a claim that is immediately undermined by his hasty retreat and abandonment of Hermione. He also attacks Peleus' defence of Andromache and her son as defending barbarians who caused Achilles' death. Peleus' lack of the Greek chauvinism that Menelaus displays, his promise to his great-grandson that he will raise him 'to be a great enemy to these people' (724, i.e. the Spartans) stands in antithesis to Menelaus' anti-barbarian rhetoric and creates a lack of clarity in identifying who is friend or foe. Peleus' victory over Menelaus is enhanced by the third stasimon (766–801), in which the Chorus sing his praises.

In the fourth episode (802–1008), the plot returns to Hermione, who, abandoned by Menelaus, tries, according to the Nurse, first to hang herself, then to use a sword upon herself. Hermione treats her intention to kill Andromache and her son by Neoptolemus as an actual deed, although she knows that it did not happen (860, 926–28). The incongruity between Hermione's perceived world and the real one, as well as between intention and deed, noticed in Hermione's first entrance, continues in her second appearance. She fears that upon his return Neoptolemus might either exile her from his house or kill her for this 'deed', which did not actually take place. Hermione's reappearance is rather shocking. Unlike her earlier entry as a queen parading in her gold-spangled dress, the spectators now see her tearing her luxurious apparel and showing her breasts, while removing her veil from her hair. These acts would seem improper to both the on-stage and the off-stage audiences. While the Nurse tries to calm Hermione down, Orestes enters. Hermione begs him to take her to her father's house. Orestes, unlike Hermione, is fully in control of his words and deeds, but adheres no more to the truth than his cousin does. Orestes claims that Hermione was promised to him, but eventually given by Menelaus to Neoptolemus as a prize for sacking Troy. Orestes had begged Neoptolemus to release her, claiming that since he is a matricide, no one else would give him his daughter to wed, but Neoptolemus refused. He predicts that Neoptolemus will be killed in Delphi, without revealing that he himself had set up a trap to ensure Neoptolemus' death.

In a brief fourth stasimon (1009–46), the Chorus sing of the common sufferings and toil of Greek and Trojans as a result of the Trojan War, a topic that informs the entire play as it sheds light on the human cost of this War on both sides.

Peleus arrives in the *exodos* (1047–288). In a bizarre enough answer to his question as to what Hermione was so afraid of that she has fled her house, the Chorus mention only her fear of being expelled and omit her fear of being killed by Neoptolemus. It is unclear why they provide the old man with only half of the information. The Chorus do, however, warn Peleus of the lurking danger to Neoptolemus from Orestes, who has whisked Hermione away. A Messenger then arrives and announces the death of Neoptolemus, describing how boldly and courageously he fought his attackers in Delphi. Neoptolemus' body is finally brought on stage and lamented bitterly by Peleus and the Chorus. In his boundless grief Peleus considers himself bereft of descendants. Oddly enough, Andromache's son by Neoptolemus is utterly forgotten. Peleus blames his grandson's death on his marriage to Hermione. Andromache is not mentioned at all. Finally, Thetis appears *ex machina* and tells Peleus to bury Neoptolemus in Delphi, as a reproach to the Delphians, because he was slain there in the ambush planned by Orestes. Andromache must migrate to the Molossians and be married to Helenus, Hector's brother. Thetis recognizes Andromache's son as 'the last of the line of Aeacus' (1246–47). Not only will he continue her own and Peleus' line, but his descendants will rule over Molossia in unbroken succession. Greece and Troy combine in this boy forever. Thetis also promises immortality to Peleus, saying they will dwell together in the deep in the house of Nereus, which will also enable him to see their son Achilles in his home on the island of Leuke in the Euxine Sea.

Theatre and Performance

Introduction

Having reviewed the plot structure of *Andromache*, we now move on to consider various aspects of the background and setting of its production and early performances. The fifth century BCE, when Euripides wrote *Andromache*, is regarded as a time when, despite being embroiled in various wars, ancient Athenian society reached the pinnacle of its cultural and political development. The groundwork for a written constitution, enforced by law courts to replace oral traditions based on blood feuds, had already been laid by Draco in the seventh century. The seeds of democratic rule sown in the sixth century with the introduction of citizens' assemblies, which decided matters involving the daily running of the city, had been refined by the constitutional reforms of Cleisthenes in 508 BCE, which removed tribal influence by dividing the city into regional *demes* and granted equal rights to all male citizens. This was also the time when theatrical competitions became more important in Athens as well as in rural areas.

The three tragedians whose plays have survived to the modern age, Aeschylus (*c.* 525–456 BCE), Sophocles (*c.* 496/5–406/5 BCE), and Euripides (*c.* 485/80–406 BCE), have left their indelible mark on theatre, with their plays continuing to inspire new creations in the plastic and dramatic arts to the twenty-first century. Aeschylus is credited with introducing the second speaking actor, and Sophocles the third, while Euripides is considered to have introduced a plethora of plot innovations, including taking the romantic drama of tragedy, as seen in *Andromache*, to new heights. The magnificent poetry, complex characterization, and sophisticated plots have also resulted in numerous revivals of the original plays from the fourth century to the present day.

Many of the Athenian plays were initially copied and preserved in the library of Alexandria, along with many other documents. A process of selection occurred, so that some of Euripides' tragedies were preserved in ancient collections, whereas others seem to have been lost, having been either discarded or destroyed. Eventually during the third century CE, a definitive selection of ten plays was made, to which *Andromache* belongs.[4] Seven of these plays also retained their scholia (annotations). It is not entirely clear how the ten plays were chosen, to the exclusion of the other extant eight plays.[5] The assumption is that the choice was influenced either by school requirements, or by the dramatic opportunities that these plays offered popular actors. By whatever means they were selected, ten of Euripides' plays were performed several hundred years after they were written in a revival of Greek tragedies during the third century CE, and *Andromache* was selected as one of these ten.

Ongoing discoveries of papyrus fragments, some being palimpsests with new texts inscribed over the original writing and stored particularly in monasteries in Greece and the Middle East, attest to the manuscripts of tragedies having been preserved and copied in the Hellenistic period and beyond. While some of the many texts stored in the famous library of Alexandria were destroyed by fire, or discarded in selections, others were stored in monasteries in ancient Greece, especially in the monasteries on Mount Athos, in the Santa Caterina monastery in the Sinai desert, and the Byzantine Monastery of Catellion St. Sabas in the Judean hills. Twenty-first-century technology has enabled scholars to discover the ancient texts hidden for centuries under the later additions in these monastery collections. Surveys of what has been termed the *bibliosphere*[6] base an assessment of the popularity of an ancient text outside Alexandria on the number of surviving fragments. For example, Plato's *Phaedo*, discussing the death of Socrates, and his *Phaedrus* on rhetoric have more surviving fragments than might be expected from the length of the texts, with only the much longer *Republic* having more surviving fragments.

If we accept surviving fragments as indicative of the popularity of Euripides' plays, the four best represented works of Euripides' are: *Phoenician Women* (twenty-eight fragments), *Orestes* (nineteen), *Andromache* (twelve), and *Medea* (twelve). While *Hecuba* is also fairly well represented with nine fragments, there are for example only three surviving fragments of *Alcestis*, *Iphigenia at Aulis*, and *Trojan Women*; and only two for each of *Electra* and *Helen*. When discussing later the critical analysis of the play, and its notable reception through the ages, we may bear in mind that *Andromache*, like many of Euripides' plays, does seem to have been a work of increasing popularity after the fifth century.

Date and locale of the first performance

Many aspects of *Andromache*'s first performance are cloaked in mystery. The fate of the theatre or theatres where the play was performed is not much different, with the locale and the exact date of the first performance of *Andromache* in the fifth century BCE still shrouded in uncertainty. A scholiast's note on line 445 tells us that the first production occurred outside Athens but fails to say where. Neither the title nor its *archōn* was listed in the *Didaskaliai* (performance records), circumstances which gave rise to suggestions that it could have been premiered in Argos, Thessaly, Molossia, or Sicyon.[7] However, since the *Didaskaliai* are incomplete, a play's absence from the list cannot serve as a positive argument against production in Athens.[8]

As far as the date is concerned, the only ancient testimony is the same scholiast's comment referring to the fact that Euripides uses Andromache as a mouthpiece to revile the Spartans because of the war that was in progress at the time, and that the play seems to have been written at the beginning of the Peloponnesian War. Thus, Andromache's attack on Spartan treachery and their practice of injustice (445–52), Peleus' grudging admission of Spartan military renown (724–25), or Menelaus' declaration that he is going to punish a city that escaped the alliance with Sparta (733–36), all served scholars as allusions to concurrent events, but none of them could pinpoint an exact year for the play's composition or production.[9]

The various other clues included in the note offer but limited help for dating the play. Scholars have looked for a recent historical incident that could be referred to by Andromache's attack on Spartan treachery, but nothing specific can be proven beyond doubt. Stevens is certainly correct in his scepticism on relating the play to contemporary politics: 'I am, however, sceptical about the extent of Euripides' preoccupation with diplomacy and propaganda.'[10] This is not to say that Euripides was not as patriotic as other playwrights, but a general attitude does not necessitate references to specific concurrent events. Furthermore, one needs to take into account the span of time that it takes to write a play, have it approved for a competition, and manage its production. It seems that it would have been almost impossible to orchestrate a specific time relation between concurrent historical events and the production of a play.[11]

Although we do not have a certain date for the first performance of *Andromache*, we can date the play on metrical and stylistic evidence. Statistical analysis of the iambic trimeters of the play places it in a group with Euripides' *Hecuba* and *Suppliants*; that is to say it was composed and performed between 425 and 418 BCE, with scholars favouring a date closer to 425 BCE.[12] This indicates that *Andromache* is probably the fifth of Euripides' extant plays. Nineteen of his plays came down to us (eighteen tragedies and one satyr play), out of an opus that has been calculated at about ninety-two dramatic works. As mentioned, Euripides himself is one of only three classical

Greek tragedians, along with Aeschylus and Sophocles, whose plays have survived at all, with plays of Aristophanes alone among comic playwrights surviving from the fifth century. The many others who plied the dramatists' trade in fifth-century Athens left only their names, in obscure historical documents and scholarly writings.[13]

With regard to the location of the first performance, the assumption in this book is that *Andromache* was indeed first produced in Athens. There simply is not enough evidence to rule out a premier production there, and no clear evidence to support a premiere elsewhere such as Molossia, Thessaly, Argos, or Sicyon. Furthermore, nothing in Euripides' *Vita* suggests that he travelled to any of these locations to produce the play there.[14] If he did not travel to any of these places, we may ask who trained the chorists, which was usually done by the tragedian himself. It is also noteworthy that the strongly Athenian sentiment and anti-Spartan commentary would likely have been somewhat irrelevant to a foreign audience of whose cultural associations the playwright would have been less aware (see also the section on Andromache, Peleus, pp. 4, 5, 9).[15] If the play was performed first in Athens, it most probably was put on stage at the City Dionysia (or Great Dionysia) of Athens, the largest and most magnificent, annual, state-sponsored religious festival.

Dramatic competitions

Held in late March, the City Dionysia celebrated the life and deeds of Dionysus, the god of wine and vegetation, along with the coming of spring. In the fifth century BCE, no play was mounted for more than a single performance at this festival. By the time the *Andromache* was performed, the Dionysia had become a major Greek festival with an international audience, second only to the Olympics.[16] Although popular plays were reproduced in local *deme* (township) theatres in the fifth century, as well as in Athens throughout the following century, most plays probably saw only one performance in all, a fact that helps explain why so few have come down to us. The plays were put on over several days, as part of formal competitions. Three days were allotted to the tragic competition, one to the comic. On each of the three days of the tragic competition, a different playwright mounted three tragedies followed by a satyr play. The three tragedies, referred to as trilogies, could tell a single story (only one of the extant trilogies, Aeschylus' *Oresteia*, does this) or different ones, as most probably did. The satyr play was a raucous production, rife with obscenity, whose title refers to the satyrs, half-goat, half-man, who made up its Chorus.[17] These plays provided relief from the emotional intensity of the tragedies, served as vehicles for social criticism, and exemplified the spirit of Bacchic revel befitting the god to whom the festival was dedicated.

We do not know with what other plays *Andromache* was produced or what position it occupied in its trilogy. However, a fragment of the preface (*hypothesis*) to the play by Aristophanes of Byzantium (*c.* 257–180 BCE), librarian at Alexandria from *c.*195, gives the scene, the identity of the Chorus and of the first speaker, and some critical comments. The most striking of the critical comments is his statement that the play is 'of the seconds', which probably means 'of second-prize quality' rather than 'second rate'.[18] It could however also have indicated that it was the second play in a trilogy. This preface would originally have contained useful information (now lost) about the first performance of the play (e.g. date, result of contest).

Like the rest of the festival, the tragedies were sponsored by the state. Playwrights who wished to have their plays performed had to submit them the previous spring to the chief magistrate of Athens, the *archōn epōnymos* (so called because the year in which he held office was named after him; *epōnymos* meaning 'giving one's name to'), who selected the three tragedians for the year from among the many applicants. The *archōn epōnymos* also chose the *choregoi*, literally chorus leaders, who were in effect the plays' producers and footed most of the production costs.[19] To each playwright, the *archōn* assigned his own *choregos* and, beginning later on in the century, the actors who would perform in his plays. From the mid fifth century on, the state paid the lead actors and the tragedians. Although the playwrights were not quite state employees, they were not independent of the state either. While the state's involvement may not have had the stultifying effect one might expect, it may have defined the outer boundaries to the questioning, criticism, and protest found in many of the plays.[20]

The plays were produced before large audiences. The estimate of the number of spectators at the Theatre of Dionysus ranges from 20,000 to a relatively conservative 4,000–7,000.[21] The first few rows of the theatre were occupied by the elite: Priest of Dionysus, Athenian magistrates, and visiting ambassadors from various states.[22] Most of the audience, however, consisted of the ordinary citizens of Athens – by definition male. Women, who some claim were not permitted to watch the comedies, were allowed to attend the tragic performances;[23] and boys attended with their *paedagogoi*, slaves who brought them up when they were young and accompanied them to their tutors when they were older. From the middle of the fifth century, tickets to the festival were subsidized for those who could not afford the price.

The plays were part of the formal competitions that were held at the festival. They were judged by a panel formed through a combination of selection and lot.[24] The purpose of selection by lots was to diminish the risk of bribery and corruption. Given the important role of the City Dionysia in the life of fifth-century Athens, it is likely that the judges would have been chosen on the basis of some criteria of education and discernment, meaning that they would have come from the elite. Yet the documentation that has come down to us contains tell-tale grumbling that the judges were often swayed, or even intimidated, by the reactions of the audiences.[25] Put differently, it tells us that the winning playwrights were those who were likely to have been appreciated by the ordinary folk as well. From the public records of the plays, we can calculate that Euripides (and his *choregoi*) won altogether only five prizes in the course of his career.[26]

Thus, even though classical Greek drama was state supported, we can surmise that it was popular drama, in the best sense of the term: drama written not for the elite, but for the entire *polis*, drama that moved the ordinary Athenians of the time, addressed their concerns, and was fairly congruent with their thinking and world-view.

The theatre

The plays must have provided breath-taking spectacles for the Athenian audiences, mounted as they were in the open air at the Theatre of Dionysus, on the southeast slopes of the Acropolis. The audiences may well have been spellbound, not only by the tragic plots, and visual elements of performance, but also by the dancing and musical aspects. The successive performances began in the early morning and continued, with breaks, throughout the day. The performing area, located on a levelled space at the bottom of the hillside, consisted of a large *orchēstra*,[27] or dancing place, for the chorus and, probably, a narrow, elevated platform that served as a stage for the actors and was connected to the *orchēstra* by several steps in the centre. In *Andromache*, the *orchēstra* contains an altar and shrine to Thetis with her statue, where Andromache sits as a suppliant.

At the back of the *orchēstra* stood a flat-roofed building, probably with double doors, about twelve metres long and four metres high, where actors changed their costumes and masks. It was termed the *skēnē* (tent) after its origins as a tent or hut, with actors making their entrances to the stage from the *skēnē* and returning to it when exiting the stage.[28] When *Andromache* was produced, the *skēnē* was probably still a temporary wooden structure that could be removed after the festival. Most of the action of the Greek tragedies took place in the outdoor space in front of the stage building, with off-stage actions occurring within the building. According to Aristotle (*Poetics* 1449a16–17), it was Sophocles who first introduced scene painting (*skēnographia*) for his plays, with the artwork having been painted either on cloths draped over the stage building or on wooden panels placed or hung in front of it. While the painting probably depicted the type of location (e.g. urban, rural, seashore) and buildings in the plot setting, most of the audience would have been too far away to see any details. The setting for *Andromache* is the front of Neoptolemus' house at the Thetideion, not far from Pharsalus in Thessaly, so we may assume that this would have been painted on the *skēnē*. On either side of the *orchēstra*, running up to the stage building, were two broad aisles, usually referred to as *eisodoi* or *parodoi* (side paths), which served as entrances for the chorus and characters arriving from the outside. In the play, *eisodos* A represents the road to Pharsalus and other parts of Thessaly, from where Peleus and Orestes arrive. *Eisodos* B represents the way that leads to Sparta, Argos, and Delphi. These pathways could also be used by the spectators.

One of the stage devices connected with the stage building was the *mēchanē*, a 'flying machine': a crane used to fly in gods who take part in the play. Hence the term *deus ex machina* 'god from the machine'.[29] Thetis is flown through the air and alights on the ground at the end of *Andromache* as *dea ex machina* to console Peleus and predict what will happen to their line in the future (1226–30).[30]

Andromache and conventions of performance and plot

Greek tragedies can be described as verse musicals. Song and dance were essential components, along with speech and recitative (declamatory song or chanting in the rhythm and tempo of speech). The entire script was in verse, and the dance, song, and recitative were all accompanied by the music of double reed flutes. Every Greek tragedy featured a chorus, initially of twelve members, later fifteen, who danced and sang, whether alone or in dialogues, termed *kommoi*, with the main characters. Scenes are generally divided from one another by antiphonal choral odes termed *stasimons/stasima*. The choral songs and monodies (lyric solos), both accompanied by a double reed flute, were written in a great variety of meters and rhythms. The characters spoke mostly in iambic trimeter, which, according to Aristotle, is the metrical rhythm closest to spoken cadence (*Poetics* 1449a18–19). The recitatives were in other meters. Song or recitative punctuates the spoken dialogue and monologues throughout a tragedy.

The structure of a Greek tragedy is fairly predictable. The play typically begins with a prologue, spoken by a god or one or two of the characters, which sets the scene and provides the background to the action. In this play, as discussed at the start of this chapter, Andromache explains her situation while sitting as a suppliant at the shrine of Thetis. The prologue comes to an end with the *parodos*, which may be translated 'the accompanying song' and usually marks the chorus' entrance. In addition to providing more background information, the *parodos* generally strikes the play's key emotional chord. In *Andromache*, this is pathos in the form of sympathy that the Chorus express for Andromache, while addressing her directly and at the same time reproaching her for her useless resistance to necessity. The *parodos* is followed by three to five *epeisodia* (episodes or scenes) separated, as noted above, by *stasimons* (antiphonal choral odes). Euripides' *Andromache* has four *epeisodia*.

The plot action in *Andromache* is unusual in that there are several main sections to the play, the unity among which has been hotly disputed. As described above, after the action is brought to a height with Menelaus threatening both Andromache and her son, they are saved by Peleus. At the end of line 765, Andromache leaves the stage and does not return. However, a new drama plays itself out after this point, with the distraught Hermione threatening to kill herself, out of fear of Neoptolemus' reaction upon hearing that she and Menelaus had planned to kill his son. The arrival of Orestes in line 881 brings relief to Hermione, when he provides a perhaps too convenient solution to her troubles by offering to take her to her father's home, where Menelaus can decide whom she should marry. Orestes already knows at this point that a trap has been set for Neoptolemus in Delphi. Hermione and Orestes leave (1009), and only after the choral ode (1010–46) does Peleus return. The final episode of the plot occurs when the body of Neoptolemus is carried on stage, received by his grieving grandfather (1166). The plot tension is finally relieved only when Euripides introduces the goddess Thetis, Achilles' mother, who foretells the fate of Neoptolemus' son with Andromache. Andromache will marry Hector's younger brother Helenus, but it is her son with Neoptolemus who will establish a dynasty ruling over Molossia. In *Andromache*, as with most other tragedies, the play ends with a brief choral song as the chorus exit the *orchēstra*.

The tragedians also tended to observe conventions of plot and character. The plots were nearly all based on myth. The main characters were larger than life mythical figures, usually great warriors or members of ruling houses. The chorus consisted of characters from all walks of life; in *Andromache* it consists of women of Phthia. Speaking with one voice, the chorus provided information, commented on the action, and sometimes participated in the action as well. Their comments were to be taken as the normative view – which may or may not have been the view that the playwright wished to advance. The action, as Aristotle would observe a century later, was generally compacted into the span of a day and usually restricted to a single place. The action of the play was generally the culmination of events that had occurred before the play started and which were usually explained in the prologue. Violence as a rule was not displayed on stage, but recounted by a messenger, as happens in *Andromache*.[31]

Early Greek tragedies were performed with two speaking actors and one or two mute characters. Aristotle credits Sophocles with adding a third speaking actor (*Poetics* 1449a16). All parts of a tragedy are divided among the *protagonist* (first actor), the *deuteragonist* (second actor), and the *tritagonist* (third actor). All roles of characters or chorus were played by males, who wore masks. The actors wore the same masks of whatever characters they played with the same fixed expression throughout either the whole or most of the play; as a result, facial expression could not be used to show emotion at all, and gesture only to a limited extent. In the absence of these vehicles of emotional expression, the ability to convey feeling through variations in vocal tone and cadence became essential. Of all the qualities required of an actor, the most important was, therefore, a strong and versatile voice.[32]

The huge size and open-air venue of the Theatre of Dionysus meant that the actors had to project very well in order to be heard. To play multiple roles, actors also needed to have a voice versatile enough to endow each character – of whatever age or gender – with his or her distinct vocal signature. Versatility of voice was required to compensate for the limitations created by the use of masks. Since the tragedies routinely had more characters than actors, actors would have to play more than one role. The masks were obviously an advantage here. The protagonist was not necessarily the actor with the most lines, but the one whose part required the greatest flexibility of voice. He was expected to manage all the meters: the lyrics, which are sung, the recitative elements, and the spoken meters. In lines 501–14 and 523–36, for example, both Andromache and her son sing their lines. The second and third actors usually did not have roles that exacted much vocal versatility, but they also had to be able to sing.[33] Thus Hermione engages in an *amoibaion*, in which she sings lyrics while the Nurse answers in iambic trimeter (825–65). Peleus sings a *kommos*, a lyric exchange between an actor and chorus (1173–225), but his part is metrically less elaborate.

Nine characters appear in *Andromache* in addition to Andromache's son and the corpse of Neoptolemus. There is more than one way to distribute the roles, but the most probable is to have the protagonist play Andromache, Orestes, and Thetis; the deuteragonist play Menelaus, Hermione, and the Messenger; and the tritagonist play the Maidservant, Peleus, and Nurse. A child actor and a mute adult character would have been needed as well. In addition, non-speaking extras are mentioned in some scenes. Menelaus has at least two slaves on each of his appearances (425–26, 547); Peleus has at least one slave on each of his appearances (551, 1066–67); a male slave tries to restrain Hermione (841–45); slaves bring on Neoptolemus' corpse (1166–72) and remove it at the end of the play.

The Greek tragedies have come down to us without stage directions.[34] Since the poets directed – and often acted in – their own plays (tradition has it that Sophocles had to stop performing because of a weak voice) and were on the spot to give instructions, written stage directions would have served no purpose. Thus, for us, the plays' staging is a matter of surmise, based on deduction from information that the protagonists provide about themselves and other characters so that the audience would know who they are, where they are, and what they are doing.

Masks and costume

Classical Greek tragedy was formal, stylized, non-realistic, and consciously removed from everyday life. The masks worn by the actors and the members of the Chorus completely covered their heads in front and back, with openings only for the eyes and mouth. The tragic costume consisted of a tunic and two mantles, one long and one short, and was worn by nearly all the characters, although they were not necessarily uniform. The masks and costumes identified the plays as tragedies, as opposed to comedies, and as dramas, as opposed to depictions of 'real life'. Along with the minimalist scenery and props, the formal structure, and the mythic background, they announced that the events portrayed took place in another realm, beyond the mundane.

Andromache makes use of the costumes to heighten the visual drama of the play. Hermione's finery and jewellery are contrasted with the probably unadorned costume that Andromache wears. Hermione's first words focus on the elaborate costume of luxurious gold that adorns her head and neck, and the spangled gown that graces her body (147–48). Nothing is said of Andromache's costume, but as a captive and suppliant, she probably wore a simple costume that may have been faded and worn out to boot. Hermione would also use a thin veil to cover and uncover her hair (830–31).

Orestes' garment ought to have some mark that distinguishes his garb from the clothing usually worn by the Phthians because the Chorus of the Phthian women point to him as looking foreign (879–80).[35] In terms of props, Menelaus appears equipped with a hoplite's gear, which included primarily a shield, linen body armour, a spear, and a second weapon (458). The same weaponry is described as being used by Neoptolemus, who will snatch it down from a nail in the temple of Apollo in order to defend himself against his attackers (1122–3). The play also probably used a bier for carrying

Neoptolemus' corpse and a rope of some sort by which Andromache's and the boy's hands are tied. Peleus carries a sceptre with which he threatens Menelaus (588), and which he later throws away in despair (1223). The props are overall scanty but described in detail for dramatic effect.

Imagining how the spectators would have followed the roller coaster of emotions portrayed by the masked actors through song and dance, as the fortunes of *Andromache*'s main characters rise and fall in quick succession, we gain some impression of the excitement they must have felt. The following chapters deal with the mythic origins of the play, plot unity and themes, the characters involved, and the reception of the play in more detail. It is hoped that the introduction to these topics, together with the outline of what is known about early Dionysian performances appearing in this chapter, will help provide a rich context to the following discussions.

2

The Myth

Writing about the mythical background of *Andromache*, or any other extant Greek tragedy, entails an unavoidable dilemma; although the tragedians borrowed their characters from well-known myths, most of what we know about these myths today comes from the tragedies themselves.[1] Attempting to unravel which plot elements or character features are novel, and which would have been familiar to the poets and their audiences, may appear at first sight to be an impossible or fruitless task, when at best we can only make educated guesses as to precisely which mythic stories Euripides would have been aware of. When scholars write of the mythical background of *Andromache*, or of any other Greek tragedy, what they really mean is the myth, in its multiple versions, that *may* have been available to the playwright. The 'may' should be emphasized. The mythical background that scholars present is actually a reconstruction based not on direct evidence but on an assortment of clues, ranging from Homeric epics (where these are relevant) to the treatment of the myth by other fifth-century playwrights and extrapolations from later texts.

Those parts of the myths with which we are familiar today have come down to us through a variety of literary genres including epic and lyric poetry predating Euripides, the Athenian tragedies, and later compositions such as the *Library* of Apollodorus, which may or may not have been influenced by any of or all the former works. The works we know of that relate to the myths surrounding the Trojan War, and that predate Euripides, include the Homeric epics, the *Iliad* and the *Odyssey*; the no longer extant *Cypria*, *Aethiopis*, *Little Iliad*, *Nostoi*, *Telegony*, and *Iliou Persis*, collectively referred to as the Epic Cycle; and some of the pre-Classical lyric poetry, including a poem by Sappho (fragment 44). The Homeric and non-Homeric epics would have been performed for generations by rhapsodes before they were known as written texts.[2] However, neither the *Iliad* nor the *Odyssey*, nor any of the epic cycle poems we know of give a continuous account of the Trojan War, or of the mythic past within which it is described as occurring. There may have been many other 'sub-cycles' including works unknown to us, and there would have been a loose collective understanding of the story of the Trojan War.[3]

While no extant written works represent the entirety of the traditional myths, both Euripides and his audience would have been familiar with the 'pervasive tradition of the Trojan War . . . that cut across lines of genre, media, class and gender'.[4] The myths which together told the stories of an imagined past developed long before any of the extant epics telling of them were composed.[5] Epic poems are highly stylized renditions of selected stories chosen from Panhellenic myth, just as the tragedies are carefully crafted dramatizations of mythical stories, some of which had been represented in epic poems.[6]

Euripides introduces many divergences from the *Iliad* in his tragedies. One example is the circumstances of the death of Polydorus, the youngest son of Hecuba and Priam. In the *Iliad* (20.407–18), Polydorus is slain by Achilles while showing off his fleetness of foot on the battlefield, while from Euripides' tragedy *Hecuba* we learn that he was sent to Thrace with an abundance of gold when the War started, in case Troy should fall. He appears to Hecuba as a ghost in a dream after the fighting is over, having been killed by Polymestor, who had promised Priam to safeguard his youngest son. This innovation allowed Euripides to focus on the depths to which human beings may descend as a result of the atrocities of war, with Hecuba exacting a horrific revenge on Polymestor.[7] In his *Trojan Women*, Euripides also places the suffering of the women after the end of the War on centre stage. The fact that Euripides chose to change the well-known elements of myth in these ways may indicate a humanitarian message about the universality of suffering. The 'barbarian' Trojans are just as human as the Greeks; while the Greeks themselves are viewed under a critical lens, rather than simply being glorified.

An illustration of the difference between the Homeric portrayal of women and Euripides' approach is their treatments of two 'spear brides', Andromache and Briseis. Andromache becomes the concubine of Neoptolemus, after his father killed Andromache's husband. Briseis becomes the spear bride of Achilles, after he himself killed her husband. Although the *Iliad* begins with the wrath of Achilles against Agamemnon, who demands Achilles' spear prize, the 'fair cheeked' Briseis be taken from him, we hear little about what Briseis has to say about her situation. Although Briseis does lament the death of Patroclus in the *Iliad* (19.282–300), she never challenges the men who control her life. Briseis is mentioned again towards the end of the poem (24.676), as she sleeps next to Achilles after he agrees to return Hector's body to Priam. Although the *Iliad* features this young woman, from a royal family but taken into captivity, both near the beginning and close to the end of the epic, she is treated merely as a possession to be argued over. By contrast, Euripides' *Andromache* opens with Andromache delivering the prologue herself, then engaging in rhetorical combat with all the other main characters, although she is also an enslaved spear prize. The play ends with her future made clear by Thetis, although the audience hear no more from Andromache after she leaves the stage with Peleus and her son (after line 765). The *Iliad* does conclude with laments by Andromache (24.725–45), Hecuba (24.748–59), and Helen (24.762–75) over the body of Hector, which has been returned to Troy. However, it is Helen who has the last word, and she seems to be grieving mostly for losing the protection Hector had offered her from other Trojans, rather than any real concern for her fate or for the fate of any of the Trojans.

For Euripides, when composing *Andromache*, the pervasive familiarity with myth would have posed challenges and provided opportunities. The most basic challenge was to transform the myths about Andromache from epic narrative into staged drama in a way that was interesting and convincing. The myths about Andromache describe her as a Trojan princess, the wife of the famous warrior Hector, who has lost her parents and brothers after her hometown was sacked by Achilles. She is the mother of Hector's baby son, Astyanax. Andromache's appearances in the *Iliad*, when she beseeches her husband not to return to the fighting (6.394–502) and her later laments for him after he was killed by Achilles (22.477–514, 24.725–45) created the enduring image of a devoted wife and mother in tragic circumstances. After Troy was sacked by the Greeks, Andromache experienced further grief as Astyanax was thrown from the ramparts of the city, before it was burned to the ground.[8] Andromache was taken captive and given as a war-prize to Neoptolemus, the son of Achilles.

In this chapter, I will discuss allusions or references to the myths about the various characters appearing in other dramatic and non-dramatic sources in an attempt to determine what these tell us about the mythic lore that may have been available to Euripides and about the choices he made. There is no attempt at an inclusive analysis of the many ancient references to the myths or of later literary renditions in the ancient world. My hope is that, in addition to providing information, my approach will convey the difficulties and uncertainties of exhuming the play's mythic background.

The discussion of significant allusions will be followed by a more general discussion of the ways in which the key figures in the play may have been viewed in the fifth century. Most of the specific allusions to the myth focus on the action: on what happened to whom and who did what. They tell us very little about the personalities of the figures involved. Yet the personalities with which the playwrights endowed the mythic figures are what enabled the audience to identify with and be moved by them, and the playwrights to convey the meanings that they found in or built onto the mythic action. Just as they could draw on a mythic tradition for the action of their plays, the playwrights had at their disposal a rich mythic lore with which to flesh out their characters. The chapter will end with a very brief look at elements of the lore that pertain to the personalities of Andromache, Hermione, Neoptolemus, Menelaus, Peleus, and Orestes.

When reviewing references to the myths in other plays, we are initially challenged by a problem similar to that relating to the Epic Cycle: many works are no longer extant. For example, there remains one single fragment which could be attributed either to Sophocles' *Andromache* or to *Andromeda*, which is therefore not of much help. We do know of plays titled *Hermione* composed during the fifth century by Sophocles, by Philocles – Aeschylus' nephew – and by Theognis.[9] However, we do not know for sure whether Sophocles' play, about which we know somewhat more than those by Philocles and Theognis, preceded Euripides' *Andromache*.[10]

Allusions to Andromache's myths found in plays postdating Euripides are also of interest, as they not only indicate Euripides' influence on later works, but also reveal elements of mythic background no longer extant. Obviously, however, it is not possible to be certain what is innovation and what is derivative. From the Roman stage we know of a play *Hermione* by Livius Andronicus (*c.* 284–*c.* 205 BCE) in which Andromache was a character along with her son by Pyrrhus (Neoptolemus), a son she feared might be turned against her. Having Andromache as a character in the play on this myth points to the influence of Euripides rather than Sophocles, since Andromache played no part in any of the known fifth-century plays other than Euripides'.

There is also a *Hermione* by Pacuvius (220–*c.* 130 BCE) about which we have somewhat more information. It does not follow the plot of any of the known Greek plays, but does have reminiscences that can be traced to Euripides: Pyrrhus being killed by Orestes, a quarrel between Peleus and Menelaus, and reconciliation of the two by the intervention of a goddess, Minerva, who also bestows immortality on Peleus, who, however, in this play has no heir.

It is interesting to see how Euripides' treatment in *Andromache* of the marriage between Hermione and Neoptolemus differs from what we know of Sophocles' *Hermione*. Only two actual quotations have reached us from this play, one of a line, and one of a single word (*TrGF* iv. 202–3, Radt). While Euripides presents Neoptolemus rather positively compared with the hero's other portrayals both in later literature and in the Epic Cycle, where he either kills Priam at the altar of Zeus Herkeios, or drags the old king to the doors of his palace before killing him (*Little Iliad* frag. 25 West),[11] Euripides nevertheless has Neoptolemus act quite thoughtlessly in *Andromache* in the matter of marriage.[12] As the Chorus sing, it is not wise to have two women vying for one man in one household (*Andr.* 465–70). Taking a wife while keeping a concubine in the house was not the accepted norm in the minds of the Athenian spectators. While it was socially permissible for a husband to have extramarital liaisons, having a concubine cohabit with a wife was not acceptable.[13]

We do know that all the *Hermione* plays of the fifth century dealt with the betrothal of Hermione to both Neoptolemus and Orestes.[14] According to the scholia on *Odyssey* 4.3–4:

> Sophocles in *Hermione* says that while Menelaus was still at Troy, Hermione had been given in marriage by Tyndareos to Orestes, but when Neoptolemus came home, according to [Menelaus'] promise she was taken away from Orestes; later Orestes lived with her again, after Neoptolemus had been killed at Pytho by †Tyndareos†, and then Tisamenus was born.[15]

Sophocles is exceptional among the tragedians in presenting Hermione as living with Orestes prior to her marriage with Neoptolemus. According to the Euripidean *Orestes*, although Menelaus had given her to him before the Trojan War, Hermione has never lived with him. And when Menelaus ultimately gave her to Neoptolemus as a reward for sacking Troy (*Andr.* 967–70), Orestes had no means of preventing the marriage apart from attempting to convince Neoptolemus to give her up, which Neoptolemus refused to do (*Andr.* 971–81). There is in the scholia no mention of Sophocles' Hermione failing to conceive a baby, which would have been a stark contrast to Euripides' portrayal of her as childless, and which he made a primary cause of friction between her and Andromache. While there is some confusion in what we have of the fifth-century sources about when Hermione became Orestes' wife, it is clear that the union with Neoptolemus was effected by Menelaus, a fact underscored by Euripides when he makes Hermione insist that she will become Orestes' wife only if her father so decides (*Andr.* 987–88). Hermione's statement is rather odd in its context. It is unclear whether she intimates that she is not that eager to marry Orestes, or why she is saying this, while at the same time she begs Orestes to take her with him. It may be that the tale of Neoptolemus' direct seizure of Hermione from Orestes, which appears only in later sources, was already circulating in the fifth century, and Euripides is answering it.[16] Euripides himself denies Neoptolemus Hermione in his later play titled *Orestes*. In this dramatization, Orestes and Pylades hold Hermione hostage on the palace roof. Orestes puts the tip of his sword to Hermione's throat, threatening to kill her if Menelaus does not save him, Electra, and Pylades. Apollo appears *ex machina* and tells Orestes that he is going to marry Hermione, and that Neoptolemus, who thinks he is to marry her, probably because of Menelaus' promise, never will (*Orestes* 1653–55).

There are also differences between Euripides' and Sophocles' accounts of the death of Neoptolemus. In his *Commentary on the Odyssey* (1479, 10), Eustathius gives more information about Neoptolemus' death, as described in Sophocles' *Hermione*:

> ... But when he [Neoptolemus] had been killed at Pytho by Machaereus, when he was trying to avenge the slaying of his father by punishing Apollo, she [Hermione] was restored again to Orestes; from which union was born Tisamenus, meaningfully so named after the 'vengeance (*tisis*) with power (*menos*); because his father Orestes had taken vengeance on the murderers of Agamemnon.[17]

Sommerstein enumerates most of the following differences between Euripides' and Sophocles' accounts of the death of Neoptolemus:[18] the Sophoclean Neoptolemus is killed 'when ... trying to avenge the slaying of his father'; the Euripidean counterpart did also go to Delphi to demand reparation from Apollo for the death of Achilles (Eur. *Andr.* 53, 1107–8), but this happened prior to the timeline of the play. At line 1095 it is implied, although by Neoptolemus' enemies, that Neoptolemus wanted to plunder the temple on his first visit but left unharmed. It was on his second visit, when in fact he came to make atonement for his previous act of 'madness', i.e. his attempt to plunder the temple, that he was killed (Eur. *Andr.* 51–55, 1002–4, 1106–8, 1112–13). The second difference is that in Sophocles, Neoptolemus is killed by Machaereus, while in Euripides by the Delphians in a plot devised by Orestes (Eur. *Andr.* 993–1008, 1074–75, 1114–16) with the support of Apollo (*Andr.* 1147–49, cf. 1005–6, 1161–65, 1213). Thirdly, according to Sophocles' version, it was during Menelaus' absence when he was away at Troy that Tyndareus gave Hermione to Orestes; in Euripides' treatment Menelaus was the one who gave his daughter to his nephew before the War began (*Andr.* 968–69), but then gave her to Neoptolemus as a reward for the young's man effort in sacking Troy. Fourthly, in Sophocles, the agents were Tyndareus and Menelaus, and while Orestes does not try to resist Hermione's marriage to Neoptolemus, Euripides inserts the idea that Orestes tries to persuade Neoptolemus to withdraw from the competition. And lastly, both the scholiast's and Eustathius' words seem to imply that in Sophocles, Hermione remained in Neoptolemus' house until after he was known to be dead. In Euripides, afraid of being punished on Neoptolemus' return for her attempt to murder Andromache and her child by Neoptolemus, she begs

Orestes to take her home to Sparta, although she knows he is plotting to kill her husband, and leaves with him before the fatal news from Delphi is announced.

The death of Neoptolemus is also told in non-dramatic sources. The better known is by Pindar (*c.* 518–438 BCE), who wrote choral lyric poetry. In his *Sixth Paean* (100–120), an ode composed for a performance at Delphi, Pindar says that Neoptolemus was brought from Scyros and sacked the city of Troy, but he did not escape Apollo's revenge for having killed Priam at the altar in Troy. In his *Seventh Nemean*, however, written in honour of a victor from Aegina, the birthplace of Aeacus, Neoptolemus' great-grandfather, Neoptolemus is rehabilitated. The ode tells (35–49) that after Neoptolemus sacked Troy with other Danaans, he sailed for home but missed Scyros, his birth island; after further wandering, he and his men reached Ephyra, the capital of Thesprotia, a district of Epirus. There in Molossia he was a king for a short time, but his descendants held this privilege of his forever. His kingship ended with his death at Delphi. Pindar says (Sandys' translation[19]):

> Now the hero himself had gone to consult the God bearing with him precious things from the choicest of the spoil of Troy; and there, while entangled in strife concerning the flesh of his victim, a man smote him with the sword; and grieved, beyond measure, were the hospitable men of Delphi. But he only fulfilled his fate, for it was doomed that one of the royal race of Aeacus should, for all time to come, dwell in the heart of that primeval grove, beside the fair walls of the God's own temple, and, dwelling there, should preside over the processions of heroes, which are honored by many sacrifices, for enforcement of auspicious guest-right. Three words will suffice; no false loon is the witness that presideth over doughty deeds. (40–49)

That is to say, Apollo's favour testifies to Neoptolemus' greatness. This account praises Neoptolemus and has no mention of reparations Neoptolemus demanded from Apollo. This praise of Neoptolemus in *Seventh Nemean* is thought by some scholars to be an apology for his supposedly unflattering treatment of Neoptolemus in the *Sixth Paean*.

There is also a fragment (*FGrH* iii. 64a. 78) attributed to Pherecydes of Athens (*fl. c.* 465 BCE) that tells of Neoptolemus visiting Delphi to consult the oracle about his wife's barrenness and how he was killed there due to a disagreement with the Delphians over the portioning of sacrificial meat. He was buried under the threshold of the temple.

In summary, there are several mythic innovations that Euripides includes in his dramatic treatment, as opposed to those appearing in other works.

Most strikingly, he introduces Andromache as a third party in the marriage between Hermione and Neoptolemus and makes her the protagonist. The thematic *mise-en-scène* is thus the presence of a concubine and a wife sharing the same residence and the conflict between the two women. In none of the other *Hermione* plays is there another female protagonist besides Hermione. Menelaus' role is elevated to direct interference in the quarrel between the two women, while his function in allotting Hermione to Neoptolemus is side-lined. The child-theme changes focus from a son of Hermione and Orestes to the child of Neoptolemus and Andromache, and a completely new theme of Hermione's childlessness is introduced. Neoptolemus is rehabilitated with respect to his former accusation of Apollo, by making him go to Delphi to offer reparations. He is still killed, as in the other treatments, but by the Delphians and not by one of the priests. His murder is instigated by Orestes out of revenge after Neoptolemus has refused to relinquish Hermione and has nothing to do with Neoptolemus' misdoings against the Temple of Apollo. Peleus and Thetis are also newcomers to the dramatized myth, as is the future rule of Molossus over the Molossians. The criticism of Apollo for allowing Neoptolemus to die in Delphi also seems to be an Euripidean innovation.

Now we turn to indications of how the key characters in Euripides' play may have been viewed in the fifth century. Although **Neoptolemus** appears only at the end of the play and as a corpse, the entire dramatic situation is due to his foolhardiness in having a wife and a concubine reside together in his house. We can gather what the spectators were likely to know of him from the fragments of the Cyclic accounts of Troy's fall, where he is rather prominent. He is also mentioned by name in *Iliad* 19.326–33, when Achilles laments Patroclus, and identifies Neoptolemus' home as Scyros.

As part of the Greek force, Neoptolemus was one of the heroes who helped vanquish the city; and the killings done by him, like those by the other Greeks, were the work of a warrior and a source of honour. However, several of the killings attributed to him were particularly horrific in that the victims were not soldiers, but elderly men, defenceless young women, and vulnerable children whom he killed in particularly violent ways. These included Troy's aged king Priam, whom Neoptolemus killed at the altar of Zeus in the courtyard where he had sought protection, or as *Little Iliad* (frag. 25 West) states, at the palace doors, which seems to somehow reduce the sacrilegious nature of Neoptolemus' actions. The *Little Iliad* also describes Neoptolemus snatching the infant Astyanax from his nurse, seizing him by the foot and casting him from one of Troy's towers, and then taking Andromache and Aeneas in the division of spoils (frags.18, 29, 30 West).

The view of Neoptolemus as a noble and heroic warrior is salient in book eleven of the *Odyssey*, where Odysseus, in his visit to the Otherworld, tells

Achilles about his son's valour in the last days of Troy (*Odyssey* 11.505–37). In this account, Odysseus describes Neoptolemus both as a skilled speaker at the warriors' councils and an intrepid fighter who killed innumerable fine warriors (*Odyssey* 11.516–22). Neoptolemus' eagerness to fight, his fearlessness, and the slaughter he wrought are all to his credit. After the sack of Troy, he went on board his ship with his share of the spoil and a goodly prize. As usual, the Homeric muse refrains from the horrors the Epic Cycle told of the young man, choosing a more noble and positive portrayal of the son of the main hero of the *Iliad*.

It is possible that fifth-century audiences were also aware of a harsher view of Neoptolemus as reflected in later sources which were not so kind to him. The view of Neoptolemus as a brutal murderer appears, for example, in Virgil's *Aeneid*, written in the first century BCE, which expounds at length on his savagery (2.662–70). Comparing him to a snake fed on poisonous plants, Virgil describes how the brutal and degenerate warrior broke into the intimacy of the royal home and, 'insane with blood', slaughtered all who got in his way. Virgil describes his bloody murder of Priam's son Polites in front of his parents, and his ruthless killing of Priam. Neoptolemus' violent nature is also recorded in later sources portraying him taking Hermione from Orestes by force, or quarrelling with the Delphians over the portioning of the sacrificial meat, which brought about his demise (see above). For a more nuanced and ambivalent view of Neoptolemus, see the two odes of Pindar discussed above.

A nuanced view is also evident in Euripides' *Hecuba*, performed most probably in the second half of the 420s BCE, close to *Andromache*. In this play, Neoptolemus is described as slashing the throat of Polyxena, the daughter of Priam and Hecuba, in a public execution after the sack of Troy. By nature, this is a brutal act and the entire play presents it as unjust. However, the Messenger, who may be considered a normative voice, does not present Neoptolemus as a brute, but recounts a scene wherein Neoptolemus is hesitant about the sacrifice: 'And he, for pity, ... both willing and reluctant' (*Hecuba* 566, Kovacs[20]). Overall, the play presents Neoptolemus as torn between his duty to his father (who demanded the sacrifice) and the state, on the one hand, and his compassion, on the other.

Sophocles in his *Philoctetes*, performed in 409 BCE, also depicts Neoptolemus as torn between conflicting obligations and values, but seems to manipulate the different perspectives on him. He depicts him as a young man before his brutal exploits at Troy, and makes only passing reference to them. Yet, there is an inherent tension in his choice of a mythic figure with a reputation for brutality to serve as his representative of youthful idealism and as a spokesman for pure heroic values. We may well wonder how Neoptolemus' objections to deceiving Philoctetes and his moments of compassion for him struck those in the audience who recalled him as the man who killed the aged Priam and his infant grandson, or how his reputation for brutality coloured the audience's assessment of his stated preference for using force, rather than deceit, to wrench Philoctetes' bow from him.[21] From Pindar's *Seventh Nemean* and Euripides' *Andromache* 1243–49, we learn that Neoptolemus' son by Andromache will found the Molossian ruling dynasty.

Andromache must have been a very familiar character to the fifth-century audience. Hector offered a generous bride price and brought her to Troy (*Iliad* 22.471–72), where she gave birth to their son Astyanax. Achilles sacked her city of Thebe while on a raiding mission, then killed her father Eëtion and her seven brothers, and took her mother captive. He released the queen for ransom, but she died shortly afterwards. Andromache's tender encounter with Hector at the Scaean Gate in *Iliad* 6 (392–502) was famous. It is the last family meeting of a husband, wife, and their baby. Hector will return to the War, while both he and Andromache hold little hope for a Trojan victory. Both know that he will be killed and Andromache will be led into captivity. Hector lovingly tells her that of all the Trojans and his family members he grieves most over Andromache's loss of freedom (6.450–55). Andromache as a weeping and loving wife begs Hector to defend the city from within the walls, which Hector of course cannot do. The audience do not hear of Andromache again until we meet her in her chamber working at her loom, unaware of her husband's death by the hand of Achilles (22.437–46). Her devastation at the news is complete. In her first lament for Hector (22.477–514), she bewails her own and her child's loss. As a devoted mother she envisages the sad future for Astyanax, who will have no father to guide and protect him and as a youngster will be dismissed from gatherings since his father does not partake in them. She fully realizes there can be no good future for the boy. Andromache's funeral lament twelve days later encapsulates the pain of widowhood (24.725–45). In her second lament she expresses her realization that she along with other wives and children will be put on board ships sailing to their captivity. She sees a clear possibility that Astyanax will be hurled form the walls of Troy because his father has killed so many of Troy's enemies. This is the last we see of Andromache in the Homeric epics.

Euripides seems to be taking the character of his Andromache straight from the *Iliad*, where she is a loving wife of a loving husband, a devoted mother, and where she is depicted as brave and resourceful. She is not reluctant to give strategic advice to Hector: 'And set the men by the wild fig-tree, where the city is most accessible, and the wall is open to assault' (6.433–34). It is clear that she was watching the Greek attempts to scale the walls with a vigilant eye: at this particular place the Greeks have already tried three times to climb the battlements of Troy (6.435–39). This courage to express herself is appropriated by Euripides, who shows her vehemently attacking Menelaus. Her strategic resourcefulness also serves Euripides, who shows her trying to hide her son from Hermione. In fact, her shrewdness must have been known, since Menelaus boasts of being more astute than she is (*Andr.* 313).

Not only does Euripides base his characterization on the Homeric presentation of Andromache, but he also follows the Iliadic path in portraying her as the female victim *par excellence* of the Trojan War, with Andromache representing all the wives of the warriors, whether Trojan or Greek, who lose their husbands, family, and children.

Menelaus is another character who would have been well known to the spectators from the Homeric epics. The Homeric muse was kind to this hero, portraying him as courageous but neither appreciated nor respected by either Agamemnon or Nestor, who accuse him of lack of initiative. He is a respectable warrior who also possesses softer qualities. Menelaus feels pity and grief for the fallen Greek fighters (e.g. *Iliad* 5.561, 13.581), is acutely aware of his own responsibility for the death of Patroclus (*Iliad* 17.91–93), and responds to others' calls for help on the battlefield. After apprehending Adrastos, he is moved by his plea for mercy and would have allowed him to be ransomed were it not for Agamemnon (*Iliad* 6.37–44, 55–65).

All in all, in the Homeric epics Menelaus is portrayed as something of a pathetic figure, about whom Agamemnon is always anxious, since if he were killed, there would be no reason for the War to continue (*Iliad* 4.169–75).[22] Tragedy, on the other hand, capitalizes on the negative characteristics of Menelaus, for which, in fact, there is no basis in the Homeric epics. He appears in six extant plays. In Sophocles' *Ajax*, which precedes Euripides' *Andromache*, he is portrayed as cruel and vengeful. Euripides' plays, *Andromache, Trojan Women, Helen, Orestes*, and *Iphigenia at Aulis* all fail to cast any positive light on him: he is cowardly, treacherous, conniving, indecisive, arrogant, and a bit foolish. The pathos inherent in Menelaus' always taking the back seat, especially in the *Iliad*, has been transformed into uncommon cruelty and vengefulness in tragedy. Euripides follows Sophocles' characterization of Menelaus as a small man prying into others' affairs and abusing those who cannot defend themselves.

Peleus and Thetis, the revered parents of the hero Achilles, would always be respected and loved. In *Andromache*, Peleus defends Andromache and his grandson against the arrogant Hermione and her father Menelaus.

After examining the innovations in Euripides' *Andromache*, we may come to certain conclusions as to the playwright's message to his audience. Ambühl suggests that *Andromache* and the other Euripidean tragedies 'rewrite the Homeric tradition through selecting, re-focusing, and re-interpreting, and even at times self-consciously reflecting on the process'.[23] By focusing on the perspective of the victims, particularly women, Euripides reinterprets ancient myths. He does so by making explicit moral comments and by his sympathetic portrayal of Trojan characters, encouraging his audience to identify with the Trojan side. In so doing he 'deconstructs the ideological opposition between civilized Greeks and "barbaric" Trojans'.[24] Troy does not represent Athens or any other particular city, but 'functions as a transhistorical symbol, a paradigm for the fragility of human existence in the face of war that can only partly be compensated for by the enduring memory in poetry'.[25]

3

Themes and Unity of the Play

Introduction

Andromache is a fascinating play, presenting an unusual array of themes. These range from domestic topics most often associated with the *oikos* (household) and female characters, such as marital love, loyalty and jealousy, marital status and attire, parenthood and childlessness; to concerns such as war and dynasty, which are more typically considered the domain of men, who hold power in the *polis*. However, the boundaries between the two domains are not clear cut, as seen in themes such as the suffering due to the ravages of the Trojan War, which includes memory, grief, and loss affecting both *oikos* and *polis*, male and female alike. Themes which cross over gender lines also include the bravery of those assaulted and the buffoonery of the attacker, deceit and revenge, death and survival, legacy and heritage. While these themes and others, together with the highly dramatic and complex nature of the plot, have invited much scholarly attention, the organization of the play has left many critics baffled when searching for the unity essential to a good tragedy according to Aristotelian criteria. Some have criticized the play harshly, as they concluded there is no unity between the various parts of the play, while others claim that the play is indeed divided into two parts, but that these respond to each other, thus providing balance: the plight and rescue of Andromache and the plight and rescue of Hermione (1–765, 766–1288).[1]

To date, a fair number of ideas have been put forward suggesting a unifying character or theme, although none has been universally agreed upon. Some scholars suggest that the figures of Andromache[2] or the absent Neoptolemus, or the woes of the House of Peleus,[3] serve as lynchpins holding the play together. Other scholars have proposed diverse unifying themes. Kitto maintains that the unity of the play rests in the play's overall conception rather than in the details of the story.[4] He identifies the unifying idea as a complete denunciation of Sparta for *Machtpolitik*; in particular for the Spartan qualities of arrogance, treachery, and criminal ruthlessness. Stevens sides with Aldrich in arguing that 'the real theme of the play is the disastrous war, its trivial origin, and its tragic aftermath.'[5] Storey suggests that the unifying theme binding the various parts is 'domestic disharmony'; he also offers a useful overview of the unifying themes suggested in the past.[6] Critics who failed to discover unifying themes pervading the play as a whole have sometimes gone so far as to denounce *Andromache* as having little worth.[7] Allan, by contrast, suggests a different approach, claiming: 'The play has no unifying theme: it presents a variety of issues. It works through a plurality of action and a shifting of focus.'[8]

While examining these themes in this chapter, we will attempt to unite those associated with the two realms of *oikos* and *polis* so that they work together to provide a novel unifying thesis for the play. If we accept that the devastating aftermath of the Trojan War, made even more tragic by its trivial origins, is a major theme,[9] and combine with the suggestion that domestic disharmony is also a central idea,[10] we may regard the domestic situation in *Andromache* as representing a microcosm of Troy's larger-scale tragedy. Even though myth does suggest a 'weighty' reason for the necessity of war, that is, to relieve Earth of the burden of the rising human population, the Trojan War's origins are more often associated with the beauty competition set in motion by introduction of the apple of discord at the marriage of Peleus and Thetis.[11] Indeed, the Chorus refer to the 'Judgement' as being the origin of the War:

> The son of Zeus and Maia did indeed, it seems,
> begin great woes when he came to Ida's glen,
> bringing the beautiful trio of goddesses,
> armed with hateful strife about beauty,
> to the cow-stalls
> and the solitary young herdsman
> and his lonely hearth and home.
>
> (274–82, Lloyd)[12]

Myth relates that when Aphrodite offers Helen as the prize to Paris for choosing her as the fairest of the three goddesses, the wheels of war are set in motion. In this reading of the events, no mortals ever really control their own fates, whatever appearances may be. Menelaus conveniently leaves Helen alone with Paris, and the two abscond. Even more conveniently, Tyndareus had previously required all the suitors of the beautiful Helen to commit themselves to a treaty requiring them to join forces should anyone kidnap her from her rightful husband. Instead of admitting the folly of his decisions and accepting the results, Menelaus, together with his brother Agamemnon, activates this treaty, and the thousand ships are brought together to bring Helen back home. Euripides will later describe in *Iphigenia at Aulis*, how

Menelaus and Agamemnon, the sons of Atreus, also set in motion one more chapter in the history of deceit and treachery that had cursed generations of the House of Atreus, when they agree to sacrifice Agamemnon's daughter Iphigenia at the outset of the War. Their actions also ultimately endanger the dynasty of another great family, the House of Peleus. The ruse luring Iphigenia to Aulis was a fictional wedding to Achilles. Furious at having his name used in such a treacherous plot, Achilles offers to risk his life to save Iphigenia, but she decides to sacrifice herself willingly to prevent this.

In *Andromache*, after so many lives had been ruined or lost in the War, it is once again Menelaus who rushes into action to right something he perceives as a wrong. Once more, charging into a place where he has no right to be, he attempts to save a marriage, albeit this time not his own but that of his daughter; in so doing, he has no concern about destroying other people's lives. This time he is not trying to reduce a whole city to ashes, killing the men and enslaving the women, but he threatens to bring to an end the dynasty of the House of Peleus, inadvertently also endangering the life of his own daughter. Menelaus' unnecessary War has already deprived Peleus of his son and heir, Achilles. During *Andromache*, Menelaus' nephew, Orestes, will bring about the death of Peleus' grandson, Neoptolemus. We may remember that it was Menelaus who gave Hermione to Neoptolemus, after she had already been promised to Orestes. Menelaus' daughter is left to decide the fate of Peleus' great-grandson, Molossus, but Menelaus advises that he too should be put to death. Once Peleus rescues Andromache and Molossus, the distraught Hermione threatens to take her own life.

Two great dynasties are almost destroyed, but eventually, going their separate ways, each finds a path forward, with the legacy of each house secured. Just as the wheels of fortune in the War seemed to turn almost regardless of man's actions, so too in *Andromache* the fortunes of each of the major characters rise and fall, at an almost staggering speed, with a sequence of plot twists and turns keeping the audience perched on the edges of their seats. In the end, we learn that the House of Peleus will have a future through Molossus, the son of Neoptolemus and Andromache. Thus, the legacy of Peleus is preserved. Likewise, the legacy of the House of Atreus will continue in myth through the future offspring of Hermione and Orestes. Although this is not stated in the play, the legacy of the House of Priam may continue, too, through any children Andromache may bear with Helenus.

With these ideas in mind, in this chapter we will not only review the major themes in *Andromache*, but will also develop the theory that it is the theme of *legacy* that connects all the sections of Euripides' intriguing play. While this theme is a universal one, it can also be connected to the narrower themes relating specifically to the Trojan War, as well the theme of domestic disharmony put forward by Storey.[13] The themes of marriage, parents and their children are also woven into that of legacy. It is the theme of legacy that hovers over the dispute between the Houses of Peleus and Atreus. Although, as stated above, in his later play *Iphigenia at Aulis,* Euripides will bring Achilles into conflict with Agamemnon before the fighting of the Trojan War, this feud has its literary origins in the *Iliad,* when Achilles son of Peleus refuses to fight for Agamemnon son of Atreus after Agamemnon has taken Achilles' concubine from him (1.148–71, 222–44). In fact, the vehemence of some of Andromache's vitriol against Menelaus is reminiscent of Achilles' verbal onslaught against Agamemnon, especially regarding the cowardice of the opponent (1.223–44).[14] The intense dislike of Spartan villainy, a unifying theme suggested by many,[15] when voiced by Peleus and Andromache, may also be seen as part of the feud between the two dynasties, reactivated when the treachery of the Spartans threatens the legacy of the House of Peleus.

As will be argued below, each section of the play can be connected to the ultimate aspiration of achieving a degree of immortality, as parents and grandparents hand down the legacy of their heritage through their children to future generations; or in the case of childlessness, the absolute impossibility of achieving this goal.[16] As we progress through this chapter, we will note how the themes of parenthood and protecting one's children are closely related to all of the other recurring themes in *Andromache.* We believe that these themes ultimately provide a long sought-after key to dramatic unity for the play.

While presenting this unifying theme, and the related idea of the tension between the dynasties of the House of Peleus and the House of Atreus, we also focus on the experimental nature of Euripides' work in *Andromache.* As suggested by Papadimitropoulos,[17] Euripides may have been trying to redefine tragedy by extending the boundaries of the genre. Even if there is a unifying theme, there is certainly not a central hero, and the action can be split into several different sections. *Andromache* could be regarded as one of Euripides' 'problem plays', falling somewhere between melodrama and tragedy. While the trauma faced by Andromache and the ultimate death of Neoptolemus might place *Andromache* firmly amongst the tragedies, Euripides' often-used device of *deus ex machina* allows the play to end on a more optimistic note.

Before discussing how legacy, handed down from parents through their children, may serve as *Andromache*'s unifying theme, we will consider other prominent themes arising in the play. As some aspects of the theme of marriage are closely tied in with these unifying themes, these will also be discussed in the final section. Throughout the chapter, discussions will also focus on how the various themes which heighten the drama during the twists and turns of the play, while also enhancing characterization, are all ultimately connected to the unifying themes of legacy, parents, and children. The themes discussed will include (alphabetically arranged): aftermath of the Trojan War; age (youth and old-age); appropriate and inappropriate attire; deceit and betrayal; Greeks versus barbarians; marital love and loyalty; marital strife and jealousy; marriage and status; memory, loss, and grief; misogyny and gender; Neoptolemus' absence/*nostos*; revenge; royalty, slavery, and lost status; Spartan villainy; struggle and rescue.

Themes

Aftermath of the Trojan War

The entire plot of the play, which takes place in the aftermath of the Trojan War, is affected by the War. As explained above, the plot has many similarities with the War's events, but on a smaller scale, within the home of Neoptolemus. Indeed, the War has set in motion an ongoing cycle of suffering. As some of the traumas of the War seem about to repeat themselves, one cannot help but be reminded of the roles played in the War by the characters in *Andromache* and their families. There is no glory associated with the events of the play, and the Trojan War is also stripped of its lustre, while its grim effects keep resurfacing throughout the play. Because of the War Andromache lost her husband and first child, as well as her status as a free, royal citizen of Troy. If not for the War, she would be a legal wife and not an enslaved concubine. Had the War not taken place, it could be assumed that Hermione would never have been married to Neoptolemus, but instead to Orestes, as originally planned either by Menelaus himself, or by her grandfather Tyndareus. Peleus would also not have lost his son, Achilles.

Troy is mentioned five times early in the play by Andromache (3, 11, 15, 103, 105), and she recalls the death of her husband Hector at least fifteen times. With each mention of Hector, the Trojan War comes to the spectators' minds (4, 8, 9, 97, 107, 112, 203, 222, 227, 399, 403, 456, 523). Even as Andromache's life is threatened, she is spirited enough to humiliate Menelaus by reminding him of his retreat from Hector. The accusations Peleus casts at Menelaus include his cowardice, his ineptitude in the face of Helen's elopement, his role in Iphigeneia's sacrifice, and his part in causing the many war deaths, all of which emphasize the toll of the Trojan War (590–95, 610–15, 624–31, 693–705). The Trojan War also shows up the tensions between the Houses of Peleus and Atreus. The end of the play presents a possible conclusion to the upheaval brought about by the War and the start of a new era.

Age

The themes of youth and old age are present in the background throughout the play. Focusing on this theme, we may feel that the play resembles a condensed version of life beyond the stage. Youth and old age form part of the cycle of life, with our strength increasing as we grow from infancy to our prime, and then ebbing and waning as we pass from maturity to old age. Then as one generation recedes, the next generation rises to maturity; thus, life progresses forward driven by the wheels of time. As will be discussed in the section on struggle and rescue, the play, like the ups and downs of the cycle of life, has an episodic structure, as tension builds up and is released when the crisis each character faces is resolved, as the plot moves forward. Andromache's son, Molossus, on whom the future of Neoptolemus' line rests, is very young and therefore, for the time being, completely helpless. His youth mirrors that of Andromache's first son Astyanax, who was slaughtered by the Greeks when he was an infant. Andromache recalls how Astyanax was 'hurled from the high battlements when the Greeks had captured the land of Troy' (10–11, Kovacs), but never mentions him again, even when she lists all she has suffered in the past (96–99) after the Maidservant departs, and in her monody (113–16). Although the death of Andromache's previous child with Hector is not dwelled upon, sometimes silence is more powerful than any words could be. The audience would have been aware from the beginning of the play that when the life of the young Molossus is threatened, Andromache would be reliving her earlier horrendous trauma. The youth of both Astyanax and Molossus heightens the poignancy of the threats to them. What human heart is not moved by the plight of a newborn babe or young toddler? At this stage of life, when the mother holds and feeds her child, she is still full of hopes and dreams for their future. Anything is possible. As the child grows and becomes independent, the mother has less say in what their future holds. While the mother of a newborn or young infant dreams of her child's future, she also sees in them a means of continuing her own life and legacy into the future. A threat to the child is a threat to her own ability to nurture and preserve something of herself and her ancestors.

The old age of Neoptolemus' grandfather Peleus, contrasting with the youth of his great-grandson, Molossus, frames the play nicely. When the old man hears of his grandson's death, he is devastated. He has already known great sadness in his life, following the death of his son Achilles. Achilles' passing, however, in Greek terms carried great glory as he died a heroic death on the battlefield. Achilles also left his son Neoptolemus behind, to continue his dynasty and that of Peleus. The death of Neoptolemus, orchestrated by Orestes, whose men ambushed Neoptolemus by the altar in Delphi, carries no such glory, even though Neoptolemus fought valiantly for his life.[18] The old grandfather is bereft:

> O woe, woe! What sorrow for my house do I see here
> and receive with my hand!
> O woe, woe, alas!
> O land of Thessaly, I am utterly destroyed,
> I am no more. No longer do I have a family, no children
>   are left in the house,
> What sufferings I must endure!
> †What loved one shall I have the joy of looking
>   upon?†.

> (1173–80, Lloyd)

Peleus sees himself facing old age and the end of his life with no son or heir surviving him. It is this loss of legacy, beyond the personal grief, that he finds so devastating.

Peleus is indeed old, as Menelaus emphasizes, calling him an 'old, old man' (678, Kovacs). Earlier, Andromache's Maidservant (80) had suggested that his age would prevent him from helping Andromache. The Chorus leader introduces him as 'hastening his aged steps' (546, Kovacs). However, despite his oft-mentioned old age, Peleus does come to the aid of his great-grandson, Molossus. Not only does he show up, he also faces Menelaus man to man, and through his courage and rhetoric, determined as he puts it, to become young again, 'to recover the strength of my youth' (552–53, Kovacs), he gains the upper hand over his younger adversary. First Peleus orders Menelaus to unbind the hands of Andromache, who has been trussed up ready to be killed. He is not cowed by Menelaus' threats; rather, he calls Menelaus a coward (590) and accuses the Spartan king of being the murderer of his son, Achilles, and of having caused Agamemnon to sacrifice his own daughter, Iphigenia, while Menelaus himself a 'nullity' came back from Troy unscathed (590–641).

Menelaus' attempt at a rebuttal relies heavily on Peleus' age, stating that Peleus is not wise in spite of his old age (645–48, 678–79). However, Menelaus is quickly quashed by Peleus, again emphasizing Menelaus' lack of brave feats (at least compared with Achilles) that could have brought him glory in the War. Even the Chorus mention Peleus' age, though associating it with quick temper, attributing his angry words against Sparta to a generic lack of control in old men (727–28). This does not prevent them from singing his praises in their next choral ode (766–801). It seems that in spite of his age, on this occasion Peleus was more than a match for Menelaus, even if in defeat

Menelaus still calls his elder a powerless 'shadow' (745). The question of his age resurfaces once more when Andromache suspects that due to his old age Peleus might not be able to prevent Menelaus' men from kidnapping her and her son (750–56). However, Euripides successfully chips away at Menelaus' assault on old age, when he makes the younger Menelaus shamelessly retreat from Phthia under some unclear excuse about the immediate need to attack some city that has become hostile to Sparta, as if this need had not existed beforehand (732–36). Peleus, on the other hand, retains the upper hand at the end of the encounter.

The theme of age is also important in the characterization of Andromache herself as well as Hermione and her father Menelaus. On her first entrance, Hermione attacks Andromache in the way a modern-day spoilt teenage 'Prom Princess' might verbally assault another girl she is jealous of, despite her opponent's lower status, and in this case limited power, as Andromache is a slave. Having boasted of her own glorious attire (see below) and powerful connections, being the daughter of Menelaus, King of Sparta, Hermione accuses Andromache of every possible evil. Despite Hermione's intolerable behaviour, Andromache replies with restraint, highlighting Hermione's youth: 'Yes – youth is indeed an evil for mankind' (184, Lloyd); 'Tell me, young woman, what valid reason induces me to oust you from legitimate marriage?' (192–93, Lloyd); 'You are young, and you speak about shameful things' (238, Lloyd), as well as referring to her youth when speaking to Menelaus later in the play: 'of the words of your child-like daughter' (326, Lloyd).

Hermione's rashness and injustice as well as her impropriety and inclination to discuss sex *viva voce* is imputed to her youth by the more mature Andromache. Although the latter is older than her tormentor, she is still of childbearing age, so cannot be many years older than the youthful Hermione. Excusing Hermione's conduct due to her youth does credit to Andromache. In spite of her misfortune, she finds in herself the willingness to understand her opponent, rather than assigning Hermione's injustice to sheer cruelty, while her sexual openness is attributed to her Spartan upbringing. In seeking to tone down the tension, Andromache blames Hermione's conduct on inexperience. Unfortunately, this kind of sympathetic consideration on Andromache's part also points to a certain naiveté. The spectators must have known that the young are rash, seldom admitting to a mistake resulting from their own lack of knowledge or experience. Hermione sounds almost like a wealthy, privileged millennial, who knows better than her elders and everyone else.

The factor of age is also interesting if we compare the 'love triangle' of Neoptolemus, Andromache, and Hermione with that of Heracles, Iole, and

Deianeira in Sophocles' *Women of Trachis*, which probably preceded *Andromache*. In Sophocles' play, the legitimate wife Deianeira is the older woman. She resents the arrival of the younger, beautiful Iole, but the path she chooses is completely different from that taken by Hermione. Instead of attacking Iole, Deianeira focuses on her husband, and decides to send him a robe smeared with what is supposedly a love potion but which tragically brings about his death. The play's focus is on the older wife, Deianeira, rather than the young concubine, who remains silent; but age is shown to be important. It is significant that Deianeira has already given Heracles children, thus securing the familial heritage. Her ill-thought-out behavior inadvertently results in her own violent death by suicide and that of Heracles, who suffers agonizing toxic burns only relieved in a funeral pyre, but she directs no violence towards the younger woman. Age and confidence in her legacy may both have been significant in directing Deianeira's choices. The young, childless Hermione would have experienced very different emotions. The rashness of youth, the desperation of being rejected sexually by her husband, and her childlessness may all have contributed to her vicious assaults on her perceived rival, and her impulsive decisions after her father's departure.

Attire

The theme of attire, or, more specifically, inappropriate attire, appears several times in *Andromache*. Hermione's costume has been noted by scholars as having particular significance in her characterization, in her first and later entrances in the play.[19] While it may be assumed that Andromache is wearing simple clothing, or a servant's rags, Hermione is clothed from head to toe in luxuriant finery. She is not, however, wearing the dress of a Phthian queen, but that of a Spartan princess, as she carefully explains immediately on her entrance, her golden accoutrements having been part of her dowry. According to Hermione, it is these clothes that entitle her to behave as she sees fit. Her attire thus plays a role in presenting Hermione as a self-centred, spoiled young woman with no proper upbringing. It also connects her to her Spartan legacy and emphasizes her heritage. Although she is Spartan, Hermione is also a descendant of the House of Atreus through her father. The emphasis on her attire as coming from her father's house may also focus our minds on the enmity and distrust between the House of Peleus and the House of Atreus. The marriage between the two seems to have been ill-fated from the beginning.

Hermione's appearance in golden Spartan splendour is a forerunner of Euripides' depiction of her mother, Helen, dressed in glory in his *Trojan Women* (415 BCE, lines 1022–23), which contrasts so sharply with the rags of the Trojan captives. Euripides adopts a similar theme in his later *Orestes* (408 BCE), when he emphasizes Helen's golden sandals (1467). While in the first section of *Andromache*, Hermione is the arrogant young wife, flaunting her status over the concubine and planning the latter's demise, in the second half of the play, Hermione has become terrified of losing that status or worse. When out of fear of reprisal, Hermione threatens to kill herself, she casts off her veil and tears her gown, exposing her breasts.

However, different or inappropriate attire is not only important in the characterization of Hermione and Andromache. Menelaus' inappropriate apparel when he appears in full hoplite armour to face a helpless slave woman and young child is significant in his depiction as a coward, and Orestes' apparel is what marks him as a foreign newcomer to ancient Phthia. Hermione's rich Spartan attire draws attention to her father's appearance on stage. There is no good reason for Menelaus to enter dressed as a hoplite, but the armour invokes the devastating Trojan War in a round-about way. Additionally, such a costume gives Andromache an opportunity to mock a man who needs to dress as a warrior to kill a woman, when previously during the War he fled to his ship to escape Hector's onslaught (456–59). The devastating effects of the Trojan War are still impacting all of the characters in *Andromache*, but the fact that Menelaus, who played an important role in initiating it, came out relatively unscathed cannot be avoided. His armour emphasizes this further. As Peleus will point out, Menelaus took his armour in its fine covering to Troy 'and brought it back in the same condition' (617–18, Kovacs), that is to say he has not used it for fighting. Furthermore, in spite of the frightening armour, Peleus is able to threaten Menelaus, simply by holding up his sceptre. When ordered to release Andromache immediately, Menelaus can only reply with a double dare (588–89). Not only does Menelaus appear cowed at the prospect of a thrashing by an old man with a sceptre, but he also stands there equipped for a hoplite fight while facing a defenceless enslaved woman. Menelaus is of course acting on behalf of his daughter and the purported threat to her marriage, as he waged war on Troy for the sake of his daughter's mother. The allusions to the Trojan War and its toll reverberate throughout the play.

The theme of attire is also connected to the topic of chastity and the difference between Athens and Sparta. Peleus claims that a Spartan woman could not be chaste even if she wanted to, because 'They leave their houses in the company of young men, with bare thighs and loosened tunics' (595–98, Kovacs). Athenian spectators would doubtless think of the contrasting conduct of Athenian women, who were confined to their homes and certainly did not share running tracks and wrestling places with men, as young Spartan women did (599–600).

Deceit and betrayal

Menelaus' heartless manoeuvring of the desperate Andromache away from the altar of Thetis under the pretext that if she steps out and gives up her own life, her son's life would be spared, was nothing more than a deceitful ploy.[20] As soon as Andromache leaves the altar, Menelaus announces that the fate of her son is in Hermione's hands, but he would recommend killing the boy (431–32, 517–22). As a Spartan, Menelaus is marked as a master liar and murderer by Andromache, with this view probably being welcomed by Athenian audiences (445–52).

On hearing Menelaus' threats, Andromache sums up the feeling of a parent: 'If he survives, he bears my hopes, while not to die for my child would be a reproach to me!' (409–10, Kovacs). She steps away from the altar only to learn that her death might not save her son. Menelaus is supposedly acting to safeguard his daughter's marriage, but Andromache's first reply to Menelaus (319–63) highlights the nonsensical nature of the strategy he is employing. She points out that if Hermione kills her son, Neoptolemus will surely expel Hermione. With murder on her hands and denunciation by her husband, Hermione's chances of being remarried are slim at best; she might then remain unmarried in Menelaus' house as long as she lives.

Andromache also employs deceit when, after Peleus' arrival, she accuses Menelaus and his men of 'dragging' her away from the altar of Thetis, which did not happen (565–67). There is no explanation given for Andromache's deceitful tale. One plausible explanation is that stepping out perforce was equal in her own mind to having been dragged. However, it is also possible that as women are traditionally described as using deceit, this could accord with Andromache's own misogynistic statements (85). Finally, it is likely that she thinks this may be the most decisive claim to ensure Peleus' help, because the altar is sacred to his wife.[21]

In addition to these two cases that the spectators watch in real time, the play refers to Menelaus cheating Orestes of his bride. It was this deception that led to the 'love triangle' between Orestes, Neoptolemus, and Hermione, and will ultimately lead to the themes of marital loyalty and jealousy. Even though he had promised Hermione to his nephew, Menelaus ultimately gave her to Neoptolemus. Orestes is also guilty of deceitful scheming. He set out to plot Neoptolemus' murder and claim Hermione as his bride, but upon his arrival, he offers a completely different explanation for his presence in Phthia. His innocent-sounding story that while in Phthia on his way to visit the oracle of Zeus in Dodona, he has incidentally come to call on his kinswoman to check on her wellbeing (885–89), is nothing but brazen lies. He first admits that he had 'learned of the turmoil in this house' (959, Kovacs) and had waited to see whether Hermione would talk to him, hoping he could escort her away from there. After telling Hermione that she had been his to start with, before her father gave her to Neoptolemus, he finally admits that there is a cunning trap awaiting Neoptolemus. The Chorus later inform Peleus that Orestes has planned for Neoptolemus to be murdered at the shrine in Delphi. Orestes' deceit is finally proved by the Messenger's description of how Orestes strategized the ambush in which Neoptolemus was murdered (994–97, 1085–160).

Greeks versus barbarians

From the first line of the play, Andromache proudly claims her Asian (or barbarian) descent: she was the daughter of the Theban king Eëtion in Cilicia before she became the wife of the Trojan prince, Hector. However, the rift between Greeks and barbarians is mostly brought up by Hermione and her father. Hermione repeatedly refers to barbarian customs (real or imagined) and calls Andromache a barbarian woman. She accuses barbarians of committing a slew of perverted sexual behaviours that are unacceptable in Greece and not substantiated as occurring anywhere else (173–76). Menelaus feels indignant for being reproached on account of a barbarian woman. He would be willing to help Peleus to expel her because she is from Asia, where so many Greeks fell (649–53). Menelaus fails to acknowledge his part in the many deaths of the Greeks in Asia for which Peleus blamed him (605–15). Thetis' prophesy that Molossus will be the founder of Molossia, and heir to Peleus' and Thetis' line joins the two races for the future and cancels the rift. Thus, as with many of the other themes of the play, this theme becomes connected with the theme of children and legacy.

Marital love and loyalty

Andromache, who together with Penelope is the epitome of loyal wives in Homer, has become the grieving widow and the 'other woman' in her eponymous tragedy. Although her status has changed, she still displays the same trait of loyalty, protecting Neoptolemus' son (her son) to the extent of being prepared to give up her life to save his. While Andromache never indicates having feelings for Neoptolemus, she does say that she has faith in him, even though the comment is a taunt to Hermione, whom Andromache does not trust (269).[22] By contrast, Hermione's main emotions in the first half of the play appear to be jealousy and hatred towards Andromache, and the wish for revenge. There is no indication at all that she feels any loyalty to her husband – instead, she is prepared to betray him by murdering his concubine and, far worse, his son. As discussed below, Hermione's wish to save her marriage with Neoptolemus seems more concerned with the status it affords her than with any feelings she may harbour towards her husband. The same may be said about her connection with Orestes. He serves a purpose in providing her with an escape. Later these emotions are replaced by fear. Loyalty, love, and loss are also experienced by Peleus, but these are related to his grandson Neoptolemus and will be discussed below. Even the re-entry of Thetis into his life has more to do with offspring than any other marital concerns. The only explicit discussion of marital love in the play occurs when Orestes asks Hermione whether her husband loves another, and she asserts that he loves Hector's bride (908).

Marital strife and jealousy

As suggested by Papadimitropoulos,[23] marital strife and jealousy lie at the very heart of the play, although this theme alone cannot unify all of its parts. Andromache and Hermione find themselves 'in bed' with the same man, although Andromache claims that since Neoptolemus' marriage with Hermione he has spurned her bed (29–30), while Hermione claims that he hates her because of Andromache, which might suggest that he spurns her bed as well. As with the other themes, this theme is inexorably bound with legacy through parenthood and children. Hermione's jealousy of Andromache, who has obviously proved attractive enough to Neoptolemus to have borne his child, while she herself remains barren, appears to know no bounds. It is highly possible that sexual frustration and undermined self-esteem caused by her husband's absence from her bed have contributed to Hermione's distressed state of mind. These, together with her jealousy, seem to bring Hermione almost to a state of delirium, imagining Andromache has poisoned her womb and is plotting to throw her out of her home (156–58). Andromache's logical and intelligent response to the accusations against her would be welcomed by the off-stage audience: let Neoptolemus judge if she, Andromache, is the cause of Hermione's childlessness (355–60).

Throughout the first half of the play the theme of abject misery resulting from one man having two wives continually re-occurs, with the Chorus making disparaging remarks about two women fighting over the attention of one man (117–25; 465–70). This continues despite Andromache's consistent claim that she seeks no attention from Neoptolemus, and has never done so. In the second half of the play, marital strife seems likely to threaten the lives of most of the main characters. In addition to the pointed comments about two women sharing a husband, the Chorus also make blanket statements linking women with jealousy (181–82). Andromache does not remain silent, but accuses Hermione of being impossible to live with, and worst of all, lacking respect for her husband.

Marriage and status

Various marriages form the backbone to the play. Each is mentioned here, though none is the overarching theme.[24] Instead, as will be discussed further below, it is the theme of children and the legacy they entail that is at the heart of the play, although different characters see the issue with different eyes.

While Peleus and Thetis do not express emotions towards each other, their marriage underlies the play as a whole. Andromache is taking refuge at the altar of Thetis at the start of the play, and at the play's conclusion Thetis herself appears to soothe Peleus' grief after the death of their grandson, Neoptolemus. At times the marriage of Menelaus and Helen resurfaces as well, but never positively. The looming marriage of Orestes and Hermione plays a role, too, symbolizing a potential return to normalcy after the devastation of the Trojan War. Hermione presents her unfortunate marriage to Neoptolemus as unsuccessful because she failed to give him children. However, it is noteworthy that Neoptolemus does not seem to be perturbed by this fact, and his trip to Apollo's temple is for another reason altogether.[25] Andromache claims that Neoptolemus' distancing from Hermione is not on account of her childlessness but because she is unfit to live with. Menelaus explains his involvement against Andromache and her son by claiming he is trying to save his daughter's marriage, but it is his own marriage to Helen that Peleus brings up as the cause of all the miseries suffered by Greece. Menelaus is also implicated in Hermione's marital troubles by having promised his daughter's hand to two different suitors.

One important aspect of marriage in general and those marriages mentioned in particular is that they confer status. In Greece, the foremost purpose of marriage was the production of children. In Athens, being a wife in the fullest sense meant being an Athenian woman who had borne a child to her husband. The world of the play does not talk of citizens versus non-citizens in Athenian terms, but free versus not free, Greek versus barbarian. As such, Hermione counterbalances Andromache as being both free and a legitimate wife, versus Andromache's concubinage. Both of them, however, claim to have status. In the prologue, Andromache clearly and eloquently refers to her former status as a free woman, and a Trojan princess. She was richly dowered and married in order to bear children, and entered her husband's *oikos* (1–4) much as an Athenian bride would do. The mention of dowry is as important as the mention of giving birth to children. These two facets announce that a woman is a legitimate wife whose children will be legitimate as well. Indeed, she gave Hector, her husband, a son, Astyanax. Although she lost her freedom, her husband, and her son from Hector (8–10), she is still called *despoina*, mistress, by her Maidservant, whose queen she once was (56–65).

Hermione's struggle to save her marriage is obviously connected with the social status that a married wife holds. Even if this is not explicitly mentioned in the text, it would be understood by the spectators.[26] The importance of being a wife, and more particularly one who has not been expelled by her husband, is clearly stated by Andromache in her argument with Menelaus. She points out that if she or her son is killed, Neoptolemus is apt to expel Hermione for her complicity in the murder. 'Who will marry her?' asks Andromache, remarking that Menelaus will have to keep Hermione husbandless in his house until she is grey-haired (347–48, Lloyd). That being a wife is a coveted status can be seen when Hermione accuses Andromache of trying to supplant her as one. Furthermore, in her regally dressed appearance Hermione claims that the fact that she brought a large dowry from Sparta allows her freedom of speech, a right that differentiates a free person from a slave (151–53). The richness of her dowry also guarantees her power and status in her marriage, as her Nurse tells her later: 'You are not his as a prisoner taken from Troy: he has received you with a large dowry, and you are the daughter of a man of importance and come from a city of no ordinary prosperity' (871–73, Kovacs). Hermione's psychological disintegration after being abandoned by her father and her fear of being exiled by her husband indicate her fear of losing her status as a wife. Her casting off her veil, a mark of a Spartan married woman,[27] and tearing her spangled dress, part of her rich dowry, are symbolic acts indicating explicitly that she knows that her status as a wife has been lost. Orestes' wish to marry her gives her an opening to reclaim that status.

Menelaus is also very conscious of his status, as his appearance fully clad in hoplite gear indicates. He wants to be considered as the hero of the Trojan War, but Peleus does not let him, accusing him of sitting puffed up over Troy, where his generalship capitalized on the toils and labours of others on the battlefield (678–79, 693–705).

Memory, grief, and loss

The play is saturated with the memory of what and whom Andromache has lost. Starting with her hometown, the city of Thebe, which Andromache left to become Hector's bride, and continuing through her losses in Troy, memory and loss accompany Andromache throughout. She only mentions Astyanax once, in line 10, but refers to Hector repeatedly by name (4, 97, 107, 203, 222) or as her glorious husband (456) or as Priam's son (525). Peleus, too, repeatedly refers to the loss of his son, Achilles. However, the play is not entirely focused on the past, but looks forward to the future that may be secured through children.

Misogyny and gender

As we will see, negative statements about the female gender are woven into the drama, especially by women, including Andromache and Hermione, throughout the play. The extreme misogyny of these statements is puzzling in the light of Euripides' other multi-layered characterizations of women, which may not have been entirely sympathetic, but rarely descended to the blanket condemnation of the entire sex found in *Andromache*. Even within the play itself, his characterization of Andromache as a rational woman, remaining calm while facing grave danger, prepared to sacrifice her life to save that of her son, seems to belie the sweeping condemnation included in many of her comments. It is possible that Euripides was working on two levels, as has been suggested in connection with his *Hippolytus* and some other works.[28] In this case, on the explicit level, the comments indicate across the board misogyny, but on a more subtle level, the behaviour of his female characters may indicate Euripides' intentions. As Norwood has noted: 'In describing the sorrows of women … Euripides shows a knowledge of the female heart which excited the liveliest interest and wonder.'[29]

Andromache voices denigrating comments about her gender from the outset of the play when she claims that women enjoy lamenting their misfortunes, as she is about to groan over her own (91–93). In other words, women like to complain. She tells Menelaus that in his defence of Hermione he should not bring about great evils for small reasons 'nor, if we women are a ruinous evil, should you men imitate our nature' (353–54, Kovacs). Although this is not the sole misogynistic statement by Andromache, it can be explained not only as a rhetorical ploy to try to gain some sympathy from Menelaus by claiming that her disagreement with Hermione is not as dire as he might suppose, but also as representing the views of the spectators. The Chorus also make misogynistic statements (181–82). Andromache continues criticizing women while debating both Hermione and Menelaus. While on the one hand defending herself against Hermione, Andromache for some reason agrees that although not all women may be sexually insatiable, women suffer from this propensity more than men (218–21). By having her espouse this Greek male ideology about women – that is, their insatiable sexual desire, destructive nature, and so forth – Euripides makes Andromache, an Asian barbarian, more appealing to the Athenian audience, a well-known, subversive strategy of Euripides.[30] How should one view this? On the one hand, these are the current views of the spectators. On the other hand, does the fact that they are espoused by a barbarian lend them support or does it detract from their validity?

In the second part of the play, when Hermione seeks an excuse for her unjust onslaught on Andromache, she blames the women who came to visit her. She accuses these women of being unchaste and emphasizes the bad influence they exert on one another. Her attack on her own gender culminates in her advising husbands to lock their wives in seclusion from mischievous, interfering female outsiders who mean no good, an opinion which the Chorus reject as extreme (930–56; cf. *Hippolytus* 645–46).[31] Menelaus also presents the female gender as being weak and in need of male protection (668–77). Here views acceptable to the audience are given to a villainous character. Could this possibly indicate something about Euripides' own opinion of these views?

Female gender is also connected with deceit, and both are connected to childbirth in Hermione's accusation against Andromache of using 'drugs' (*pharmaka*) to poison her womb (155–58). Ample scholarly observations, both of the tragedies and of the behaviour of Athenian women, point to numerous associations between 'femininity' and deceit, as well as to the anxiety that women's purported deceitfulness aroused in men.[32] Viewing women as *a priori* deceptive would obviously make them appear unreliable and, by extension, necessitate their restriction to the home, where their actions could be supervised. It is assumed that when hostility motivates a woman to act, her weakness compels her to act by guile or poison (*pharmaka*), avoiding a direct trial of strength.[33]

Andromache's direct attack on Spartan villainy as well as her denigration of her own gender both reflect the views prevalent among the Athenian spectators. It is rather unsettling that Andromache's astute and quick-witted replies to Menelaus are criticized by the Chorus as 'spoken too much as a woman to a man' (363, Kovacs). Andromache keeps repeating statements that are far from flattering to her gender, but these statements always must be considered in context. Pointing out Hermione's attempts to humiliate Neoptolemus, she states: 'A woman, even if given to a low-born husband, must respect him and not contend with him in pride' (213–14, Kovacs). It is true that she is espousing an essentially male-generated ideology,[34] but one also needs to admit how well this is woven not only into the fabric of the immediate context addressing Hermione's pride, but also how well it meshes with the overarching topic of legacy found throughout the play. The legacy of Thetis and Peleus, a goddess and a mortal, the parents of Achilles, eventually prevails through their great-grandson, born to a concubine. Her comment on nursing Hector's bastards 'so as to cause you [Hector] no offence. By doing this, I drew my husband to me by my virtue' (225–26, Lloyd) – a *topos* of the excellent wife taken straight from *Iliad* 5.70–71, where Theano, Antenor's wife, is said to nurse Pedaeus, Antenor's bastard son, as if he were her own son in order 'to do pleasure to her husband' – also ties into the all-embracing theme of legacy.[35]

Neoptolemus' absence

Neoptolemus' absence and his final return (*nostos*) to Phthia form the backdrop to the entire play.[36] Neoptolemus has left for Delphi in the hope of atoning for his former demand that Apollo give satisfaction for the death of his father Achilles.[37] Neoptolemus is exquisitely aware of his father's legacy, and the memory of his heroism. This theme is therefore connected to the theme of parents and their children. While Andromache tries to save her own life and that of her son from the machinations of Hermione and her father, Neoptolemus tries to gain justice for his father Achilles. Although he is presented as a loving and loyal son, Neoptolemus could appear as a deficient father if he were aware of the tensions in the household he left untended. It is doubtful, however, that the audience would have perceived him in this way. Greek men, who were frequently away from home fighting battles or engaging in trade, would often have been unaware of the goings on in their homes. However, some of Andromache's utterances do raise the question of how Neoptolemus could have left his son exposed to danger in this way.

It is Neoptolemus' absence that provides the opportunity for Hermione and Menelaus to act against Andromache and Molossus. In the prologue, Andromache states she had to hide her son because 'His father is not here to protect me and is no use to his son since he is away in the land of Delphi' (49–51, Kovacs). When she learns that Menelaus has found the hiding place of Molossus, she exclaims: 'those two vultures will take you and kill you, while the man who is called your father tarries in Delphi!' (74–76, Kovacs). It becomes clear as the plot advances that had Neoptolemus not left for Delphi, neither Hermione nor her father could have threatened Molossus' life. We must assume that Neoptolemus was either utterly ignorant of the schemes Hermione was concocting against Andromache and the jealousy she felt, or he did not care, possibilities that would mark him not only as an indifferent husband but also as a detached, indifferent, and maybe negligent father. As for Andromache, who has already lost one child to Neoptolemus' cruel disposition, there is a potential, horrific repeat of another loss of a child due to his lack of attention.[38]

Neoptolemus' absence from home, and more specifically his presence in Delphi, also give Orestes the opportunity to exact his own revenge. In short, Neoptolemus' journey is a primary requirement for all of the play's action to take place. However, a condition that allows the rest of the play to proceed is not necessarily a unifying theme. Neoptolemus' absence is taken for granted for most of the play, in that it sets the scene. His absence is also distinct from most of the play's other themes. While he has gone to Delphi out of his sense of duty as a son, he is not there to try to rectify any aspect of his problematic marriage with Hermione.[39]

Revenge

Hermione's plan to murder Andromache and Molossus is an act of revenge for what she believes to be Andromache's malicious attacks on her. Hermione assumes she has been made barren by Andromache, claiming that Andromache has been poisoning her womb. Hermione also insinuates that Andromache wants to have Neoptolemus to herself, and that the concubine will cast the legitimate wife out of her home, allowing Andromache to take her place (29–35). In Hermione's deranged mind, her revenge may seem justified. If Andromache is preventing Hermione from having children, Hermione will prevent Andromache from having children – by killing Andromache's child. Even though Andromache says that after marrying Hermione, Neoptolemus shunned her own bed (29–30) and that Neoptolemus shuns Hermione because she is so hateful, Hermione is still set on revenge. When Orestes plans Neoptolemus' violent murder, it is to take revenge on Neoptolemus for having stolen his betrothed bride, and for refusing to return her.

Royalty, slavery, and lost status

Both Andromache and Hermione were given to Neoptolemus as war-prizes, but in very different ways. Andromache, the daughter of a king, and previously the wife of Hector, son of King Priam, has lost her royal status. She has become a slave, awarded to Neoptolemus as a spoil of war after Troy's defeat. By contrast, Hermione, daughter of King Menelaus, has retained her status, and was awarded to Neoptolemus as his legitimate wife, in recognition for Neoptolemus' efforts in sacking Troy (969–70; *Odyssey* 4.5–7).

Hermione stresses her royal status on every possible occasion. However, as she learns, even being a princess is not sufficient for obtaining happiness. No matter how often she claims superiority over Andromache, she obviously feels inferior, due to her childless status. Also, her father has not ensured her safety. Once challenged by Peleus, Menelaus withdraws, leaving Hermione vulnerable to what she supposes will be the wrath of her husband, once he discovers what she had plotted. If Neoptolemus were to throw her out of her home, Hermione would have lost all status.

Spartan villainy

Some critics see the play as a sort of political pamphlet of anti-Spartan propaganda,[40] especially for the purpose of dating it (see Chapter 1, pp. 9–10). As with the extreme misogyny found in the play, the hatred of Sparta is in some ways puzzling. While there is no doubt that Athenian audiences might have welcomed the inclusion of anti-Spartan propaganda on stage, would Euripides have built an entire drama to publicize this sentiment? It is possible, as suggested with regard to misogyny, that the play works on several levels. First, the anti-Spartan views are voiced only by Andromache and Peleus in connection to specific occurrences of the plot, not outside of it.[41] Even while appreciating the condemnations of Menelaus' and Hermione's behaviour in association with blanket condemnations of Sparta, the audience would have been very aware that mythic archaic Sparta had little to do with the classical *polis*. The widespread reforms in Sparta, many of which might have been deemed threatening by other Greeks, had created a fifth-century entity far removed from the notions of luxury referred to in *Andromache*. Although Spartan women may have had certain freedoms not enjoyed by Athenian women, these were aimed at encouraging women who took part in athletics alongside their menfolk and were devoted to bringing up warlike sons. The fifth-century Spartan hoplite warriors would have been as far removed from the portrayal of a cowardly Menelaus, as the warlike mothers were from a hysterical Hermione. This being said, the threat presented by modern Sparta would have made the opportunity to laugh at archaic Spartans all the more welcome.

Andromache's taunts to Menelaus and Hermione, while upholding Greek *mores*, serve this purpose well. She repeatedly emphasizes Spartan villainy versus accepted Greek standards of virtue. She is a former Trojan princess who in spite of being foreign recognizes 'ideal Greek behavior and denounces those who do not, suggesting that she is more Greek than those born as such'.[42] She takes shelter at the altar of Thetis, as a pious Greek would. She describes her marriage to Hector in Greek terms. She was richly dowered, and came to his house to give him legitimate children, which she did. She never privileged her father's *oikos* over her husband's, as Hermione does (213–14). Athenian spectators would support her wifely devotion to Hector, which included nursing his illegitimate children (224–25). She invokes the Greek notions of restraint and modesty when telling the Spartan woman that sexual matters are best kept quiet (220–21, 238, 240). She protects Molossus as best she can, and her willingness to sacrifice herself to save his life paints her as beyond reproach as a mother (409–10). By her conduct, Andromache exhibits the Greek *mores* of the primacy of husbands and children as well as the notions of piety, justice, and self-restraint. In addition, she is able to bear children. Hermione's failure to do so disqualifies her from being a proper wife, as she is depriving the House of Peleus of a legitimate heir (708–14). Andromache, therefore, is not only very Greek in her thinking but also exemplifies the ideal Greek wife and mother. Her virtue is contrasted with the Spartan villainy of Hermione and Menelaus.

When Andromache leaves the sanctuary of Thetis' shrine, she learns that her death might not save her son, because Menelaus, while claiming to be a good father, nevertheless deflects the pollution of the boy's bloodshed onto his daughter, Hermione. No reason is given as to why. At this point, Andromache bursts into a tirade about the villainy of Spartans (445–52). She blames the Spartans for deviousness, countless murders, greed, and for saying one thing while intending something else. The on-stage Greek audience who lost their loved ones to the War would have welcomed Andromache's response to Menelaus when she advised him not to opt for the kind of rash and radical solution that he adopted after the loss of Helen and which brought about the destruction of Troy (361–63, cf. 387).

What is usually seen as anti-Spartan propaganda or Spartan villainy is mostly addressed by Andromache, but Peleus also adds indignant remarks about the immodesty of Spartan women (595–601). Peleus has prevented the murder of an innocent concubine and her son by two Spartans, which speaks volumes about what other Greeks may think of Spartans and their *mores*. He also concisely but eloquently states that other than their successful contests on the battlefield, the Spartans are of no account (724–26), which does not contribute to the Spartan reputation, but gives the spectators further insight into the Greek view that military prowess is not the supreme human value. The poor behaviour supposedly characterizing Sparta is immediately proven when Menelaus, all of a sudden, retreats from his confrontation with Peleus, deserts his daughter, and goes to attack a city that turned from friendship to enmity with Sparta (733–34).[43] In other words, Menelaus proves what Peleus has just stated: the value of happiness and security of a child do not trump Spartan narrow interest in military activity, and more specifically their desire to interfere in the affairs of neighbouring states.[44] The Spartan Menelaus may also be seen to trespass on an individual level when Peleus condemns Menelaus' outrageous interference in the domestic affairs in Phthia while its ruler Neoptolemus is away.

Struggle and rescue

Throughout the play there are episodes of dramatic tension built up as a character is struggling with some kind of threat, with the tension then released as the character is rescued in one way or another. This episodic structure, with the rise and fall of the fates of each of the characters, creates an intense experience when reading or watching the play. Philosophically, one may relate these cycles to the ups and downs of fortune occurring on a larger scale, either in time or place, across a person's lifetime; or in the fate of a nation as occurs in wars. Often it seems that the fortunes of an individual or of a country are not only dependent on their own actions, but on the whims of others, or the mercies of fate. It may seem that any control we think we have over our destinies is an illusion. Just as this held true during the Trojan War, it also applies during *Andromache*. At the start of the play, Andromache hides at the shrine of Thetis in the hope that the goddess will save her. In this case the tension is diverted rather than removed, as Andromache's concern shifts to her son when she realizes the danger he is in. However, Andromache has no control over her own destiny or over that of her son: Menelaus deceives her, just as the Greeks had deceived the Trojans. Andromache then tells her son to supplicate Menelaus not to kill him, but Menelaus heartlessly rejects his pleas (528–44). While Andromache struggles with Menelaus, using biting rhetoric, it is only the arrival of Peleus that ensures their rescue. In the second half of the play, when she is no longer the aggressor, Hermione realizes that she may now be in danger herself. Having threatened the life of Neoptolemus' son, she could be exiled from her home or worse. This is a particularly strange aspect of the play. In essence, the fact that Andromache and her son were saved by Peleus changes nothing about Hermione's actions. In fact, Peleus' timely arrival prevented the deed she could have been punished for. Hermione's illogical histrionics at this point could be viewed as part of the misogyny of the play (see above), although one must allow for the possibility that were he to return, Neoptolemus could have learned about her nefarious machinations. However, we can also see Hermione as being in a state of transition. She is moving away from Neoptolemus and towards Orestes, with whom she will ultimately achieve her goal of becoming a mother, although this is not specified in the play. Hermione does not know that Neoptolemus is already dead and that she has no reason to fear him, but her struggle allows Orestes to be framed as her saviour. Lastly, Peleus, the saviour of Andromache and her son, struggles with his intense grief on hearing of the death of his grandson.

When all seems to be lost, the fragility of human lives is brought to the forefront of Peleus' mind. The thought may occur to the audience that perhaps there is a foolish aspect to our lives. We labour under many misconceptions. We think that if we behave well, we should be rewarded, while if we behave badly, we should be punished, but as seen in *Andromache*, neither might be the case. Both Menelaus and Orestes behaved atrociously, yet they seem to come out of the play unscathed. Peleus has behaved heroically, but momentarily appears to have lost everything. At that moment, as in *Ecclesiastes* (1.2), everything seems to be nothing but vanity (literally as insubstantial as thin air), or as Shakespeare put it, life 'is a tale told by an idiot, full of sound and fury, signifying nothing' (*Macbeth* 5.5.26–28).

In the final scene, it transpires that Peleus has actually saved his legacy by rescuing Molossus from Menelaus. However, it is Thetis who rescues Peleus, with Euripides allowing man's destiny to be decided once more by the gods, as he often does, using the device of *deus ex machina*. She orders Andromache to go with her son to the land of the Molossians, where she will marry Helenus, and together they will bring up Neoptolemus' son (their great-grandson) so he and his descendants will rule over the land of Molossia. In this way, neither is the line of Thetis and Peleus 'laid to waste' nor is the line of Troy, as the descendants of Andromache and Neoptolemus will go forward in time to fulfil their destinies. This brings us to the overarching theme unifying the play: that of continuing the *legacy* of the ancestral line as expressed through *marriage, parenthood*, and *children*.

Symmetry and Balance between the Sections

Before moving on to the unifying themes, we reiterate the symmetry and balance with which Euripides arranged his individual themes. As is noted, each theme is mentioned in what scholars call the first half (1–765/801) and then balanced in the second part (766/802–1288) of the play. Andromache seeks sanctuary in the shrine of Thetis, when the aftermath of the Trojan War has left her and her son vulnerable to Hermione's plots against them, and in the end, it is Thetis who sets straight the lives of those who have survived. The helpless child Molossus is rescued by the aged Peleus, who in turn is promised immortality with his son Achilles by Thetis, while Peleus' legacy on earth is ensured by the young lad he saved. Hermione boasts of her rather inappropriate attire – the spangled robe and golden headdress from her dowry in her first appearance, while tearing them up in her second one. Menelaus' deceit against Andromache to preserve his daughter's marriage to Neoptolemus is counter-matched by Orestes' trap for Neoptolemus. Orestes' plot brings Hermione's marriage to Neoptolemus to an end, but will allow her to start a family with her cousin (although this is not specified), in a marriage which had been agreed to by Menelaus before she was given to Neoptolemus. The play opens with Andromache's grief at her loss of Hector, and her loyalty to his memory remains steadfast throughout. In the closing scene, she is given a future with Hector's younger brother Helenus. The suffering caused to Andromache and other Trojan victims of the War finds its counterpart in Peleus' loss of his son Achilles during the War, and now of his grandson in its aftermath. While Menelaus and Peleus had been part of the Greek alliance, their interests are no longer aligned. Peleus' fierce verbal assaults on Menelaus form a transition from this Panhellenic alliance to bitter attacks on Sparta, although the enmity between Greeks and barbarians also remains a theme throughout. Gender issues *per se* and misogyny in particular occur throughout. Andromache and Hermione refer frequently to their gender in the first half of the play, while Menelaus brings up women's need for protection from a man. Both Andromache and Hermione also make misogynistic statements in the first half, but Hermione surpasses herself in the second half, blaming gossiping women for her ill conduct towards Andromache, even going so far as to suggest that married women should have no female visitors in their homes!

Unifying Themes

Legacy: Marriage, parents and their children

While each of the themes discussed above is important, only the theme of legacy, supported by the closely related themes of marriage, parents and their children, unifies all the parts of the play. Legacy here is concerned with the continuance of the ancestral line of the two great Houses of Peleus and Atreus. This theme serves as a continuous subtext to which all the other thematic threads bind themselves intrinsically as sub-topics. Legacy is often regarded as being realized through children. Andromache's chief concern is for the survival of her son by Neoptolemus. Peleus arrives on the scene to defend the house of his grandson Neoptolemus, and eventually finds his own peace of mind through his great-grandson, who will carry forward the line of Neoptolemus and Achilles. Parent-child relationships also abound in the story of the Trojan War and its aftermath, with the tragic relationship between Agamemnon and Iphigenia eventually followed by Orestes' murder of his mother Clytemnestra, which in turn led to the Furies tormenting Orestes, and his resulting desperation at not being able to find a wife and have children.

These themes also lie at the heart of Euripides' *Ion* (produced in 413 BCE), which revolves around Creusa's quest for motherhood, and her determination that only a child descended through her from Erichthonius, carrying her autochthonous heritage, should inherit her ancestral throne. Interestingly enough, both plays also have a connection to Apollo's temple at Delphi. In *Andromache*, none of the characters has quite the same concern for an heir to continue their line as Creusa does in *Ion*, but it is Peleus who comes closest. Andromache is more concerned with preserving the life of her child, rather than his particular heritage. She has lost Hector's son, and only refers to him once throughout the play. Likewise, Hermione wants a child to give her the status of being a mother and a proper wife, as discussed above. Orestes seeks a wife, but does not seem concerned that Hermione may be barren. Maybe he suspects that this is not caused by Hermione's natural sterility but by

Neoptolemus' sexual distance from his wife, as his question as to whether Neoptolemus loves someone else indicates. Notwithstanding these qualifying comments, the themes of marriage and parenthood remain in the forefront of all the other major characters' attention, ensuring that they remain constantly in the forefront of the spectators' minds.

Legacy

The theme of a family's legacy becomes explicit with the entrance of Peleus, who regards Molossus as his descendant 'even if he is a bastard three times over' (*nothos*, 636, cf. 711–14, Lloyd).[45] Andromache's son is fully accepted into the Greek *oikos*, and Peleus has great hopes for him: 'I will bring you up in Phthia to be a great enemy to these people' he tells Molossus (723–24, Lloyd), who will eventually be divinely decreed to found eponymously the Greek Molossians, uniting the royal Houses of Troy and Phthia. Peleus' concern about his legacy is clearly seen in his anguished exclamation when he sees the corpse of Neoptolemus brought back from Delphi:

> I am no more. No longer do I have a family, no children
>   are left in the house!
> (1177–78, Lloyd; cf. 708–14, 1205–7, 1216)

The question of legacy forms the backbone of the play and is intrinsic to the recurrent topic of parents and children. The story is not just about Hermione's childlessness, but about the offspring that will continue the House of Peleus and Thetis. In a subversive way so characteristic of Euripides, the legacy of Achilles, who brought about the death of Hector, from which Troy has never recovered, depends on a child of Andromache, Hector's wife. It is also noteworthy that Neoptolemus, Achilles' son, is not presented as being concerned about the childlessness of his wife. The only reaction the play notes on his part to his wife's barrenness is distancing himself from her, but he is not going to Delphi to find out why he has no children as, for example, Laius did. The issue does not seem to be of concern for him. Is it because he has Molossus? We cannot know. He is more concerned about what happened to his father than having or not having offspring. In a way, Neoptolemus has never matured into full adulthood. He is always the son overshadowed by his heroic father. His steadfastness is Achilles' legacy. In this respect, he differs from his grandfather, who intensely cares about his heirs, and also from Menelaus, who does not express any care for his legacy, but at least partially cares about his daughter and her unhappiness.

Marriage

The marriage of Peleus and Thetis frames the play. It was during their wedding that the apple of discord appeared at the feet of the three goddesses, resulting in the beauty contest which is mythically associated with the beginnings of the Trojan War. The Chorus allude to the prize of beauty the three goddesses competed over (279) and which Paris was to judge. Helen, his reward for choosing Aphrodite, is of course Hermione's mother. So, in this play, when Euripides pits Helen's daughter against the widow of Paris' elder brother, he is to some degree re-enacting the discord which began at the marriage of Thetis and Peleus. While on the one hand Euripides ensures an element of symmetry by balancing themes between the two parts of the play, he is also closing certain thematic circles. It is Peleus who directly invokes marriage towards the end of the play, when he discovers that Neoptolemus has been killed.

> O marriage, marriage, you have destroyed my house, destroyed my city! Alas my child! Would that you had not cast upon our family and house this ill-famed marriage and on yourself a union with Hermione that was death, my son!
>
> (1186–91, Kovacs)

Marriage is usually a welcome occasion of uniting two houses, but in this case, it led to disaster. It seemed that Peleus had a premonition that this marriage would not be blissful for his family. Hermione's mother Helen and her aunt Clytemnestra brought only anguish to their husbands. The men and women of the House of Atreus should marry apparently only within the house itself. Orestes can only marry Hermione; the Farmer in Euripides' *Electra* is better off when she is married off to Pylades, her cousin. The future union of Orestes and Hermione thus completes another cycle, with the House of Atreus also finding a way forward. Thetis and Peleus, the parents of Achilles, the grandparents of Neoptolemus, are also the great-grandparents of Andromache's son, in whom there is a degree of synthesis between Greek and Trojan. Their return to 'married life', living together as a couple, closes the play, just as their descendant finally closes the generations of suffering caused by the Trojan War.

Parents and their children

How dear children are to their parents is well expressed by Andromache after she leaves the altar of Thetis, facing as far as she knows a sure death, but ready to forfeit her life in order to save her son. In a way, her words can serve as a motto for the play:

All mankind, it seems, find children their very life. Whoever has no children and disparages them, though he may have less pain, has sorry happiness.

(418–20, Kovacs)

Peleus' outburst of grief on hearing of the death of his grandson, when he had previously lost his son (see above), further emphasizes children's crucial importance to their parents. The appearance of Molossus on stage, and his piteous pleading with Menelaus, would also have emphasized this theme.

The reverse relationship of parenthood and 'child of' also plays a vital role in *Andromache*. As Phillippo has pointed out, the use of patronymics for Neoptolemus, Orestes, Andromache, and Hermione outnumbers the use of their names almost two-to-one (twenty-eight patronymics compared with fifteen uses of the name).[46] This rather frequent use of patronymics enhances this relationship,[47] while also emphasizing the themes of children, parents, and legacy.

The theme of parenthood links all of the characters. While it is dealt with in fairly straightforward terms in relation to Andromache, who exemplifies motherhood, and Hermione, who bewails her childless condition, it is more complicated where Menelaus is concerned. To begin with, Menelaus is only present in Phthia out of concern for the wellbeing of his daughter. However, what mostly features in the second part of the play is Menelaus' failure as a father. He not only deserted his daughter in the midst of what he boasted of as bringing aid to her suffering, but we also learn from Orestes that he betrothed her to two different men.[48] Orestes tells his cousin: 'For you were mine to begin with, and you are married to Neoptolemus only by the baseness of your father. Before he attacked Troy, he gave you to me to be my wife, but later he promised you to your present husband as a reward if he sacked Troy' (966–70, Kovacs).

Menelaus did not have to abandon Hermione; he could have followed Peleus' advice and taken her home to Sparta. Instead, he left her to the mercy of Neoptolemus and Peleus (639, 708–9). By embarking on this road, Menelaus connects his poor parenting with the themes of marriage, deceit, murder, effects of the Trojan War, Spartan villainy, Greeks and barbarians, gender, and old age. He sees his involvement regarding Hermione's charges against Andromache as having to do with his daughter's successful marriage. 'I have come to the aid of my daughter, for I think it is a serious matter to be deprived of one's mate. Any other misfortunes a woman may suffer are secondary, but if she loses her husband, she loses her life' (370–73, Kovacs), he says when challenged by Andromache. On the face of it, as he explains himself to Peleus, he is concerned about the well-being of his daughter: 'The man's strength lies in his hands, while the woman's interests are defended by her parents and kin. Am I not right then to come to the aid of my own?' (675–77, Kovacs). He sees his daughter as in danger of losing her husband because of a barbarian concubine, and is therefore coming to her aid. He taunts Peleus for being willing to allow children of barbarians to rule over Greeks (663–66, cf. 655–59). Furthermore, he accuses Peleus of helping a woman whose family killed his own son, Achilles (650–54).

The abandonment by her father (805, 854–55, 918) leaves Hermione defenceless, exposed, and understandingly hysterical. Interestingly enough, when Orestes tells Hermione that he would take her home to her father in hope of marrying her, she does not commit to marrying him but says: 'My father shall take care of my marriage, it is not for me to decide this' (987–88, Kovacs). Is Hermione's absolute acceptance of her father's control over whom she is to marry a reflection of gendered social expectations inculcated in her since childhood, or is it her realization of the cold calculation of Orestes, who, consulting his own expediency, makes it clear that he cannot marry outside his family since no one would let his daughter marry a matricide (974–76). Hermione is Orestes' only chance at marriage. Eventually she will be married not only to a matricide but to a murderer as well, imitating closely the charge she mounted against Andromache (170–73). For those in the audience who might have remembered the mythic version in which Hermione was raised by Clytemnestra after the elopement of Helen, the fact that Orestes has murdered her caring aunt must have added a further horror to Hermione's future, although the play certainly does not portray her in a positive light overall.

While Menelaus' poor performance as a father almost causes his daughter to lose her mind, and inadvertently causes the death of his son-in-law, the play remains silent about Helen, Hermione's mother. Where is she at this crucial moment in her daughter's marriage? Why is Euripides silent about her? In *Helen* (412 BCE), Euripides has sent Helen off to Egypt for safekeeping for the duration of the Trojan War, while her *eidōlon* went to Troy, while in *Orestes* Euripides spirited Helen up to the heavens. There is no real connection between the plots of these two plays and *Andromache*, but it seems possible that in Euripides' mind Helen either was not in Sparta or not amongst the living.

The absence of Helen is especially underscored by the early appearance of Menelaus and his fatherly demeanour. In the very beginning, he exhibits fatherly traits not to be found in Neoptolemus, and thus serves as a good example of a parent. On the other hand, Helen is only presented as an example of how not to behave in a marriage, and by extension, we can perhaps assume that she is also an example of an unfit mother, or at best, an absentee mother. Some of the other ways in which the theme of parenthood emerges are not so straightforward. Hermione is allowed by the playwright to conveniently forget that in her own close family Orestes killed his own mother, and she was promised as a wife to her cousin, which she will ultimately become, and that her cousin Electra also married another cousin of hers, Pylades, who willingly assisted in the killing of his own aunt Clytemnestra.

Conclusion

Andromache ends with a reiteration of the theme of legacy, supported by the themes of marriage, parents and their children. Thetis comes to console her husband. Even she, although a goddess, lost her child, the swift-footed Achilles. After giving Peleus instructions about the burial of Neoptolemus, she prophesies how Andromache will marry Helenus, Hector's younger brother, and how the son of Andromache and Neoptolemus will found a dynasty that will rule over Molossia. Thetis and Peleus lost their son and grandson but they both can look forward to their legacy continuing through the establishment of their own dynasty. Thetis not only goes on to bestow immortality on her husband, but also divulges to him that Achilles became immortal and lives on Leuke, the White Island. Once transported to the deep to dwell with her, Peleus will be able to see their son. The announcements of Thetis also bring forward the topic of marriage. While the marriages of Hermione, Menelaus, and Agamemnon, mentioned or alluded to in the play, were failed ones and unhappy, Thetis' and Peleus' marriage, like that of Andromache and Hector in a subtext, is wholesome and loving. The play thus ends as it began with the themes of legacy: marriage, parents and their children.

4

Characters

Andromache

Introduction

Andromache is of royal birth, the daughter of Eëtion of Thebe, ruler of Cilicia; however, the spectators would know her first and foremost for having been the wife of the heroic Trojan prince, Hector. From Homer onwards, she was the iconic wife and mother, and in tragedy she became the 'victimized' heroine *par excellence*. Euripides inherited this image of a loving, devoted but suffering wife and widow. After her childhood family was butchered by Achilles, she sees her husband as her 'father and queenly mother, you are brother, and you are my stalwart husband' (*Iliad* 6.429–30). The poignant episode in the *Iliad* (6.369–502) in which Andromache begs her husband to remain on the walls of Troy with her, rather than going back into the battle, which will most likely leave their son an orphan (6.431–32), and Hector replies by insisting he must part with her, while going on to predict the fall of Troy and Andromache's future captivity (6.447–65), would have been etched into their collective memory. In the last book of the *Iliad*, Andromache appears again, lamenting Hector, whose corpse lies on a bier. In her dirge she also foretells the city's destruction and herself being led to captivity with her baby son, who might either grow up to be a slave or be thrown from the walls of Troy for being the son of Hector (24.723–45). Euripides features Andromache in two extant plays, *Andromache* and *Trojan Women*, whose chronological sequence is the reverse of the mythic order of the events they dramatize. In both plays, the path of her suffering is similar. In *Trojan Women* she passes from being a widowed mother to a childless widow after Astyanax is thrown from the battlements of Troy. In *Andromache* she is 'widowed' again, if we regard Neoptolemus as her husband, and almost becomes childless a second time.

In all these literary works Andromache is drawn as a long-suffering, and at times helpless, figure, as well as a victim of trickery. From among the various tragic female protagonists, she shares only with Alcestis the portrayal of a woman who is powerless to steer the course of her own destiny.

Furthermore, she suffers from masculine deception, and in spite of the best possible intentions, she fails to protect her child. As if applauding the ineffectiveness of her actions, the play presents her in a highly positive light as the preferred type of feminine woman who, despite her use of some guile, may easily be thwarted.

Andromache delivers the prologue, highlighting from the outset her important position in the play's cast, with her prominence continuing throughout the first half of the play. She starts by mentioning Thebe, the city of her birth, located in Trojan Cilicia in Asia Minor, which her father Eëtion had ruled, until Achilles killed him and all of her brothers. Andromache had gone to Troy to be wedded to Hector and give him legitimate children. By introducing herself in this way, Andromache is portraying herself as a woman who once was envied (5), but in spite of this auspicious start she has become the epitome of misfortune. She has seen her husband killed by Achilles and their son Astyanax hurled from the ramparts of Troy. She does not state that Neoptolemus killed her son, but this would have been the connection the audience was likely to have made. After seeing Troy sacked, she was given as spear-booty to Neoptolemus. She now lives in Phthia, as Neoptolemus' concubine, having shared his bed perforce, although she clearly states that since his marriage to Hermione, he has spurned her bed (30). Before this marriage, Andromache bore Neoptolemus a son, whom other sources, but not the play, call Molossus.

The nexus that connects her fate with that of Achilles is peculiar.[1] When we first meet Andromache in Euripides' eponymous play, she is huddling at the altar of Thetis, the mother of Achilles, the man who had killed her father, her seven brothers and her husband. Achilles is also the father of Neoptolemus, who in some versions killed Astyanax. This is the destructive part of Achilles' legacy. On the other hand, there are his parents. While Andromache hopes Thetis will save her life, it will be Peleus who will indeed rescue her and her son. The parents of one of the most famous heroes will be the ones who will save her life, while preserving their own legacy. Ironically, Andromache, the barbarian, the daughter, daughter-in-law, and wife of the arch enemies of the Greeks, is also the means through which Peleus and Thetis will be able to preserve their line. No wonder that, as will be discussed below, in spite of her ethnicity Andromache is portrayed all along as if she were a Greek woman.

Neoptolemus' absence has left Andromache in a dire situation: Hermione and her father plan to kill her and her son. Despite being defenceless, Andromache is portrayed as a woman who does not despair but can strategize and plan. When her Maidservant tells her that Menelaus has found the hiding place of Molossus, Andromache begs her servant to go by herself and fetch Peleus, even though her former requests sent by messengers to the old man have failed, perhaps never delivered. It is noteworthy that Andromache does not consider her son unworthy of a 'Greek' rescue even though she is a slave, and is not a Greek. In spite of her current lowly status, Andromache radiates the self-confidence of the princess that she had always been. Her royal and free status is mentioned on four occasions by her and by her Maidservant (1–5, 12, 56, 65). Even though she acknowledges her current servitude (12, 25, 30, 64, 99, 110, 114), Andromache's demeanour suggests that her thinking is that of a free person. It is also noteworthy that even while she states that after marrying Hermione, Neoptolemus stopped their sexual relationship (30, 37), the Chorus of Phthian women and the people in the palace still think of Andromache as Neoptolemus' consort, referring to her by the adjective *syngamos* (σύγγαμος), which literally means 'married' or 'wedded' (182, 836).[2] This elevated status might result from the fact that she is the mother of Neoptolemus' only son. It is extremely unlikely that they would have had an intimate relationship distinct from the sexual interaction,[3] since Neoptolemus murdered Astyanax. Andromache has no warm words for Neoptolemus other than identifying him as the father of her son, although an absent one. However, her status in the household is clearly higher than that of a simple slave. There is also no question that Andromache, who claims to have belonged in the past to 'a house most free' (12), behaves in a manner befitting a woman who was once a princess. The Chorus have noticed her haughty demeanour and tell her: 'Know your fate, consider the present ill-fortune into which you have come' (126, Kovacs), before Hermione speaks along similar lines (164–68, see below).

Andromache and ethnicity

> Glory of Asia, city of Thebe! It was from you that I once came,
> dowered with golden luxury, to the royal house of Priam,
> given to Hector as lawful wife for the bearing of his children.
>
> (1–4, Kovacs)

Andromache's first sentence locates her birthplace in Asia and categorizes her as a barbarian in Greek eyes, and yet at the same time it furnishes her with Greek customs. Her ethnicity as a non-Greek is emphasized in the prologue by the repeated mention of Troy and her connection to the city (3, 11, 15, 58, 103, 105). However, apart from her geographic origin, nothing in her behaviour or in the views she espouses differentiates her from a Greek. As Vester points out: 'Andromache's account of her status past and present leads to the matter of civic identity.'[4] She came richly dowered to the palace of Priam, married Hector in order to bear children, and entered her husband's *oikos* (204), much like any Athenian bride. Andromache not only had royal status in Thebe and Troy, but as a lawful wife in Troy she fulfilled all aspects of her role as a spouse. She gave a male heir to Hector, while the Greek Hermione is unable to do the same for her husband, Neoptolemus.

Andromache's views on what constitutes a good wife conform in every aspect to what would be acceptable to the Athenian male audience. She preaches utter submission to a husband, showing no jealousy even if the husband has strayed, to the point of nursing his bastard children.[5] The husband's happiness is what matters. She is well versed in Greek mores, as she shows upon her encounter with Peleus, falling in supplication in front of him although she is unable to touch his chin as the custom prescribes, because her hands are bound (572–74).

Andromache is far removed from everything that Hermione brings up as 'characteristic' of barbarian behaviour: 'Father lies with daughter, son with mother, and sister with brother, nearest kin murder each other, and no law prevents any of this' (174–76, Kovacs).[6] In fact, mentioning the incestual relationship of a son and a mother would bring to the spectators' minds their *own* myth of Oedipus and Jocasta. As Hermione does not provide any examples of actual unacceptable barbarian sexual liaisons, she neutralizes her own allegations.[7] Hermione's other charge against Andromache – that is, sharing the bed of the son of the man who killed her husband and bearing a child to a family which has killed her kin – is utterly accurate. However, on this occasion she conveniently ignores the fact that Andromache is a slave who has to do her master's bidding (36, 171–73), while everywhere else she insists on Andromache's servitude. Furthermore, the audience will soon see the irony in this accusation when it becomes apparent that Hermione will eventually do the same thing. She will marry Orestes, who brought about the death of her husband Neoptolemus (and murdered her aunt Clytemnestra), only she will do this without being a captive.

Andromache and misogyny

The use of stock arguments devaluing women by Andromache, Hermione, and the Chorus reflects male patriarchal values and derive from internalized psychology.[8] While the text offers two misogynistic comments by Hermione (see under Hermione), and one by the Chorus (181–82), it is Andromache who utters repeated statements that sound as though they come from internalized misogynistic thinking. Unlike Hermione and the Chorus, whose misogynistic remarks are integral to specific situations, Andromache's comments are mostly gratuitous, free of a context demanding them but nonetheless would be clearly welcomed by the off-stage, predominantly male audience.

Thus, for example, in her first appearance after hearing from her Maidservant that Menelaus has discovered the house where she had hidden her son and is on his way to fetch him, Andromache launches into a lament about which she immediately feels the need to apologize: 'It is in the nature of women to take pleasure in always having their present troubles on their lips and on their tongues' (93–95, Lloyd). Not only is this comment uncalled for, but its proverbial nature is not entirely suited to Andromache's present misfortune. It is as if she is saying that she is *always* preoccupied with dirges, laments, and tears (91–92), not only now in her present misfortune. However, this degrading comment about her gender is not intended to be representative of Andromache herself, but rather to ingratiate her with the off-stage audience (or at least part of it) from the beginning of the play.

Similarly, when Hermione reveals her sex-oriented nature, Andromache broadens her criticism of the princess to the entire female gender, who she implies fall prey to sexual insatiability but know how to veil this from sight (218–21). There is no immediate need for this comment, but she scores a point with the off-stage audience. By claiming that all women are guilty of this malady, she includes herself, but unlike Hermione, her conduct conforms to the accepted patriarchal values: she screens her lust successfully.

There is also no contextual need for her vicious assault on her gender at the end of her encounter with Hermione:

It is strange that a god gave mortals remedies (*akē*)
for savage snakes, but as for what is worse than viper or fire, no
one has yet found a cure for a woman [who is bad:
so great an evil are we for the human race].

(269–73, Lloyd)

This is not an aside. Andromache does not try to hide her musings; she addresses everyone and no one. The remark is directed to the off-stage audience to whom this opinion was very well known. This hyperbolic accusation degrading women is superfluous in this context. Euripides gives Andromache misogynistic utterances that are well established in the male ideology in Athens and internalized by women in general. By repeating these remarks in a variety of forms, she serves as a tool for perpetuating the cultural devaluation of women. The desired effect must have been to make her likeable to the off-stage, mostly male audience in spite of her foreign ethnicity.

It should be stated that there are several cases in extant Euripidean tragedies where women express misogynistic views which must have been inculcated in them since youth, explicit and implicit messages about femininity. For example, while convincing herself that she should be prepared to lose her young life and not allow Achilles to fight for her, Iphigenia exclaims, 'It is better that one man should see the light of the day than numberless women' (*IA* 1394, Collard and Morwood).[9] However, such comments are usually inherent and contribute to the situation, while Andromache's usually are not.

Andromache and Hermione

Andromache and Hermione spar with each other in the first episode of the play, each making a single speech followed by a short stichomythia of intense invective.[10] Andromache starts her carefully balanced rebuttal of Hermione's spurious charges with a formal proem (183–91), and goes on to refute the accusations briefly and sarcastically. She mentions the disadvantage of her position: she is a slave and Hermione is young, unjust, proud, and unlikely to listen to 'superior arguments' from one inferior in status. Although Andromache's efforts will be futile, she must defend herself. This kind of proem is a rhetorical commonplace for someone who claims that they have a superior and just argument, which will nonetheless prove ineffective.[11]

Next, Andromache counters Hermione's unfounded allegations, which start by simply blaming her for being a concubine (177–80) as if it were her fault or choice, and continue by accusing Andromache of wanting to supplant Hermione as the mistress of the house. Andromache uses flawless rhetoric in the form of ironic and even sarcastic questions in which she not only demonstrates logical thinking and courage but also a level-headed calmness of spirit in spite of the great distress that she is experiencing and the danger that hovers over her and her son. She does not grovel at Hermione's feet or ask for pity, but counters the senselessness of Hermione's allegations head on. As Lloyd states, she 'uses the argument from probability, a hallmark of rhetorical sophistication in the late 5th C. . . . An. shows first that she is not able to supplant Hermione (194–8), and then that she would have no motive to do so even if she were able (199–204)'.[12] In a string of rhetorical questions (192–204) that serve as hypothetical, absurd arguments for why she might possibly want to displace Hermione as lawful wife, she completely destroys Hermione's case against her. First, she asks what would enable her to oust Hermione from her legitimate marriage. Would it be on the basis of status: because Hermione thinks that Troy is greater than Sparta, so giving Andromache higher status, or because Hermione thinks of Andromache as being a free woman with status equal to or greater than her own? Does Hermione imagine that Andromache would purposefully intend to bear children in Hermione's stead, even though they would be slaves and 'miserable dependents' to herself? That she is emboldened by her own 'youthful body' and by the power of her own city and friends who want to take possession of Hermione's house? Does she think the Phthians would tolerate these children as kings, or that the Greeks would love her because of Hector? She finishes by reclaiming her own former status even though it has nothing to do with the allegation hurled against her, but could sting Hermione: 'And am I myself obscure and not one of Troy's royal family?' (204, Kovacs). Here she once again shows her proud spirit and confidence.

It should be noted, however, that these questions, in spite of their presentation as rhetorical absurdities, highlight the plausibility of Hermione's case.[13] First of all, although admitting to being a slave, Andromache behaves and speaks not only as if she were still a free woman but an aristocratic one. This conduct must be menacing for Hermione. The Chorus of Phthian women note this and tell Andromache to be humbler. Even the adoption of the rhetorical probability structure with which she defends herself demonstrates a rather offensive rhetorical sophistication not usually exhibited by a slave-concubine. The intimation that she has no friends is untrue. Andromache has her Maidservant and Peleus as her allies, although they would not help her to repossess Hermione's house. Her body must be youthful enough for Neoptolemus to have wanted her to share his bed. Her son, in spite of being the cause of Hermione's jealousy, is her only reason to hope that Neoptolemus would save her upon his return (26–27). Finally, her children will indeed be the royal family that will continue the House of the Aeacids. Thus Euripides, subversive as ever, gives Andromache a rhetorical win, but in the eyes of a thoughtful spectator it would not be a moral one.

Having eliminated herself rhetorically as a source for Hermione's troubled circumstances, Andromache points to the real cause of Hermione's misery and by doing so reveals her views of what it means to be a good wife. She pinpoints Hermione's disposition as the fount of Neoptolemus' hatred for her: 'You are not fit to live with' (206, Kovacs). Hermione might be beautiful and young, but she lacks the qualities that make a successful wife (208). A wife should identify herself with her husband's household and not assert herself unduly. Hermione should identify herself as the Phthian spouse of Neoptolemus, rather than continuing to consider herself a Spartan, the daughter of Menelaus. Instead, Hermione taunts her husband by claiming that Scyros, Neoptolemus' birthplace, is of no account in comparison to Sparta, and that Menelaus is a greater man than Achilles (209–12).[14] By preaching total submission of a wife to her husband, Andromache must have infinitely pleased the Athenian male audience (213–14). She then goes on to lob Hermione's assertions about barbarian sexual mores back at her, accusing Hermione of being so sexually insatiable and so jealous of her husband's affections that she cannot tolerate the thought of him ever having had intercourse with another woman (215–21). Finally, Andromache offers herself as an example of a loving, submissive, and understanding wife (222–31). Even in instances when Aphrodite 'tripped' Hector, rather than showing bitterness, she nursed his 'bastards'. 'By doing this I won my husband's love', she tells her tormentor.[15] Hermione, on the other hand, is so apprehensive that she would not allow even one drop of rain to spatter on her husband's face. Thus, while condemning Hermione's conduct, Andromache lauds the standards of the perfect wife, showing herself to be the epitome of that perfection, the wife every male in the audience would have loved to have. Andromache ends her rebuttal with another sting to Hermione:

> Do not seek to surpass your mother in man-loving
> ways, woman. All children who have sense must
> avoid the paths their wayward mothers went.
>
> (229–31, Kovacs)

Hermione cannot be accused of infidelity simply because of who her mother is; however, Andromache claims that Hermione resembles her mother in her sexually oriented view of life. Helen's infatuation with Paris led her to abandon her husband's household. Hermione will eventually follow suit, if for different reasons. The same insatiable sexual cravings, *ceteris paribus* intimates Andromache, are the source of Hermione's current unhappiness. She adds that dwelling on the sexual aspect of one's marriage does not contribute to a successful marriage, but can destroy it. However, in spite of the 'good advice' included in this comment, the mention of Helen holds a sting. Bringing her mother into the argument riles Hermione, as will Andromache's mention of Helen's part in causing Achilles' death. This prompts Hermione to exclaim, 'Are you going to keep on probing my woes?' (249, Kovacs). Here again Andromache undermines Hermione in the eyes of the off-stage audience. There is no immediate contextual need to mention Helen. The following stichomythia shows that Andromache's words and advice not to speak openly about her marital sex life have fallen on deaf ears. Hermione believes that sex is 'the first interest of women everywhere' (241, Kovacs). As for Andromache's answer that 'Yes, for *chaste* women, but not for the unchaste' (242, Lloyd), Hermione sees the comment as barbarian and answers, 'We do not live in this city according to barbarian customs' (243, Kovacs). At the end of this encounter between the two women, Andromache comes out not only as a good and devoted wife who puts the happiness of her husband above her own, but as a chaste one, reminiscent of the description of a Bee Woman by Semonides of Amorgos (fl. seventh century BCE), who in Poem 7 depicts different types of women as having sprung from different species. The perfect woman is the one sprung from the bee. One of her main characteristics is that she is not prone to sexual engagement except for procreation. Andromache's views once again conform admirably to the Greek patriarchal ideal. Hermione is the one who falls outside the accepted Greek norms. The rivalry between Andromache and Hermione is thus not between a barbarian and a Greek, but between a barbarian reflecting Greek morality and an immoral Spartan woman.

Andromache and Menelaus

Andromache's interactions with Menelaus are fraught with hostility and contempt. Andromache thinks Menelaus is smug and vapid. Her encounter with him entails three speeches by her, all of them longer than those of Menelaus (329–63 to 309–18; 384–420 to 366–83; 445–63 to 425–34).

The on-stage and off-stage audiences were prepared for Menelaus' imminent arrival, together with Molossus, when Andromache's Maidservant warned her that Menelaus had found Molossus' hiding place. His speech is short and to the point, as befitting a Spartan's temperament, but also arrogant. He announces that he is smarter than Andromache and therefore has found her son. Unless she leaves the shrine of Thetis, her son will be killed. In spite of her undoubted inner turmoil, Andromache again displays her aristocratic demeanour, and maintains her wits. In spite of being trapped by the ruthless Menelaus, who presents her with a merciless ultimatum, her reaction is not one of despair and supplication, but of disdain and logical argument. She mocks him for entering into a contest with 'a poor slave woman' on the basis of the word of his daughter, 'a mere child' (326–28, Kovacs). Having thus eliminated any chance of appealing to his good graces, she presents Menelaus with a list of reasons of why neither she nor her son should be killed. Her reasoning is logical and methodical. If she dies at Hermione's hands, Hermione will be polluted, and he will be complicit in murder. If she, Andromache, escapes death, but Molossus is killed, surely Neoptolemus will avenge his son's death. He will expel Hermione from his house, and there will be no chance for her ever to remarry. She will return home to Sparta unwanted, and grow grey with age in her father's house. Her most poignant argument addresses the charge that she has poisoned Hermione's womb with drugs. If this is indeed the case, she will leave the altar and willingly submit to punishment by Neoptolemus, whom she is allegedly depriving of a legitimate child.

Andromache's argument is cogent, reasoned, and well structured. She has examined the issue from every angle and given the correct responses; however, she suspects that Menelaus is overly susceptible to the women in his family. She ends by stating, 'but as for your nature, there is one thing I fear: it was in a quarrel about a woman that you also destroyed unhappy Troy' (361–63, Kovacs). In short, Andromache does not think that Menelaus should be engaging in the matter between her and Hermione.

Menelaus' reply is full of platitudes and pointless generalities but devoid of any justification for wishing to murder Andromache, with or without her child. He sidesteps the consequences such a murder would have for Hermione's marriage, which he allegedly came to save. He reaffirms his resolve to kill Molossus if Andromache does not step out of the shrine. Realizing the seriousness of Menelaus' threat, Andromache replies with a much more agitated speech describing the impossible choice he has set before her: 'If I win my life, it means misery, if I lose it, disaster!' (385–86, Kovacs). She again presents Menelaus with a list of questions pointing to her utter innocence. She forthrightly asks him why he is killing her:

> What city have I betrayed?
> Which of your children have I killed? What house
> of yours have I set fire to?
>
> (388–90, Kovacs)

In desperation she points out that even Neoptolemus is guiltier than she is, because he forced her to share his bed, and rhetorically she asks: 'will you then kill me rather than him, the one who is to blame?' (391–92, Kovacs). She is effectively pointing out, to a man who prides himself on being smarter than she is (313), that he is overlooking the cause of the situation and only dealing with the consequences. However, Andromache is also bright enough to be aware that logic will not have any effect on Menelaus (392–93). As if preparing herself for death, she outlines what she has lost and what remains. She witnessed Hector killed and dragged behind a chariot and Troy burned. She was pulled by her hair to the departing Greek ships, and when she arrived in Phthia, she was given to Hector's murderers. The present and future hold nothing for her, 'My son here was the only light my life possessed' (406, Kovacs), so she is willing to die to save him.

After stepping out of the shrine, she asks her son to remember her sacrifice so he can tell his father about it. In a further ratification of her decision, she reflects that children are, after all, one's life. A childless person may be comfortable, but his happiness is barren. Once she realizes that she has been tricked, that her sacrificial gesture was in vain as her son will probably be killed anyway, and as she sees Menelaus' indifference to his treachery, Andromache's outburst is violent. She launches into a relentless tirade against Spartans:

Dwellers in Sparta, most hateful of mortals in the eyes
of all mankind, treacherous plotters, masters of the lie,
weavers of deadly wiles, whose thoughts are always
devious, nothing that is sound, but all that is twisted,
how unjust is the prosperity you enjoy in Greece!

(445–49, Kovacs)

There is no crime that they are not guilty of. They always say one thing but plan another. She curses them!

Because Andromache is not attacking Menelaus and Hermione by name here, but addresses herself to the 'dwellers in Sparta', the common assumption is that Euripides is using Andromache as a mouthpiece to comment on the political situation in the context of the Peloponnesian War rather than addressing the context of the play.[16] If the play was indeed performed around 425 BCE, there would be a historical justification for this criticism. For example, in 427 BCE, at the end of the siege of Plataea, the Spartans induced the Plataeans to surrender, promising that no one would be punished unjustly. However, the Spartans then massacred over two hundred prisoners for political reasons (Thuc. 3.68.2; cf. 53.1; 58.3). As was discussed in Chapters 1 and 3, the suggestion that *Andromache* is being used politically by Euripides cannot be determined as a certain fact. It might be coincidence prompted by the dramatic situation, or it might be that Euripides seized on the opportunity created within the drama to insert some political commentary. Spartan treachery was a commonplace theme among Athenians (cf. Eur. *Supp.* 187; Hdt. 9.54.1; Thuc. 2.39.1; Aristoph. *Acharnians* 308; *Peace* 622–23, 1064–68; *Lysistrata* 629).

Andromache continues by claiming that she died when both Troy and Hector fell. She does not spare Menelaus, saying that he fled from Hector's spear. Harping on his cowardice, she mocks Menelaus for arming himself in hoplite armour in order to kill a woman: 'Kill on!' (459, Kovacs) she taunts him. She won't reduce herself to flattery so he might spare her; after all, she was once quite as great in Troy as he is in Sparta, and who says that the reversal that befell her might not one day happen to him. Andromache remains defiant in facing death. However, as she and her son are led bound with ropes into the house, the cruelty of the situation produces a change in Andromache as a mother. She now sings a threnody (501–36) with a tone of despair that was not present before. The boy joins his mother in a glyconic song. Andromache's spirit is nearly broken, and she tells her son to plead with Menelaus to spare his life, which may be seen as a forerunner to Hecuba's directive to Polyxena in *Hecuba* (424 BCE) asking Odysseus to spare her young life and not to sacrifice her on the tomb of Achilles (334–41). Menelaus shows himself in his two replies to the innocent people whom he has condemned to death to be not only evil but heartless and callous. He helps only his own, he says, and although it is Hermione who will decide the boy's fate, his advice would be not to leave any enemy alive, and he sees both of them as enemies. Similar logic will be espoused by Odysseus in *Trojan Women* (415 BCE) in his recommendation to throw Astyanax from the walls of Troy (721–25), although Astyanax is only an infant. Menelaus tells the boy that he can feel no love for him because he has spent a fair portion of his life capturing Troy and his mother. Menelaus uses the moment when the young boy pleads for his life to tell him that he dies because of his mother: 'It is thanks to her [your mother] that you now go down to the Underworld' (543–44, Kovacs). It is hard to top this cruel and obnoxious man.

Until she realizes that her son will definitely be put to death, Andromache remains as calm when facing Menelaus as she was clear-headed when facing Hermione. Furthermore, she remains fearless, despite her looming execution. She proves herself to be a loving, devoted mother who is willing to give up her own life to save her son. It is only when her son is on the brink of death that her spirit nears breaking point. Her words to her son are as full of tenderness as they are of despair.

Andromache and Peleus

We hear in the prologue that Andromache has sent numerous messengers to alert Peleus to the peril she and her son are facing, but both she and the Maidservant assume that none of the messengers cared enough about Andromache to deliver the message (82). Once the Maidservant reaches him, Peleus comes immediately. His arrival is almost too late and must have created a moment of great suspense in the audience.

Upon his arrival, when he sees Andromache and her son bound by rope, Peleus ignores Menelaus and addresses Andromache, asking her on what charges these men bound her and her son (555–57). At the sight of Peleus, Andromache's bearing and confidence return. She prefaces her reply with a reproach for Peleus' tardiness: 'It was not by a single eager summons that I sent for you but by countless messengers' (561–62, Kovacs). She also assumes that Peleus has heard of the charges levelled against her by Hermione and does not answer Peleus' question, but pleads for help. It takes courage and self-assurance to refuse to answer Peleus, implying a further rebuke to the old man: he knew about the contentious rivalry between her and Hermione, but still did not come to her aid, a reality that her enemies counted on, knowing Neoptolemus was abroad and she and her son were all alone (568–70). Although Andromache is explicitly scared of deceit, as will be discussed below (752–56), she gratuitously uses some trickery and lies in order to save herself and her son. Knowing how dear Thetis' shrine is to Peleus, she insinuates in her tale to the old man that Menelaus violated the shrine, by saying that his men '*dragged*' her from the altar of Thetis (*apospasantes*, 565–67). This is not true, as she walked freely out of the shrine, albeit under duress. Neither Menelaus nor his attendants had desecrated the temple by applying *physical* force. However, this pitiful lying was unlikely to prevent the Athenian audience from sympathizing with her. Andromache must be saying this to inflame Peleus, exactly as Antigone lies to incite Ismene, when she tells her that Creon has already buried Eteocles, while Polyneices is still unburied (Sophocles, *Antigone* 23–25).[17] However, the concept of a blameless Andromache is so pervasive through the ages, that even modern scholarship looks to explain away her lying by stating that even though she does not tell the truth about Menelaus, 'the charges against him are in essence justified'.[18] However, there might be another reason for describing her as deceitful. Ample scholarly observations, both of the tragedies and of the behaviour of Athenian women, point to numerous associations between 'femininity' and deceit, as well as to the anxiety that women's purported deceitfulness aroused in men.[19] With many of the avenues of action open to men being far beyond the reach of women, the heroines of Greek tragedy need to find alternatives, one of which is deception.[20] This kind of gratuitous lying on Andromache's part can be seen as part of the playwright's attempts to make her compliant with the male spectators' expectations of a woman, springing from societal, institutionalized misogyny.

Andromache's second exchange with Peleus happens after Peleus has managed to drive Menelaus from Phthia and rescue her and her son. As Peleus takes the boy under his arm, telling Molossus to lead him to Pharsalus, and soothes both Andromache and his great-grandson, Andromache is all of a sudden fearful, an emotion she has not yet shown. She is not bashful about telling Peleus that his old age might induce Menelaus' men to ambush them where the road is deserted and recapture them (750–56). In short, she has no confidence that Peleus can protect her and Molossus. By this comment Andromache shows that she is a fast learner: she has been tricked by Menelaus once, and there is nothing to deter the conceited and devious Spartan from trying to set a trap for the old Peleus when he is most vulnerable, on an isolated road with a weak woman and a young boy. Her words also show that she feels confident enough in her past royal stature to admonish a king who has just saved her life.

Summary

In *Andromache*, Euripides builds on the Homeric image of Andromache as the iconic wife and mother, who has become the 'victimized' heroine *par excellence.* Although she is a slave and a concubine to Neoptolemus, the prevailing image of her is that of a grieving widow and a mother who lost her young son after the sack of Troy and is almost rendered childless again. She has retained her royal stature and behaves with dignity despite the threats she faces. Her one overriding concern is to save the life of her child. Tragedy inherited Andromache's image as the perfect wife and suffering widow from the Homeric epic, and no extant drama has countered this description. As Mary Lefkowitz states: 'Andromache has every female virtue: loyalty to her husband, willingness to die to save her child, kindness, good judgment and intelligence.'[21]

As a new development, in *Andromache* Euripides puts in her mouth utterances of anti-female moralizing that are usually found mostly in male expressions (e.g. 269–73, 353–54). This serves to further enhance her positive evaluation in men's eyes. Furthermore, Euripides has gifted Andromache with a sharp wit and with the ability to hold her own rhetorically with her sparring partners. Although the formal debates in the first part of Andromache's appearances are not signposted, most likely because the frequent scenes of personal conflict and passion require a natural flow of argument rather than strictly formal structuring, Andromache's masterful rhetoric comes out clearly in her debates with both Hermione and Menelaus.[22] While adroit rhetoric usually carries the negative associations of a deceitful woman displaying masculine traits, this is not the case with Andromache, since like Hecuba she fails in spite of her skilful rhetoric.[23] In the same way that Hecuba will depend upon Agamemnon's assistance, Andromache is still a 'damsel in distress' needing the physical help that a man, in this case Peleus, can provide.

Hermione

Hermione, the daughter of Menelaus and Helen, does not appear in the Homeric epics. In tragedy, besides *Andromache* she appears in Euripides' *Orestes*, where Orestes, having committed matricide, is facing a death sentence, together with his sister Electra. In a desperate attempt to gain help from Menelaus, Orestes and Pylades, who has come to the aid of his cousins, hold Hermione hostage. Amid the violence, while Orestes is holding his sword to Hermione's throat, Apollo appears as *deus ex machina* and resolves the situation for all of the characters. Orestes, Pylades, and Electra will be granted their freedom, on certain conditions. Pylades will marry Electra, and, after purifying himself, Orestes will marry Hermione. In *Andromache*, although it transpires that she had at one point been promised to Orestes,

Hermione is Neoptolemus' legitimate wife. However, she has been unable to bear children. The widowed Andromache, now Neoptolemus' concubine, has given birth to his son. Feeling intense jealousy, Hermione plans to have Andromache put to death, claiming that the concubine is poisoning her womb.

Hermione appears in two episodes of the play situated in the first and second halves of the drama. In the first episode, bolstered by her father's presence in Phthia, she bitterly wrangles with Andromache, having resolved to see both Andromache and her son die. In the fourth episode, after her plans have been thwarted by the arrival of Peleus, and abandoned by her father, she falls into a wild panic. Desperate as she belatedly imagines the likely magnitude of Neoptolemus' wrath when he discovers she had intended to kill his son, Hermione is now planning to kill herself.

Hermione is not liked by anyone. The Chorus of Phthian women express their sympathy for the Asian Andromache from their first choral song, even though they are Phthian. They show only fear of Hermione. Although Hermione herself is Spartan and not Phthian, nevertheless she is the wife of the ruler, and it is significant that a Chorus of Neoptolemus' subjects have not a good word to say about his wife. This strongly reinforces the impression of the queen's character that the two Trojans, Andromache and her Maidservant, have already created for the audience.

Hermione's apparent goal is to save her marriage, or at least the societal status granted to her through her marriage. In spite of this, she not only does nothing to improve her marriage but actually puts it in jeopardy by planning for her husband's son to be put to death. Furthermore, she does not seem particularly interested in her relationship with Neoptolemus, never expressing concern for his wellbeing. Indeed, Hermione seems hardly conscious of the needs or wellbeing of anyone around her, being solely and exquisitely aware of her own self-interest, and as far as Hermione is concerned, without marriage a woman is 'as good as dead'. She must have heard this wisdom from her father, who states that the sole reason he came to aid his daughter was because 'I think it is a serious matter to be deprived of one's mate. Any other misfortunes a woman may suffer are secondary, but if she loses her husband, she loses her life' (371–73, Kovacs).

During her first appearance, Hermione is parading in a gold spangled gown, while luxurious gold adorns her head and neck (147–48). Her emphasis on her wealth and appearance not only reflect her vanity, which might be characteristic of her youth, but also perhaps indicate her lack of self-confidence. She needs external finery to confirm her married status and rank in society. When her father deserts her and she is faced with the consequences of her actions, she disintegrates mentally. The contrast between Andromache's composure when facing death and Hermione's devastation on realizing that Neoptolemus might send her away from his household, in other words divorce her, is particularly noticeable. Hermione apparently sees no way forward once she loses the accoutrements afforded her by her marriage. To exhibit this visually, she casts away her veil, which in Sparta was the marker of a married woman, and exposes her hair which must have been covered with the veil at her first entrance (830–31, 147).[24] In addition to uncovering her head, she also exposes her breasts by tearing her gorgeous robe (832–33),[25] both symbols of her lost status and dignity as a married woman.

From the start Hermione is cast as the antithesis to the good and devoted wife represented by Andromache. Although she enters beautifully adorned with finery from her dowry (147–48), she has no internal beauty, using her wealth as a tool to degrade Neoptolemus' house.[26] Her clothes and accoutrements do not originate from the House of Neoptolemus or Peleus, Hermione arrogantly states, but are brought from Sparta together with her large dowry (149–53). The implication is not only that the house of her husband is not rich enough, which casts aspersions on Neoptolemus, but also that she is financially independent of Neoptolemus and can therefore speak freely (153), as she says to the Chorus ([ὑμᾶς, *hymās*154]). Usually, the bridegroom seeks to provide a better home for his bride than she had before, but apparently this has not been the case with Hermione and Neoptolemus. Wealth means a lot to Hermione; she believes that her expensive dowry gives her licence to behave as she chooses. Her speech displays vanity, pride, jealousy, selfish cruelty, and impiety.

Her extravagant dress, visually attesting her high status as a royal wife, contrasts starkly with the appearance of Andromache, who is a mere captive concubine and probably dressed accordingly. However, in spite of all her proclamations of superiority, Hermione has so far failed as a wife. A wife is supposed to provide her husband with an heir, assuring that his bloodline will continue. Hermione has not given birth to a child, which also differentiates her from Andromache, but to her chagrin not in a positive way. Trying to divert the responsibility for her childlessness from herself, Hermione accuses Andromache of using drugs that make her barren and thus hated by her husband. Andromache, on the other hand, while not countering the claim that Neoptolemus hates his wife, which is probably a euphemism for his sexual disinterest in her, she points out that Hermione is impossible to live with (205–6), hence Neoptolemus' sexual disinterest. Indeed, later myth gives Hermione and Orestes a son, Tisamenus, she is not marked as sterile.[27] Her barrenness might just be a matter of conjecture on her part, and blaming the Asian captive might be a good excuse to explain her childlessness to those outside the house, like Peleus, who is aware of his grandson's failure to produce a child with her (709–11). The entire stichomythia between Andromache and Hermione, in which Andromache directs Hermione to refrain from speaking of 'shameful things' and to 'suffer in silence your troubles in love' (238, 240, Kovacs), is in fact referring to Hermione's sex life with Neoptolemus, about which Hermione obviously feels that she should be able to speak freely (242). In her confusion, the young woman somehow mixes up the two ideas of Neoptolemus shunning her bed and the possibility that she is barren. She finds an easy solution for both problems by blaming Andromache firstly for attracting Neoptolemus' attentions away from his legitimate wife and secondly for poisoning her womb.

With its repeated references to the intrigue or rather dishonour, sordidness, and suffering resulting from two women sharing one man's bed, *Andromache* is Euripides' 'tragedy of sex' as much as *Women of Trachis* is that of Sophocles.[28] *Andromache*, however, depicts a young woman yearning for her husband's attention, unlike the older Deianeira, who feels threatened by the young and beautiful captive, Iole. Blaming a woman for using poison against her foes is a recurrent theme used against women. As is the case with Hermione, such accusations may be made by an angry or hostile woman, who lacks the ability to fight her adversary in a direct trial of strength.[29] Hermione's accusation smacks of internalized misogyny, even though it is very well suited to the context within which it occurs.

It seems that Hermione is irked by Andromache's lack of humility, compounded by the elevated status the concubine must hold in the House of Neoptolemus (see p. 63). She says to Andromache, that '... if ... some god or mortal should decide to save you, you must abandon the pride of your former wealth, and cower abjectly and fall at my knees and sweep my house, sprinkling Achelous-water with your hand from golden jars, and recognize where you are in the world. This is a Greek city, and there is no Hector here nor Priam with his gold' (163–69, Lloyd).[30] Hermione's youth and unformed personality are well presented in her lack of clarity about what is to be done to Andromache. On the one hand, Hermione has decided to kill Andromache before Neoptolemus returns, either by making Andromache leave the altar or by setting fire to the altar (161–62, 245, 255, 257). On the other hand, Hermione allows for the possibility that Andromache will in the future be sweeping the floors of the house.

Hermione's immature and unformed personality resurfaces in the second half of the play, when she finds herself abandoned by her father. All of the confidence she exhibited in the first half of the play, which evaporates in the second half, must have derived from Menelaus' presence. Hermione's mental collapse is preceded by the third stasimon, in which the Chorus start with a general strophe claiming they would prefer not to be born unless they had noble parents and lived in an exceedingly wealthy home because 'if one were to suffer something beyond remedy, there is no lack of resource for the well-born' (767–71, Lloyd). The Chorus then continue, turning the epode into an encomium for Peleus, noting his past heroic achievements. Euripides, however, then abruptly shatters the comparative tranquillity reached during the choral ode. In sharp contrast with the idyllic notion of a wealthy princess who has abundant resources at her fingertips, the audience learn that the high-born Hermione now wants to commit suicide after suffering adversity. She seems to have no personal resources at all to fall back on to save herself.

Menelaus clearly has not followed Peleus' directive to the letter. He left, as he was told, but he neglected to take Hermione with him. Now bereft of her father's protection (805, 854) Hermione is at her wit's end, having lost any capacity for logical and sequential thought: she wishes to die out of fear of dying. She wants to kill herself by a sword, a noose, a fire, or to leap from a cliff out of fear that her husband might kill her. The Nurse must be correct in thinking that in actuality she is afraid of being banished by Neoptolemus, in other words being divorced (809). Following her father's logic, a woman without a husband is as good as dead; and Hermione is certain that Neoptolemus will not forgive her for planning to kill his concubine and his son. Tossing off her veil and ripping her dress, thereby exposing her breasts, are the visual gestures of her realization that she has lost the status of being a married woman (829–35, 857–58). The Nurse, understanding Hermione's real fear, tries to console her by arguing that Neoptolemus will not reject his marriage with a daughter of a noble man so quickly, just for the sake of a barbarian, but her words fall on deaf ears. Hermione is utterly shattered by having been abandoned by the father whom she trusted (869–76).

While both the Nurse and the Chorus assume that Hermione feels remorse and a moral sense of guilt for what she intended to do to Andromache and her son (805–6, 814–15, 822–23), Hermione dwells not so much on the evil she intended, as on the retribution that she will suffer. That she continues to resent Andromache whole-heartedly, without any self-recrimination, is betrayed by her comment to Orestes that Peleus prevented her from killing the slave-woman 'by honouring those who are weaker' (*kakionas*, 914, Lloyd). The departure of her father has led her to reflect not so much on the crime she and her father intended to commit, as on her current situation. She knows that there can be no forgiveness for an attempted murder, as is evidenced by the fact that she begs Orestes:

But I beseech you in the name of Zeus the god of kindred, take
me from this land, as far as possible, or to my father's palace.

(920–22, Lloyd)

Both Hermione and her father are inclined to shun responsibility for their acts. Hermione seeks to put the responsibility for her crime upon other women. When Menelaus puts the life of Neoptolemus' son in Hermione's hands, Hermione claims innocence through temporary 'foolishness' (*mōria*, 938) that allowed her to listen to the incitement of evil women and act upon it. The women were relentless, she claims, in inciting her:

> Will you put up with that wretched captive slave-woman in your
> house sharing your bed? By Hera, in my house she would certainly
> not have enjoyed the use of my bed and lived to see the light of day.
>
> (932–35, Lloyd)

Whether the event happened or not, the story is a good one.[31] It works in her favour in her current situation with regard to the on-stage audience, namely Orestes, but less so in terms of the well-read spectators, who might have remembered Semonides' poem in which a wife who sits among women where they talk about sex is the opposite of the man-beloved Bee Woman who makes the house of her husband prosper (9.90–91). The gossiping women sparked her jealousy of Andromache and prevented her from thinking rationally, she claims. She now realizes that she had possessed everything she needed: she had wealth, she was the mistress of the house, 'and I would have borne legitimate children, while she would have borne bastards with half-slave parentage to serve my children' (939–42, Kovacs). It is noteworthy that Hermione, who might be looking forward to marrying Orestes and bearing children with him, now offers a different reason for her childlessness. She still blames Andromache for her situation, but not for having poisoned her womb. Rather, she claims that the concubine enticed Neoptolemus away from the bed of his legitimate wife (904–8). Facts have a way of shifting in Hermione's mind.

It is amazing how Hermione, who was only a step away from hysteria a few moments earlier, suddenly gains sufficient control over her nerves not only to concoct a good excuse about being riled by gossiping women, but also to deliver a coherent speech advising husbands about closeting away their wives. There is no reason to suppose that her hysterical anguish and supposed remorse prior to Orestes' arrival were contrived for the sake of Neoptolemus, so that he would hear of her anguished contrition upon his return. It is not that upon seeing Orestes, who is her potential means of rescue, she sheds her hysterical pretence, but rather that she is so volatile that her mindset changes from one instant to the next. She instantaneously moves from a state of collapse to feverish explanations of her behaviour, assembling a rational and acceptable explanation for her former criminal plotting.[32] Euripides excels in portraying young women who, when confronting danger, become utterly unstable.

Hermione's unbalanced and volatile behaviour is similar to the Electra Euripides will later create, whose anxiety while awaiting the news as to whether her brother has succeeded in killing Aegisthus and has himself survived brings her to such a frenzy that she wants to commit suicide, assuming the worst. Once Orestes returns, Electra recovers from her inner turmoil immediately, going on to sing Orestes' praises, and has sufficiently collected herself moments later to participate in her mother's murder (*El.* 746–70).[33]

Hermione's reaction, on coming back to her senses upon seeing Orestes, is to try to avoid any blame for her actions, by delivering a disturbingly misogynistic attack on her own gender:

> But never, never (for I will not say it only once)
> should married men, if they have any sense, allow
> women to visit their wife at home. For they are teachers
> of evil: one helps to corrupt the marriage for gain,
> another because she has fallen and wants someone
> to share her shame, and many because of
> wantonness. The result is that men's homes are
> afflicted. Guard well the doors of your homes
> against this with bolts and bars; for the visits
> of women from outside accomplish nothing
> wholesome, but many evils instead.
>
> (943–53, Lloyd)

While some of what she says was heard from Hippolytus on the dramatic stage only three years earlier (Euripides, *Hippolytus* 616–68), the novelty here is that it is now a woman who is hurling vile accusations against her own gender. The monstrosity of this is felt by the Chorus of Phthian women who reprimand her:

> You have hurled your tongue too violently at your
> own sex. To be sure, this is pardonable in your case,
> but still women ought to cover up women's frailties.
>
> (954–56, Kovacs)

It is noteworthy that the Chorus do not oppose the accusations that Hermione mounts against women, but only the fact that she 'tells' on them. This is another example of internalized misogyny, but again unlike Andromache's, it is well contextualized.

After Orestes shamelessly explains to her why he would like to marry her, Hermione is *compos mentis* enough to tell him that it is her father's decision as to whom she will marry; but nevertheless, she asks him to remove her quickly from her house so her husband won't come and 'catch her'. She also fears that if Peleus hears that she is about to leave her home, he will come after her with horses in hot pursuit (987–92), although it would be unclear to the off-stage audience why he would do this. They have already heard Peleus say that he objected to this marriage of his grandson (619–2, cf. 1186–91). Euripides does not let his audience know what Hermione's response was to Orestes' prediction that Neoptolemus would die in Delphi by falling into his, Orestes', trap. As usual, she is interested only in herself, and she leaves together with her cousin.

Summary

Hermione is depicted as a young woman entirely absorbed in herself. Her main concern is for her social status, which is conferred, in her eyes, by marriage and wealth. She seems utterly confused about cause and effect in general. She fails to see her own actions as a cause for her husband shunning her, or his absence from her bed as a cause for her inability to bear children. It is easier for her to find a scapegoat for all of her ills, with that scapegoat being Andromache. Hermione is devoid of conscience and of ethical principles. Her preferred remedy for her childlessness is murdering both Andromache and probably also her son with Neoptolemus. She is so oblivious of the effects of her own actions that she does not for one moment think about the possible consequences of such an act. She also is completely unaware of the inner workings of her own household, not realizing that since he married her, Neoptolemus has not shared Andromache's bed. While she flaunts her wealthy background, her privileges and her youth seem to have left her lacking in inner resources to fall back on in the face of adversity. It is only with the appearance of another male who can replace her husband that Hermione regains her equilibrium. In the words of Grube, Hermione is 'the Athenian conception of a typical Spartan woman: luxurious and licentious, with all her father's contempt for a mere barbarian; the immodesty of which Peleus so emphatically accuses Spartan women, is strikingly illustrated in her scene with Orestes. She is throughout the daughter of Helen, whose beauty brought so many evils – including the situation so powerfully dramatized – upon Greece.'[34]

Menelaus and Peleus

The characterizations of Hermione's father Menelaus and Neoptolemus' grandfather Peleus contrast strongly with each other, but are formed to a large extent both by their interactions with each other, and by the differences between them; and so, they will be dealt with together. Menelaus is cast as a type of a *miles gloriosus* peppered with conceit and duplicity. He is depicted as an arrogant and self-congratulating man who considers himself the paradigm of a Homeric hero, but runs away when the elderly Peleus tells him to leave. He thinks that by finding Molossus he has proven himself smarter than Andromache, for which he commends himself (312–13). However, he actually proves himself to be cowardly, indecisive, irresponsible, conniving, and treacherous. By contrast, Peleus, whose old age is the characteristic that receives the most attention in the play, displays the stalwart traits of a true, if aged, Phthian hero, refusing to be cowed by his grandson's heavily armed father-in-law, standing his ground holding only his sceptre. In his dealings with Menelaus, Peleus is relentless and shows no respect for the king of Sparta.

The contrasts between Menelaus and Peleus seem to distil the contrasts between their respective ancestral families: the House of Atreus, mythically associated with deceit and treachery over several generations, as opposed to the House of the heroic Aeacus, a just ruler, ancestor of the famed warriors Peleus, Achilles, and Neoptolemus. If we accept that, to a certain extent, *Andromache* presents a microcosm of the Trojan War, then we can see many parallels between Menelaus' behaviour in the War and in this tragedy, even if the action in *Andromache* takes place in a confined, domestic arena, rather than in the grand scale of all-out war between nations. Although there are many possible origins of the Trojan War, one potential starting point is Menelaus' rage on discovering that his wife has left, willingly or otherwise, with Paris, the young Trojan Prince, who ostensibly had arrived in Sparta to sign a peace treaty. Notwithstanding the involvement of the gods, and particularly the goddess Aphrodite, who supposedly ignited a flaming passion between Paris and Helen, Menelaus could be accused of having behaved recklessly in allowing the attractive young visitor to meet his beautiful wife at all. We may even suggest that by his lack of caution in leaving Helen unguarded, Menelaus inadvertently set the tragic events of the Trojan War in motion. Agamemnon, his brother, leads a fleet of a thousand ships on his behalf, representing a broad coalition of Greek nations against Troy. After the demands of Menelaus and his allies to have Helen and all the treasures that she took with her returned are rejected, the fighting takes a heavy toll on both sides, before the Greeks take Troy by the deception of the Trojan horse. This ruse eventually causes the destruction of an entire city. In *Andromache*, Menelaus almost sets a domestic tragedy in motion by again charging into someone else's home, this time the palace of Neoptolemus, the absent Phthian king, and insisting his demands be met. Rather than planning all-out war, he is now orchestrating the murder of a concubine and her young son, who just happens to be the son of Neoptolemus. Menelaus' rash behaviour could have caused the end of two dynasties at once: that of Peleus, if Molossus had been killed, and his own, if Neoptolemus had killed Hermione in revenge.[35]

Menelaus also serves as the representative of Sparta against whom both Andromache and Peleus utter fully justified invectives. Even before they speak, both Spartans, Menelaus and Hermione, initially stun the audience by their inappropriate appearances. Hermione comes on stage decked in finery from her dowry; a luxurious dress more fit for a formal celebration than everyday wear. Similarly, when Menelaus arrives in Phthia to help his daughter save her marriage from the menace of a captive concubine, he is attired as a fully armed warrior (458). The reason for this, as with Hermione's excessive finery, is obscure. Is he going to fight a captive woman? He knows that Neoptolemus is not at home, so it is unlikely that he has prepared himself to attack his son-in-law. In fact, his portrayal as a heavily armed soldier only offers his opponents the opportunity to mock him. Andromache capitalizes on his appearance to make fun of him, focusing on his armour, unnecessary for killing a woman (458–60, see also p. 40 this volume). She prefaces her comment by reminding Menelaus that Hector chased him from the battlefield, forcing him to take refuge on his ship (456–57).

Soon after his entrance, Menelaus stoops to deceitfully tricking Andromache into leaving the shrine of Thetis, promising her that if she does so, she will be killed but her son, whose hiding place he has discovered, will be spared (314–18, 380–83). However, once she comes out, Menelaus tells Andromache that her son's fate is in the hands of his daughter, and his recommendation would be to kill him (518–22). Menelaus is depicted as being not only dishonest, but also as having a particularly callous nature when facing opponents who are not able to defend themselves. This cruelty is effectively portrayed in his reply to the anguished pleas of Andromache's son: 'Dear friend, dear friend, spare my life!' and 'O alas! How long must I suffer pain?' (530–31, 535–36, Kovacs), to which Menelaus haughtily and emotionlessly replies:

> Why do you fall before me, entreating
> me when I am like some sea-beaten
> cliff or ocean wave? I help my kin, but
> I have no cause to love you since I
> expended a great part of my soul
> in capturing Troy and with it
> your mother. It is
> thanks to her that you now go down to the Underworld!
>
> (537–44, Kovacs)

The shameless repetition of the gist of Patroclus' famous words to Achilles in Homer, *Iliad* 16.33–35, and the appropriation of characteristics given to Achilles, immediately call for a comparison between the two heroes in the spectators' minds, greatly to Menelaus' disadvantage. In his words Menelaus proves himself to be not only stony-hearted, but sadistic too. His insufferable personality only becomes more intolerable when he takes full credit for the Greek victory over Troy. He is lucky that Peleus is not yet present (and that Achilles and Agamemnon are dead!). When Menelaus tells the child that he is about to die because of his mother, Menelaus has reached a new pinnacle of human degradation. He thus appears true not only to his adopted country of Sparta, but also to his ancestral lineage, coming as he does from the House of Atreus, whose ancestors from Tantalus and Pelops, through Atreus and Thyestes were all infamous for their deceit and trickery. Their cruelty also often involved the heartless and horrendous murder of young children. Peleus, the Phthian, demonstrates that, like his son, he too is the antithesis of these villains.

The pathetic hollowness of Menelaus' attempt to appear as a great warrior resurfaces immediately upon the appearance of the indomitable old Peleus. Peleus has arrived to aid Andromache and her son when the two have already been tightly bound, and are on the very brink of their impending death. Andromache had previously appealed many times for his help, and the audience do not discover the reason for his tardiness. While we don't know what delayed Peleus, from his conduct we might need to accept the Maidservant's view that none of the messengers Andromache had sent really cared enough about her to deliver her pleas to the old man (82). Andromache accepts her maid's opinion, and yet reproaches Peleus for his tardiness (561–62), to which Peleus does not respond. Peleus is also well aware of the frailty of his old age. As he walks towards the bound Andromache, he realizes that he has come just in time. He asks the Maidservant to lead him more quickly: 'this is no time for me to dally but, now if ever, to recover my youthful strength' (551–53, Lloyd). Immediately upon his arrival, Peleus focuses on the matter at hand. He had obviously been aware of the general situation between Andromache and Hermione and orders her to be released immediately (577–78), but the order is countermanded by Menelaus. It is only at the end of the scene between Peleus and Menelaus that Peleus himself unties Andromache's tight bonds (717–18).

Upon seeing the bound Andromache, Peleus is appalled that Menelaus dares to come to Neoptolemus' house and take his grandson's concubine as if she were his own (582). He is not willing to agree with Menelaus' claim that the house is also his, since he and Neoptolemus are related and replies with an aphorism to this claim of Menelaus: 'Yes, to treat well, not ill, and not to kill by the sword' (586, Kovacs). Bent on defending Molossus, his great-grandson, Peleus does not care that the boy's mother is not a Greek. In contrast with Menelaus, Peleus is concerned with a person's inherent value, rather than their ethnicity. He has no patience for Menelaus' tirade about the need for purity in those who rule Greece.

In response to Menelaus' arrogant speeches, Peleus launches into violent verbal assaults against Menelaus in particular and against Sparta in two speeches (590–641, 693–726). In his verbal onslaughts, Peleus makes full use of Menelaus' best-known weakness: Helen's elopement. While the Phthian king excoriates Spartan women as a group for their lack of modesty, he focuses particularly on Helen as the most wanton of all women (594–95). Menelaus should have been glad to get rid of her, but instead he inflicted the Trojan War on Greece to get her back. One can feel the deep bitterness of a father who lost a son and who now stands quarrelling with a man he considers responsible for his son's death. Peleus thinks Menelaus should not have made that much of losing such a promiscuous woman as Helen (605–13), reminding the spectators of a similar comment made by Andromache to Menelaus when she attempts to dissuade him from interfering so deliberately in the disagreement between herself and Hermione: 'You should not repay trifling injuries with great', she tells him (352, Kovacs). The message is that Menelaus tends to exaggerate everything he does, as, for example, in fully arming himself to face a suppliant woman. Peleus also brutally faults Hermione, the only daughter Menelaus has with Helen. Not only is her character blemished by having the depraved Helen as her mother, but it is further tainted by her being a sterile woman who cannot tolerate others having children. Peleus clearly states that unless Menelaus leaves Neoptolemus' house at once, together with his daughter, when he returns Neoptolemus will drag her by the hair through his house and drive her out (708–10). He proceeds to loosen Andromache's ropes, ignoring Menelaus' objection, which further minimizes Menelaus, who considers himself a great hero.

Considering the loathing of barbarians Menelaus exhibits, Peleus' reminder that 'you were deprived of your wife by a mere Phrygian' (592, cf. 602–4, Kovacs) must have stung. Peleus accuses Menelaus of gathering a great throng of soldiers and causing a massive loss of men on behalf of a wanton woman whom Menelaus should have left in Troy. Peleus also knows well how proud Menelaus is of his status as a warrior in the Trojan War and therefore focuses on 'debunking' the glorious War and thus depriving Menelaus of his cherished claim to fame. The two nearly come to blows. Even though Peleus is only armed with his sceptre when he confronts Menelaus, who is equipped with heavy weaponry, Menelaus gives in. Peleus furiously threatens to trounce the armoured warrior with his sceptre, whereupon

Menelaus, who must have stepped back, does not do much more than counter Peleus' threat with a double dare. This comic scene, in which an old man threatens to thrash the 'great Greek general' that Menelaus pretends to be, shows Menelaus as the coward he is, evincing his true nature as a spineless man with no fortitude. The grandiose armour also offers Peleus a chance to scornfully taunt Menelaus, saying bitterly that while Achilles fell fighting at Troy:

> You alone came back from Troy without a scratch,
> and you took your fine armor in its fine case to Troy
> and brought it back in the same condition.

(616–18, Kovacs)

The implication is that Menelaus failed to fight at all. Mocking someone is tantamount to dishonouring them in the value system of the Homeric hero, but Menelaus does not seem to rise to Peleus' goading on this theme. Although in the *Iliad* Menelaus is not depicted as a poor warrior, even if not one of the foremost heroes,[36] he fails to counter Peleus' accusation, even though he does later respond to accusations made regarding Helen.

Does Menelaus' arrogance make him see this ferocious onslaught as beneath him? His interest resides in the 'legality' of what he pursues rather than in the personal consequences to those around him: he is allowed to deal with Neoptolemus' household because they are related (374–76) and their property should be considered common (376–77). He sees his trickery of Andromache as justifiable revenge (438), never mind how abominable the murder of a helpless captive woman and her young son might be.[37] The lack of emotion in his reaction might be related to his realization that he is facing a man who will not accept his murderous act, and whom he does not wish to further enrage. After all, Peleus is the reigning king of Phthia with an army close by.

At the same time, Menelaus is no mean rhetorician, although he mostly uses general clichés in answer to Peleus' specific *ad hominem* accusations. He chooses first to find common ground with Peleus as a member of the best families of Greece. After all, as Peleus is the father of Achilles and husband to a goddess, he certainly is on par with the renowned Atreidae. As such he should be as prejudiced against foreigners as Menelaus. He too should wish to uphold the purity of Greek rulers and join Menelaus in hating the Trojans indiscriminately. Furthermore, Andromache is related to Paris, who killed Achilles, Menelaus states, as if Peleus did not know this. Menelaus' anti-barbarian incitement also helps him to evade Peleus' charge that he led an army on account of his disgraceful wife. By killing Andromache, he, Menelaus, had Peleus' interest at heart as much as his own:

... if my daughter is childless and this woman
has children, will you set them up as kings
over the land of Phthia, and will they,
barbarians by birth, rule over Greeks?

(663–66, Kovacs)

The thought should horrify Peleus as it does him. Peleus remains silent, because Menelaus, who otherwise considers himself intelligent, is utterly oblivious that what Peleus is most interested in is his legacy, the continuation of his bloodline (710–14, see Chapter 3). Andromache has provided this; Hermione has not. When Peleus makes no response to Menelaus' xenophobic remarks, the Spartan retreats to the most explicit point at hand, his age advantage: 'You are an old man, old man!' (678, Kovacs), he tells Peleus, as if Peleus' preference for justice in the form of sparing life over revenge (438) were a matter of age rather than morality.[38] However, despite Menelaus' taunts about his old age, it is Peleus who consistently shows the younger man what true strength of character is.

According to Peleus, Menelaus' complete submission to Helen was obvious when after retrieving her, he abstained from killing her, kissing her after she had exposed her breasts (627–31). Should the audience remember this comment when later in the play Hermione exposes her breasts? Should they conclude that Menelaus' daughter learned her behaviour from her mother, and was thinking of bewitching her husband who she believes would be willing to kill her? This does not speak well of the education Hermione received, as she appears to emulate her mother. Peleus seems to have been concerned about the possible influence of the mother on the daughter, when his disdain for Helen and for the House of Menelaus spilled into his objection to his grandson's marrying Hermione, the daughter of such a worthless woman. He admits that he warned Neoptolemus against marrying the daughter of the base mother 'for such daughters reproduce their mothers' faults' (619–22, Kovacs).

In contrast to the somewhat risible figure Menelaus presents, Peleus must be very positively received by the off-stage audience. Not only does he stand for what is 'right' in this situation, which comes down to not murdering a helpless woman and her son, but he also becomes a spokesman for the common folk when he bids Menelaus to take his daughter away, saying:

It is better for mortals
to have a good poor man as father-in-law
and friend than a bad rich one.

(639–41, Lloyd)

Peleus goes further in his second speech by pointing out the injustices of glory and honour in the army. In war, he states, generals always get far more credit than they deserve, a thought that was especially true of Agamemnon and Menelaus (693–98, 704–5). This is particularly poignant coming from Peleus, who lost his son, the greatest hero of them all, in the War. By emphasizing this concept, Peleus deprives Menelaus of his one cherished claim to fame. The victories are won by the simple soldiers, but the 'general takes the credit. He wields his spear as one among countless others, and does no more work than one, but has more renown' (697–98, Lloyd). Peleus specifically focuses on Menelaus and his brother who 'sit back, puffed up by Troy and by your generalship there, exalted by the toil and labour of others' (703–5, Lloyd), he tells Menelaus.

Peleus also brings up Menelaus' heartlessness and villainy in 'ordering' his brother Agamemnon to sacrifice his daughter Iphigeneia, so that the fleet could set sail against Troy to recover his wanton wife (624–25). The tightness of Andromache's bonds and the needlessness of such torture are indicative of Menelaus' cruelty, to which Peleus draws attention:

> Did you, villain, disfigure her hand so cruelly?
> Was it a bull or a lion you thought you were
> tying up with these knots? Or were you afraid
> That she might take a sword and avenge herself on you?
>
> (719–22, Kovacs)

Both of Peleus' diatribes against Menelaus are aggressive and violent (590–641, 693–716). He touches on every possible weakness or liability exhibited by Menelaus and his family: Helen's elopement; the multitude of lives lost in the War that Menelaus caused by insisting on bringing Helen back; manipulating Agamemnon into sacrificing Iphigeneia; Menelaus' cowardice and his final affront to all those who had lost loved ones in the War, that is, excusing Helen. After such a brutal assault, one would expect Menelaus to offer an equally heated reply. Instead, we find him calm and calculated, as if there were a hollowness of spirit at the core of his character that prevents him from getting perturbed.

Menelaus does answer Peleus' remonstration over his treatment of Helen and spins his behaviour in a rather sophistic way. He argues that Helen got into trouble not of her own accord but by the will of gods. This excuse also happens to be apt for Menelaus and his daughter, neither of whom take responsibility for their actions. However, Menelaus does not stop at exculpating Helen; he also prides himself on not having killed her as an example of his self-restraint. Furthermore, he argues, the War benefitted the

Greeks who were 'inexperienced in arms and battle, they progressed to bravery. We learn everything from meeting other people' (682–84, Lloyd). A similar logic is espoused by Helen in her self-defence in *Trojan Woman*, where she claims to be the saviour of Greek freedom. Thanks to the victory of Aphrodite, 'my relations with Paris benefitted Greece to this extent: you are not ruled by barbarians, either because of a battle or by usurpation' (*Trojan Women* 932–34, Kovacs), either of which would have resulted from Athena's or Hera's victory in the judgement of Paris. Menelaus ends his reply to Peleus by pointing out the good nature with which he answered Peleus and advising the old man to follow his lead.

Menelaus is, most probably, not afraid of Peleus' personal threats of violence, since Peleus is indeed a fragile old man, but no matter how well attended Menelaus is, he does not have an entire army close by at his disposal as Peleus does.[39] His final words to Peleus' first tirade are aimed at appeasement and compromise: 'I have confronted you on these points in good will toward you, not out of anger' (688, Kovacs), a reply which shows that the speech is indeed contrived to sound phlegmatic and emotionally inhibited. However, he has a warning for the old man: 'But if you show a hot temper, you only make yourself more hoarse, whereas my forethought is a gain to me' (689–90, Kovacs). Menelaus is very fond of his 'forethought'. He attributes his intent to kill Andromache and Molossus also to his foresight, which will prevent the rule of barbarians over Greeks (660–67). Peleus of course does not give up and keeps insulting Menelaus in his second, shorter speech (693–726), telling Menelaus to leave immediately, as noted above. Menelaus knows he must yield and once again chooses the milder and more diplomatic tone, although not very gracefully.

Menelaus ignores Peleus' second speech, claiming that he is in a hurry to leave. He suddenly realizes that he has to take care of a rebelling city, of which the spectators have not heard before, nor did they know that he is pressed for time. He then makes a nebulous threat aimed at the absent Neoptolemus: he will come back after Neoptolemus returns and will deal with him directly. With another sneer at Peleus' senile weakness, he leaves (729–46).

Peleus had spoken earlier in praise of the lowly born and the lower ranks who do the work on the battlefield. This support for the common man would have made him popular with the off-stage audience, but Euripides also wants the spectators to know that he is greatly appreciated by the on-stage audience as well. In spite of Peleus' spoken defence of the lowly born who achieve greatness by their actions, the Chorus start their ode of praise for the old man (766–801) by singing first generally of the advantage of belonging to a noble and wealthy house, possessing power and honour as well as virtue, which Peleus has just exhibited. In the antistrophe they stipulate that victory and power must be achieved by just means only, rather than violence, in which case they must be thinking of the hubristic Menelaus. In the epode they address Peleus by his patronymic, 'O aged son of Aeacus' and celebrate his past exploits: his fighting at the side of the Lapiths against the Centaurs; his sailing with the Argonauts; and his participation in the previous Trojan War. At this point he exits as a beloved figure with Andromache and Molossus, leaving the scene to Hermione and Orestes.

In contrast to Peleus' positive characterization, Menelaus' tendency to avoid responsibility, another negative trait, is exemplified by his hurried departure from Phthia without pausing to tell his daughter that he is leaving, never mind taking her with him. In doing this, he is effectively abandoning her to face alone the consequences of their shared murder scheme. From Menelaus' excuse, it seems that he has to return to Sparta to amass an army before embarking on some fight over a city, which means that he could have taken Hermione with him. Why didn't he? Menelaus seems to be a devoted father in words alone. It is true that it is unlikely that Neoptolemus will kill Hermione, as she later fears, or even chase her away from his house. She is after all Menelaus' daughter, who brought a large dowry into the marriage, as the Nurse points out to her (869–73). However, Menelaus cannot be sure that his daughter will not suffer some consequences of their scheming. A truly devoted father would take the possible risks into account, but he does not, even though Peleus has just told him that he expects his grandson to drag her out of his house by her hair. Nor can he be sure that the aged Peleus himself will not kick his sterile granddaughter-in-law out of the house. Peleus did not have one good word to say about Hermione, and, as the audience will see shortly, Hermione fancies herself in great danger from both Neoptolemus and Peleus, as she states explicitly that her father has abandoned her.

In sum, Menelaus is a repugnant human being: a failed parent, cruel, irreverent, and cowardly, but not a mean politician. Grube's words summarize him:[40]

> Menelaus does show himself a cheat, a liar and a twister, arrogant and cruel, weak before his daughter as he was before his wife. Above all, the tremendous part which the Trojan War plays in his life goes far to justify the old man's [Peleus'] sneer that if you take away the Spartan's warlike reputation, there is little left (724–26).

Indeed, to Peleus, Menelaus is 'a nobody' (641); he does not acknowledge Menelaus' departure with a single word, as if he never existed. When Andromache, still shaken from her near-death experience, expresses fear that they – a woman, a child, and an old man – are alone on the road to Pharsalus and that the Spartans might ambush them, Peleus dismisses her fears. He reminds her that he is king with an army close by, but also that though he is old, he could tackle Menelaus: 'all I have to do to triumph over a man like that is to look at him' (762–63, Lloyd). He ends his words of encouragement with 'what use is a powerful body to a coward?' (765, Lloyd). Scholars tend to see his words as 'an amusing mixture of boasting and good sense',[41] but what has just happened proves Peleus right. Menelaus is younger, most probably in better physical shape, and protected by his mighty armour, yet he fled when Peleus told him to leave.

Peleus returns to the scene in line 1047. He wants to make sure that the rumour he heard about Hermione's departure from Neoptolemus' house is true. The Chorus verify the rumour, explaining that Hermione was afraid of being expelled from Neoptolemus' home. Peleus' preoccupation with his legacy is revealed again when he asks if Hermione thought she would be expelled 'For plotting to kill the boy, perhaps?' (1058, Kovacs), forgetting completely about Andromache, of whom the Chorus need to remind him: 'Yes, and because she tried to murder the slave woman' (1059, Kovacs).[42] Peleus assumes that it was Menelaus who took her away, but the Chorus tell him it was Orestes. 'In hope of what? Meaning to marry her?' asks Peleus (1062, Kovacs). The Chorus divulge to him not only that Orestes means to marry Hermione, but that he also is contriving the death of his grandson. When the Chorus inform him that the murder will take place with the Delphians' help in Apollo's sacred precinct, the old man becomes alarmed and tells his men to hurry to Delphi to warn Neoptolemus and his people of the plot, lest Neoptolemus be killed. Peleus' order cannot be executed however, for at that very moment, a messenger arrives from Delphi with the news of his grandson's death, followed by the arrival of the corpse itself brought to Peleus for lamentation.

The chronology of this last section baffles scholars, since in lines 993–1009 Orestes speaks of Neoptolemus' murder as yet to happen, but minutes later the Messenger arrives reporting that the murder has already been committed, adding that Orestes was involved (1075, 1115–16). It is obviously unlikely that Orestes has physically gone to Delphi in the time that passed, and lines 1075, 1115–16 do not need to be interpreted as if Orestes was physically present in Delphi at the time of the murder, but rather that he was the instigator and planner of the trap, as he told Hermione he was. Although ancient tragedy takes some liberties with reality through devices such as the *deus ex machina*, the chronology of the action tends to be limited to events that could reasonably take place within the timeframe of drama.[43]

Hearing about the death of his grandson, Peleus collapses, but again his concern for his loved ones who have survived and can continue his line brings him back to his senses, as the Messenger urges: 'Raise up your body and listen to what happened, if you really do want to help your loved ones' (1079–80, Lloyd). As painful as the description he hears is, Peleus ought to be very proud of his valiant grandson, and the courage and ingenuity of his self-defence against the despicable trap laid for him by the younger Atreid. However, the arrival of Neoptolemus' corpse for burial reminds him again of the loss of his line as he sings:

> O woe, woe! What sorrow for my house I do see here
> and receive with my hand!
> O woe, woe, alas!
> O land of Thessaly, I am utterly destroyed,
> I am no more. No longer do I have a family, no children
> > Are left in the house.
> > What suffering I must endure!
>
> (1173–79, Lloyd)[44]

Peleus wishes Neoptolemus had died at Troy: a death in battle would not have made him less dead, but as the Chorus observe, it would have conferred more honour upon him and made Peleus happier (1182–85). Peleus bitterly deplores Neoptolemus' marriage to Hermione as well as his reckless dealings with Apollo. Now the death of Neoptolemus has robbed him of a grandson, and he blames Apollo for taking two children from him (1205–12). Again and again, he dwells on being left childless and lonely and calls on Thetis to see how he has fallen into utter destruction (1216–25).

Peleus' sorrow and grief have no limits. Euripides allows this beloved old man, who has lost both his son and grandson, to stay for an extensive time in front of the off-stage audience and arouse as much pity as possible, until his divine spouse, Thetis, arrives. She does not waste time but immediately attends to the matters at hand. Peleus ought to bear his grief more lightly. She points out that although she is a goddess, she has also lost her child, Achilles, their son. In short, Peleus' bereavement is not unique. Next, in an aetiological mode, she instructs Peleus to bury their grandson at Delphi as a reproach to the Delphians, who defiled the temple of the god, and to Orestes, the cause of Neoptolemus' death (1231–42,[45] 1263–64). Andromache ought to go to the land of the Molossians and marry Helenus, Hector's younger brother. Andromache's son from Neoptolemus, who is 'the last of the line of Aeacus' (1246–47, Kovacs), must go with her. The following words should give Peleus peace of mind:

... his [Molossus'] descendants, one after another,
shall live out their lives in prosperity as kings
of Molossia. Your race and mine, old man, is not
fated to be so utterly destroyed, nor that of Troy;
for the gods do indeed, care about Troy,
although it fell by the desire of Athena.

(1247–52, Lloyd)

In these lines Thetis alleviates Peleus' chief concern and resolves the main issue at the heart of the play: legacy and continuation of one's bloodline. Although in the previous scene, Peleus could not see in Molossus the heir for his house, even though he told Menelaus that he has high hopes for the boy (636–38, 723–24), Thetis sees in him the start of a dynasty that will keep alive the families of both his mother and his father, a combination of the House of Peleus and the Trojan House that will rule over the Molossians.

Peleus will become immortal and will live with Thetis for all time in the House of Nereus. His immortality will allow him to see his beloved son Achilles dwelling in his island home on the strand of Leuke in the Black Sea. But Peleus needs to stop mourning Neoptolemus, as death comes upon all mortals (1253–72). We thus leave Peleus having achieved what he believed had been lost: a promise of legacy.

Orestes

Orestes' character in *Andromache* is different from that usually presented throughout extant tragedy, in that with the exception of his independent arrival and his own scheming of the revenge for his father in Aeschylus' *Libation Bearers*, he never acts on his own initiative. In Sophocles' and Euripides' *Electra* plays, in Euripides' *Iphigenia among the Taurians* and *Orestes*, he is always accompanied, incited, or assisted by Electra, Pylades, or both. In every single Euripidean drama, he deceives others to various degrees. *Andromache* is the only play that presents him alone and left to his own devices.

In *Andromache*, Orestes lies and uses deceit twice. His arrival is a surprise: he was not mentioned at all up until his entrance. He appears as the Nurse is trying to reason with Hermione, who is situated in front of the palace unveiled and with her breasts exposed by her ripped dress. He tells the Chorus that he is on his way to Dodona (885–86), which quickly proves to be a lie. Next, he pretends not to know about Hermione's source of unhappiness although he actually knows a lot about what has been happening. Indeed, he might not know why her dress is torn and her breasts uncovered, but he does know that she has not yet borne a child (904–5), and somehow immediately concludes that her husband must desire another woman (907). From this conclusion, apparently based on conjecture alone, he also conjures up the possibility that Hermione must have plotted against that woman, as her gender would do (911).

Indeed, further along, when Hermione clutches him, begging him to save her life, he admits that his avowed ignorance of the situation in which Hermione has been living was sheer pretence (887–88, 901, 907). He learned prior to his arrival that there had been considerable turmoil and strife in the house between Hermione and Andromache (959–61). He has also been informed about Hermione's murderous attempt against Andromache, and wondered whether she might wish to leave her house with him (961–63), fearing the consequences. He may or may not know whether she was successful in killing Andromache, but he clearly knew that the murder was intended, which to a matricide like him did not disqualify Hermione as his future bride.[46] Upon his arrival, he thus deceives everyone regarding his supposed ignorance of the situation and his actual purpose for putting in an appearance. Further along we learn both from him and from the Messenger that he had already managed to devise a murderous plot against Neoptolemus in Delphi even without being present there himself.[47]

This is the only extant play that paints Orestes as a successful schemer telling his own lies independently of his sister Electra, and plotting his actions without his cousin Pylades. In the later play *Iphigenia among the Taurians*, which was probably performed sometime between 414 and 412 BCE, Pylades, Iphigenia, and Orestes need to devise a plan that will help them escape from the Taurian land. Orestes' suggestion is simple-minded, but with murderous intent. He suggests killing Thoas, the king, which immediately meets with Iphigenia's refusal. As a foreigner, she will not kill her host (*Iphigenia among the Taurians* 1020–21). In *Andromache*, he shows himself more cunning and conniving, capable of long-term planning of events that will take place even in his absence.

Orestes realizes that the matricide has disqualified him as a potential bridegroom for any other family than his own. This is the excuse that he presented to Neoptolemus earlier, when asking him to relinquish his marriage to Hermione: 'I told him of my evil fortunes and my present fate, how I could marry the daughter of a kinsman but only with difficulty one from outside, since I was in exile from my home' (973–76, Kovacs). Neoptolemus, however, refused, while taunting him for the matricide and reminding him of the madness that the Erinyes cast on him because of his crime (977–78). The crime of matricide clearly vexes him, as does Neoptolemus' insolence against him on this issue, so much so that when he describes his revenge plot against the son of Achilles, he turns the tables on Neoptolemus and says, 'If my allies in Delphi keep their oaths, I, *the matricide* [my italics], will teach him not to marry anyone who should have been mine' (999–1001, Lloyd).[48] In his boasting he wishes to show the son of Achilles that even though he is a matricide, he can still trap him. On the one hand, he understands that obtaining Hermione as his bride is his only chance of getting married because of his former crime, but his plan for obtaining her, involving the murder of her husband, also mimics his previous crime to some extent, in that both arise from a revenge motive. This time around, however, Orestes' motivation is purely selfish. As Conacher puts it: 'Orestes is a self-seeking dastard, waiting about in the wings, so to speak, for the psychological moment to make his nefarious proposals to Hermione, and even committing his murder by proxy, through his Delphian allies. Apollo plays a vital part in this murder, but, in planning it, Orestes is following his own self-interest, not the will of the god.'[49] As summarized by Grube: 'If neither Menelaus nor Hermione are subtle characters, they are tremendously alive. Not so Orestes. He belongs to the same family and is equally unpleasant, but to steal a man's wife in his absence and then plot his death, leaving others to carry it out, is merely the part of a cad. Orestes is a poor sort of cad, even with the backing of Apollo.'[50]

The Chorus

The role of the Chorus in tragedies by Aeschylus, Sophocles, and Euripides has received considerable attention over the last few decades.[51] In general, the Chorus influence the perception of other *dramatis personae*, at times offering emotional guidance to the off-stage audience by helping the spectators 'become involved in the process of responding, which may be a matter of dealing with profoundly contradictory issues and impulses',[52] as well as adding to the spectacle of the dramatic contests through movement and dance.[53] The Chorus may present an authoritative collective identity and speak in one voice, but they also express fluid opinions with varying viewpoints.[54] This fluidity in the choral utterances is manipulated by the playwright to enhance selected themes or shed light on characters.[55] However, attempting to interpret the identity of a tragic chorus is a tantalizing experience, as their lyrical odes, albeit exquisite, may only offer the faintest hints as to their characters, with the Chorus of *Andromache* being no exception. Although they may be given beautiful lines, and an authoritative voice, the often conservative values of the Chorus, who may represent the common man, tend to contrast strongly with the extraordinary heroes of tragedy and myth. Furthermore, while it may also appear from one ode that we have, if not a firm grasp, then at least a vague inkling as to the Chorus' personality, during their next ode we may realize that we have been completely wrong-footed.[56]

There may be several reasons for this. The Chorus are always distinguished from the main characters of a tragedy in several ways, but first and foremost by having primarily a group identity. In *Andromache*, we have only the scantiest information about them, being told that the Chorus are Phthian women. As such, the Chorus are not impartial observers, but have their own collective identity and, accordingly, their own sympathies and loyalties. They owe their main loyalty and allegiance to their king Neoptolemus, and his wife, Hermione. As women, they may also be expected to identify with the main female characters, but as we shall see, this is not always the case. We may surmise that these women may resent the authority held by the royal family in their home town, especially when the bride is a foreign princess who is not reticent about expressing her opinion of her childhood home's superiority over that of her husband. The Chorus in *Andromache*, as with many Euripidean choruses, share various elements of liminality, not only as women and therefore belonging to a marginal group with limited rights, but also in that they are not entirely involved in the plot action or are limited to conversing with the other characters, yet are often allowed to sing about past or mythic events in distant localities.[57]

There are three main kinds of choral performative discourse: performative utterances, gnomic statements, and those of mythic content.[58] *Andromache*'s Chorus, as often is the case in tragedy, is at one moment firmly entrenched within the play's action, present in both time and place, interacting with Andromache or other characters, offering their view of the difficulty of two women sharing one man, but a short time later they are singing about mythic events of a different era. In interweaving these three types of performative discourse the Chorus fulfil their traditional dual role of participating in the plot action together with their on-stage audience, while also having a decorative presence on stage and entertaining the off-stage audience.[59] Through their dancing and singing, the Chorus have a major impact on the spectacle provided to the audiences.[60]

As we shall see when looking at the comments made by the Chorus, even when they are interacting with the other characters, they often seem to be in a world of their own. Bearing in mind their fluid identity and unique dual role of entertaining the audience while interacting with the other on-stage characters, it is perhaps not surprising that their comments do not seem to follow any kind of logical sequence that would be expected of main characters, even without taking their complex group identity into consideration. The

Chorus may be serving as a mouthpiece for the playwright, expressing gnomic truths, or may simply be entertaining the off-stage audience, allowing a change of pace while they sing and dance before the next episode of the play can take place. Indeed, while on some occasions the Chorus may contribute to the build-up of dramatic tension in the play, as when they beg Andromache to leave Thetis' shrine, at other times their odes provide an interlude, as during their fourth ode, after the departure of Orestes and Hermione (1009–46) and before Peleus' re-entry, which while ominous in tone, slows the pace and damps the tension down.

In *Andromache*, the women of the Chorus do not seem to be particularly effective in interceding in the action. This is in keeping with the typical tragic Chorus who are often seen as failing to take action at critical moments.[61] They are largely ignored by the main characters, so we may assume that their inputs are for the benefit of the off-stage audience, rather than the on-stage one. Indeed, the degree of interaction between a Chorus and the main characters is often affected by the degree of their dependence upon them. However, the main character they would have been most dependent upon, Neoptolemus, is absent from the stage until he appears as a corpse in the final scene.

Euripides did not give his Chorus of Phthian women the task of opening the play and setting the scene, allowing Andromache to speak first instead, explaining why she sought shelter at the altar of Thetis. In their *parados* or entry song (117–46), the Chorus reflect on Andromache's decision to seek shelter at Thetis' shrine and disapprove of it, although rather mildly. They encourage her to step out of the shrine, not realizing that she will be killed if she does. They admit to pitying Andromache (they call her the 'unhappiest of women, most wretched of brides', 139–40, Lloyd), but at the same time attempt to remind her of the reality of her condition. She is a captive concubine and cannot oppose the masters of the house. Thus, the Chorus start off by regarding Andromache as a foreign slave, albeit a sympathetic character, but a woman with no rights. For the external audience, who would have been familiar with Andromache's elevated position in Troy, the harsh words from the Chorus would have brought home the dramatic changes Andromache must have experienced since leaving Troy. The Chorus, being familiar with how things stand now for Andromache, find her behavior inappropriate and initially are more concerned with advising her to accept her fate and guard her tongue rather than expressing any sympathy:

Know your fate, consider the present ill-fortune into which you have come.
Do you wrangle with your masters
when you are a woman of Troy and they were born in Sparta?

The sea goddess's shrine, receiver of sacrifices – leave it behind.
What profit is for you to mar your body with weeping in bewilderment
because of the hard constraints of your masters?
The mastering hand will come upon you:
why do you toil in vain,
powerless as you are?

                                                              (126–34, Kovacs)

However, the *parodos* is also very telling with regard to the complexities in understanding the characterization of the Chorus. Immediately after their criticisms of Andromache, they also admit their pity for her:

In my eyes you were much to be pitied when you came,
woman of Troy, to the house of my lords.
But I hold my peace from fear
(though in fact I have pity your lot)
lest the child of Zeus's daughter
learn that I wish you well.

                                                              (141–46, Kovacs)

They thus inform the audience that they may not feel at liberty to express any criticisms of the royal couple, and fear their haughty queen.

Gradually, however, a more daring nature is revealed, as they become willing to express their sympathy with Andromache, especially when she finds herself in the piteous situation of having to decide to face her death in order to save her son's life. Throughout the first episode, the Chorus continue to address Andromache directly (232–33, 364–65), on the one hand criticizing her behavior, while also pitying her for the predicament in which she finds herself. It is almost as if they are torn between their two identities, as Phthians loyal to Hermione, and as women seeing the plight of Andromache. The same apparent inner schisms are also evident in their following choral odes even while they recall the mythic background to the events taking place on the stage in their second ode (274–308) and when they add their own commentary and interpretation of those events, in their third ode (465–500). The Chorus' growing support for the Trojan Andromache while opposing Hermione, despite the fact that she is the wife of their ruler, reflects not only on Andromache's admirable character and morality but also on the Chorus' kindness and courage.

In their mistaken assumption that Andromache can leave the altar with no repercussions, the Chorus are perhaps influenced by the duality in Hermione's equivocal claims in which on the one hand she wants Andromache to die, while on the other she demands that Andromache abandon her pride, fall at Hermione's knees, and sweep the palace, as if she no longer intends to take Andromache's life (164–70). In this way the off-stage spectators are baffled and misdirected, as they are being prepared for the volatility of the princess, and Andromache's difficulty in dealing with her. In terms of adding to the characterization of the main characters, the Chorus also provide the audience with an important clue about Andromache's deportment: she is a slave, but she does not behave as one, a characteristic that we have noticed (see pp. 63, 67). We learn that Andromache might be projecting a haughtier persona to the on-stage audience than we have realized. The *parodos* thus gives the audience another perspective on Andromache's character and circumstances as well as on the character of Hermione, who is yet to appear before the spectators. The Chorus also draw attention to the cruelty of their princess when they confess that they kept silent when Andromache came to their masters' palace, out of fear of the ruler's wife. Lastly, they summarize for the spectators the problematic situation that is presented in this play: two women 'having one man in common' (124–25). As a group, the Phthian women are cast as being very brave. In spite of their fear of Hermione, they do give voice to their kind and sympathetic words for Andromache.

It is also possible that the Chorus simply do not believe that Hermione would really inflict such a terrible penalty on another woman, also originally from a royal family, although not Greek. It is only after Hermione's haughty first speech that they begin to change their tone. Even then they are at best neutral, commenting on the jealousy of women towards their love rivals, without taking sides. When they address Andromache, they advise her to reason with Hermione, still believing in their state of denial that she could reach an agreement with the tempestuous younger woman:

> My Lady, to the extent that you are able to without vexation, to that extent
> be ruled by me and come to some agreement with her words.
>
> (232–33, Kovacs)

Perhaps it is Andromache's responses to Hermione, which gradually seep into their consciousness, that change the women's attitude to Andromache. The Chorus have already heard Andromache remind Hermione that she treated Neoptolemus dreadfully. Being reminded also of the disparaging remarks Hermione made about Neoptolemus' birthplace could not have helped the Chorus to think kindly of Hermione:

> But if *you* get angry, you argue that Sparta
> is a great city and Scyros is of no account,

that you are a rich woman living in the midst of the poor,
and that Menelaus is a greater man than Achilles.

(209–12, Kovacs)

Or perhaps it was the reminder that it was Hermione's mother Helen who set
the War in motion, and in so doing was responsible for Achilles' death, that
had the greatest effect on the Chorus. When Hermione says to Andromache,
'I'll set fire upon you, paying you no heed . . .' (257, Kovacs), it could not have
helped her make a better impression on the Chorus.

The second choral ode (274–308) reviews the events that led up to the
Trojan War, starting from the beauty contest of the goddesses and the
judgement of Paris and continues with Cassandra's desperate pleas not to
allow her younger brother to live, after she foresaw the destruction and loss
of life he would bring to Troy. It ends with the ramifications of Paris' survival:
the slavery that came upon the women of Troy including Andromache and
the toll on Greece and its young men fighting Troy for ten long years.[62] In this
way, the Chorus tie together the threads that have led to the piteous situation
of Andromache and other enslaved Trojan women. As Lloyd[63] maintains,
'The ode is related to the action, but also contrasts it.'[64] Indeed, the ode is
woven well into the fabric of the play. The vehement quarrel between
Andromache and Hermione brings up the idea that this confrontation would
have not happened had the judgement of Paris not taken place. Furthermore,
the jealousy exhibited by Hermione and its potential ramifications meshes
well with the jealousy among the three goddesses and its impact on the
Trojan War, in which Aphrodite, the winner of the judgement, supported
Troy while Hera and Athena endlessly battled against it. However, the
contrast between the very realistic proximity in time of the impassioned
formal debate the spectators just witnessed and the temporal remoteness of
the judgement of Paris, make the sequence incongruous if not clashing.[65]

Immediately after the Chorus' second ode, Menelaus makes his grand
entry wearing a hoplite gear, dragging the defenceless Molossus alongside
him. After Menelaus states that he will kill either Andromache or her son,
Andromache seeks to defend herself by challenging the wisdom of Menelaus'
plan. After all, Molossus is also the son of Neoptolemus, outside whose palace
the altercation takes place. At this point, even if we accept that the identity of
a Chorus is fluid rather than cohesive,[66] the Chorus' lack of response to what
has just happened is rather surprising. As Andromache hurls harsh criticism
at the Spartan general and his daughter, all the Chorus do is to tell
Andromache that 'as a woman' she has spoken too much (364–65). At this
juncture they are criticizing their own sex as well as the enslaved Andromache.
The Chorus then witness the heart-rending scene in which Andromache

leaves the sanctuary offered by the shrine of Thetis of her own free will, in order to embrace her son and save his life, only to hear that her sacrifice may have been in vain. Menelaus immediately instructs the slaves to seize Andromache and tie her up, as he expects her to strongly if not violently protest what she is about to hear. He will kill her, but she has not necessarily saved the life of her son. He leaves Molossus' fate in his daughter's hands, while recommending that he should be put to death too.

The Chorus' initial, almost incredible, response to this contemptible betrayal is to decry the situation of 'double marriage' with two women sharing one man. Andromache has ripped into Spartans in general and Menelaus in particular, but after Menelaus leaves, leading Andromache and Molossus off the stage, presumably to be killed, the Chorus sing the most phlegmatic ode imaginable. This third ode (465–500) is almost entirely devoted to finding parallels to a marriage where a husband has two mates. They compare this with civil strife in a town ruled by two kings, with a poet led by two conflicting muses, and with a ship being steered by two different helmsmen. After claiming that Hermione's heart is enflamed against her rival, apparently not having paid any attention to Andromache's rebuffs explaining that she has not shared Neoptolemus' bed since his marriage to Hermione, they do finally condemn the murders in lines 491–93.

The Chorus, however, still only blame Hermione, keeping silent about Menelaus' conduct, or only referring to him as Hermione's father and suggesting he should make peace between Hermione and Andromache (421–24). It is almost as if they have disregarded his role in the planned murder of Andromache and Molossus altogether. This raises some questions, particularly because Menelaus' behaviour at this point is bizarre to say the least. He is supposed to have come to rescue his daughter's marriage, and it should have occurred to him that murdering her husband's son would not have helped this cause, as Andromache points out to him. There is a possible explanation for Menelaus ignoring the consequences of such an act, but it does not explain the silence of the Chorus. If Menelaus was working against Neoptolemus together with Orestes all along, he would have known that neither he nor Hermione have anything to fear from the absent king, because he is about to be murdered. Verrall surmises that another play may have preceded *Andromache*, laying out just such a conspiracy between the Atreid uncle and his nephew.[67] Menelaus may have wanted to put Hermione in the position of having to agree to a marriage with Orestes, that he knew she was reluctant about.[68] However, even if such a play existed, it would have been highly unlikely that the Chorus would have known about such a plot to murder their king. It appears in this case, as with other tragic Choruses (for example, in Aeschylus' *Agamemnon* and Euripides' *Medea*), that either they do not always fully grasp what is happening or they do not dare criticize the Spartan king. Their silence, contrasting so strongly with Andromache's verbal onslaughts, highlights Andromache's bravery. This silence also reiterates the fact that although their gnomic statements do broaden the audience's understanding of the play's context, the Chorus have no impact on the plot action.

When Andromache and Molossus reappear, and Molossus piteously pleads with Menelaus to spare him, there is no response from the Chorus, until they announce the arrival of Peleus. After Peleus' impassioned verbal onslaught against Menelaus, the Chorus make another phlegmatic response (642–44). All they can say is that mortals who are wise should not start quarrels with those who are near and dear to them. Likewise in lines 727–28 they comment on the temper of old men, before their next ode (766–801) in praise of nobility and of Peleus' bravery. The Chorus next speak in lines 879–80 announcing the arrival of a man of 'different hue', referring in this way to Orestes. Their emphasis on Orestes being a stranger different from them reinforces the Chorus' own identity, as local women, who may be at the least suspicious of strangers, particularly foreign strangers. Before the return of Peleus after Hermione absconds with Orestes, they emphasize the gods' role in man's fate (1010–46). This ultra-conservative traditional Greek viewpoint may explain some of their more phlegmatic comments throughout the play. If everything is in the hands of the gods, then who are we as mere mortals to comment or criticize? This kind of attitude seems typical of the Euripidean chorus, who can be considered to establish the relationship between man and the gods as well as reflecting on the relationships between human beings in a community.[69]

While other characters come and go, the Chorus' continual presence provides a certain unifying element. Although in *Andromache* the Chorus are not effective in influencing any of the main characters, once Hermione and Andromache have disappeared from the stage before the final scene, it is the Chorus who interact with Peleus on his return. The encomium ode to Peleus (766–801) starts as Greek lyric often does by moving from the general to the particular. Of the five odes, this seems to be the most engaged with the immediately preceding context. Peleus has just won a rhetorical and existential victory over Menelaus, who pretty much flees from the old man while abandoning his daughter. The Chorus praise wealth and noble birth, by which, as the end of the ode indicates, they mean Peleus. By recommending victory and power achieved by just means rather than violence, they finally criticize Menelaus. Perhaps in the presence of a greater authority, the old king, they now dare to state out loud what they may have thought earlier. Finally, they address Peleus directly by the patronymic 'son of Aeacus' and sing his past heroic achievements: the defeat of the Centaurs, the voyage of the Argonauts, and, with Heracles, the first sack of Troy. His defeat of Menelaus in the preceding act serves as a proof that his heroic capabilities have not waned. While their praise of wealth and noble birth is rightly based on the foregoing act, it will probably dissipate in the unfolding one in which Hermione, to whom both qualities apply, will be seen to be psychologically disintegrating in spite of her wealth.

On the face of it, one should note the wisdom in Aldrich's comment: 'The chorus cannot look ahead to realize the irony of its words, nor should we'; however, we need to ask whether this irony is in vain, or whether it has any repercussions on characterization beyond that of Hermione.[70] Indeed, it seems it has. Hermione's complete meltdown is caused directly by her realization that she has been deserted by her father and is at the mercy of her husband, who might not think kindly of her scheming against his son. This 'irony' thus reflects further on the unsavoury character of Menelaus and will remind the audience of similar conduct when Menelaus left Helen and sailed to Crete (Euripides, *Trojan Women* 938–44), an act that directly precipitated the Trojan War and the domestic suffering enacted in this play.

The fifth and last ode (1009–46) is fittingly the most general of all, as it sums up the tragic events of the entire play, and as might be expected in a drama performed in a complex celebratory ritual to a god, it pinpoints the idea that the common suffering of Greeks and Trojans originates in the divine. The Chorus reproach Apollo and Poseidon, who built the walls of Troy, for letting the city be destroyed in the hands of Ares. The focus is more on Apollo than on Poseidon because he has a part in the upcoming murder of Neoptolemus predicted by Orestes (1002–8). They sing of the murder of Agamemnon by Clytemnestra, and of Clytemnestra by her son Orestes with the blessing of Apollo. The ode also deals with the bereavement of many mothers and wives, in which they include Andromache.[71]

In addition to the five odes, the Chorus Leader, as is usual in Euripides, offers brief comments following formal debates or during the debates. There is a tendency to disregard the comments of the Chorus as not very profound.[72] However, in *Andromache* these comments are well contextualized, and their reflection and reaction to preceding events, albeit brief, contribute to the characterization of the speakers. For example, to observe that the mind of a woman is a jealous thing always ill-disposed towards rivals in a marriage-bed, following Hermione's vicious raging against Andromache, is a very apropos statement (181–82), as is their address to Hermione after Andromache's reply to Hermione's attack. In their address to their queen, the Chorus with great respect ask Hermione to come to some agreement with Andromache, only to be utterly ignored (232–33). Their comment is not only very fitting to the preceding circumstances, but the fact that they are ignored contributes to the characterization of Hermione as an arrogant and conceited youngster who thinks she has unlimited power and looks down on those of marginal status. Other comments of the Chorus are similarly relevant to the context and support it (363–65, 642–44, 691–92, 726–27, 954–56). In addition, the Chorus also fulfil their usual functions in describing what is happening inside the house, announcing and meeting strangers, as well as updating a character with necessary information (879–80, 883, 1053–66). In the final scene just before the appearance of Thetis *ex machina*, the Chorus sing a *kommos* of antiphonal lament with Peleus, in which they echo and intensify the old man's enormous grief.

It is in the final *stasimon* that the Chorus deliver perhaps their most important lines, emphasizing the 'similarity of suffering' of the Greeks and Trojans resulting from the Trojan War.[73] When Trojan grief and Hellenic grief are recognized as being one and the same thing, the Chorus finally contribute to one of the underlying themes of the play: the differentiation between the House of Peleus which is considered virtuous, and the House of Atreus, here represented by Menelaus, Hermione, and Orestes, all of whom are marked by deceit, treachery, and vile treatment of both their own family members and fellow man. Furthermore, the Chorus have aligned themselves with Andromache and Peleus in seeking to preserve the dynasty of the House of Peleus, even if only by expressing their sympathies with Andromache and distancing themselves from Menelaus and Hermione. When taking into account all of the considerations outlined above, we may conclude that the songs of the Chorus, the remarks of the Chorus Leader, and the *kommos* are excellently integrated with the action of the play, and moreover establish all through the drama a consistent and clear identity.[74]

Reception

Introduction

Exploring the reception of a piece of literature is a fascinating undertaking. One embarks on a virtual journey through time and place, meeting individuals whose creative endeavours (whether they be *objets d'art*, musical compositions, or any forms of literature) were influenced in some way by the work we are interested in, and whose work in turn influences our own understanding of the original piece, as well as those coming both before and after each artist's time. It feels a bit like exploring an imagined universe that folds back on itself, so we can travel through loops in time and space, using artistic creations as a kind of portal. The older the original piece of art, the greater the scope for adventure, so exploring the reception of Euripides' *Andromache*, dating back to the fifth century BCE, itself influenced by older literature based on the same myths and legends, promises to be a very exciting adventure – and indeed, the more we search the more exciting the adventure becomes.[1]

Our journey exploring *Andromache*'s reception necessarily starts by going further back to the time before Euripides wrote *Andromache* in the fifth century. Although Chapter 2 describes the myths Euripides himself may have received, we will remind ourselves briefly of some of the materials available to him. This will not only help us appreciate Euripides' own unique contributions as we go forward in time, but will also help us bear in mind that later texts were also influenced by these earlier materials. It is generally accepted that Euripides had a considerable collection of texts in his own personal library, the first of many to be established in Athens,[2] so he could have been influenced by many poems of the Epic Cycle, including various tales from the *Cypria*, describing the involvement of the gods in the origins of the Trojan War.[3] As Ambühl notes, even though the 'dramatic structure and their high proportions of direct speech make the Homeric epics appear as an ideal model for the tragedians', the playwrights seem to have avoided 'competing' with Homer and 'focussed instead on mythological material treated in the epic cycle.'[4] This is borne out in *Andromache*. Homer's *Iliad* mentions Andromache several times. Her name itself is interpreted by scholars as giving her Amazon-like attributes, and scholars note that there are several references to her knowledge of military affairs in the *Iliad*: the advice she gives to Hector at 6.433–37, the care she gives to his horses at 8.185–90, the care she might give to his armour at 17.207–8, and the fact that she is an only daughter with seven brothers, which naturally masculinizes her.[5] However, it is among the extant fragments of the Epic Cycle that we find a few lines of the *Little Iliad* and *Sack of Ilion* which relate Andromache's fate after the fall of Troy. These fragments recount the death of Andromache's son Astyanax, and the fact that she was taken as a concubine by Neoptolemus.[6] The lyric poetess Sappho, born about 150 years before Euripides, is known to have composed at least one poem (44 L-P) about Andromache, contained in one of the longest surviving fragments of her work found at Oxyrhynchus in Egypt. Sappho is regarded as having written mostly love poetry, so perhaps it is fitting that this papyrus manuscript is devoted to Andromache's arrival in Troy with her beloved Hector, the man she famously loved and grieved over for so many years after his death. Although we can never accurately assess all of the other works Euripides may have been aware of, it is still safe to say that in *Andromache* he created a unique plot driven by the particular characterizations he developed for Hermione, Andromache, and her son by Neoptolemus, Menelaus and, to a lesser extent, Orestes.

The Athenian fifth-century tragedies represent a crucial stage in the development of the dramatic arts, taking what had essentially been forms of stage tableaux, albeit brought to life by a chorus that sang and danced, and developing them into the beginnings of modern theatre. Even though Thespis had appeared as a main actor as far back as the sixth century, it was the second and third actors appearing in the tragedies of Aeschylus, Sophocles, and Euripides that allowed the emphasis to gradually move away from the chorus. While choral odes accompanied by double reed music and performed while moving or dancing were still an important feature, the fifth-century tragedies may be seen as anticipating modern musicals, as well as other forms of theatre.[7] Moreover, Euripides' considerable training as a musician, and great emphasis on the score for the performances of the individual actors, allowed his productions to resemble something approaching modern-day opera.[8] Indeed, vocal strengths of the main actors became critical in projecting their personas.[9] With these roles becoming more sophisticated, the chorus are gradually relegated to bystanders. In this sense, part of the originality of Euripides' *Andromache* is derived from the innovations of the fifth-century tragedians in general. Just as Aeschylus, Sophocles, and Euripides would have been inspired by Homer, modern dramatists continue to find that the staged versions of *Andromache* provide creative inspiration. In an early example, the Roman dramatist Seneca (4 BCE–65 CE) followed closely in the footsteps of the fifth-century tragedians, as far as we can judge from his extant plays.[10] In his *Trojan Women*, Seneca recreated Andromache as a powerful rhetorician, but the play is set while Troy is still burning, paralleling Euripides' *Trojan Women*. Euripides allows Andromache, rather than the chorus, to deliver the prologue to his tragedy, and Seneca, mimicking this structure, has Hecuba speak the first sixty-seven lines of *Trojan Women* as a prologue, introducing the women's grief at the loss of their city and their dear ones.

Three Varying Elements in the Reception of *Andromache*

While considering the changes in location, stages of the myth, plot and characterizations of the main personae in the receptions to come, we will bear in mind permutations in three important elements: firstly, the changes in the romantic relationships among the four main characters, Andromache, Neoptolemus, Hermione, and Orestes; secondly, how and where Neoptolemus died; and thirdly, the parentage of Andromache's surviving children, and the importance of their legacy.

The permutations of the Andromache/Neoptolemus/ Orestes/Hermione relationships

Almost every possible variation on the romantic theme exists. Who married whom seems to shift with ease from version to version. Perhaps more poignantly, how the characters feel about each other changes from one extreme to the other with time.

Several main variations occur in the relationships among Andromache, Hermione, Neoptolemus, and Orestes (all further complicated by the now-dead Hector and partially resolved by his younger brother Helenus):

1. Orestes was betrothed, or even married, to Hermione before she was given to Neoptolemus, OR Neoptolemus was betrothed to and married Hermione before Orestes announced his love to her.
2. Neoptolemus marries Hermione, OR Neoptolemus never marries Hermione and marries Andromache instead.
3. Hermione is married to Neoptolemus but is still in love with Orestes, OR Hermione is married to Neoptolemus but is jealous of Andromache, who is still his concubine.
4. Andromache is Neoptolemus' slave, and bears him a child. Once Neoptolemus marries Hermione, he immediately passes Andromache over to Helenus.

5. In almost all of the versions, notwithstanding with whom she is living, Andromache only loves her first husband, Hector, who is dead.
6. In many versions, Andromache ends up spending most of her life with Helenus, younger brother of Hector, but her heart remains true to Hector.

The level of intensity of emotions experienced in these relationships also varies greatly in different receptions. In Euripides' *Andromache*, the main emotions attributed to Hermione are first jealous rage and then terror. Both are melodramatic in their intensity, and neither seems to relate to love for Neoptolemus, but rather to Hermione's own status. Orestes coolly appears and convinces her to leave with him, almost as a pragmatic act. In Virgil's *Aeneid*, Orestes had been betrothed to Hermione before her marriage to Neoptolemus; inflamed by love for his stolen bride, Orestes is the one to experience jealous rage when he encounters Neoptolemus. In Ovid's (43 BCE–17 CE) *Heroides*, Hermione was actually married to Orestes (a marriage arranged by their grandfather Tyndareus) before she was given in marriage to Pyrrhus, another name for Neoptolemus. She begs Orestes to rescue her from Pyrrhus, who she claims is holding her hostage. In the *Journal of the Trojan War* of Dictys of Crete (late fourth century CE, a Latin translation by a certain Lucius Septimius of an earlier chronicle by a fictional Dictys of Crete, who in the narrative claims to have been an 'eye-witness' of Trojan War events), Neoptolemus has consummated his marriage to Hermione, but has left her and Andromache in Phthia while he goes to Delphi. As in Euripides' *Andromache*, Hermione is insanely jealous of Andromache and calls for Menelaus to come and 'resolve' the problem. In conjunction with the work of Dictys there is also a narrative in Latin, probably from the fifth century, professing to be the translation of a work that tells of the destruction of Troy and is attributed to a Trojan priest of Hephaestus, Dares the Phrygian. These two works form the main source for the numerous medieval accounts of the Trojan legend. Dares ends his account with Helenus sailing away from Troy with Andromache, before anyone has had the chance to marry or form jealous rivalries. In the seventeenth century, Racine's *Andromaque* takes the intensity of emotions to a fever pitch. Racine presents a Hermione desperately in love with Pyrrhus, and intensely frustrated because the two are not yet married. Pyrrhus in turn is in love with Andromache, and almost literally prepared to go to the end of the earth for her, abandoning allies and giving up friends. Yet Andromache refuses him. Hermione has no interest in Orestes, but is prepared to make use of him in a fit of rage. When Orestes arrives at the palace as an ambassador from Greece, demanding that Astyanax be put to death, his old passion for Hermione is rekindled, with disastrous consequences. Ambrose Phillips' translation of Racine's *Andromaque* in his *The Distrest Mother* (1712) adds a touch of pathos in the epilogue, wherein Andromache finally realizes all Pyrrhus attempted to do for her (see below).

The murder of Neoptolemus, premeditated or spontaneous?

In most versions Neoptolemus is killed far away from the main dramatic action, while he is at Apollo's shrine in Delphi. He may have been there to protest his father's death, may have pillaged the sanctuary and may have quarrelled with the Delphians over the apportioning of the sacrificial meat; or he may have gone to ask about Hermione's inability to bear children; or his mission may have been to offer Apollo some of the spoils of Troy (see Chapter 2 on Myth).[11] In some cases he was killed by the Delphians, while in others, Orestes either killed him personally or sent his men to do the job. However, as we will see, in Racine's *Andromaque*, a major variation is introduced. Neoptolemus becomes a major character in the play, rather than a character whose presence is felt throughout but who only arrives on stage as a corpse.

The parentage of Andromache's surviving children, and the importance of their legacy

In Euripides' *Andromache*, Astyanax, the son of Hector and Andromache, has already died in Troy. Andromache now has one son by Neoptolemus, his name assumed to be Molossus. In many Latin versions Andromache has also given birth to a child of Neoptolemus, though the child is given different names. The possibility of variations on this begin with Seneca's *Trojan Women*, when Andromache valiantly tries to outwit Ulysses (Odysseus) and protect her son, Astyanax. In this version she fails, but in later receptions her brave attempt is described as having succeeded. In these later versions then, Andromache has a surviving son born to Hector. Often this child will eventually set off on his own odyssey and become the ancestor of nobility in the poet or playwright's home country.

Receptions in Latin from the Roman Era Onwards

The starting point for the reception of *Andromache* is in the best-known adaptation of Greek epic and tragedy in Latin literature: Virgil's *Aeneid*. Written in the latter half of the first century BCE, Virgil's epic focuses on the journeys of Aeneas, a Trojan survivor of the Trojan War, who is credited with becoming an ancestor of Romulus and Remus, the founders of Rome. Aeneas' narrative of the fall of Troy, as told to Dido, queen of Carthage (who herself had to flee her childhood home, escaping her brother), starts from book 2, line 3 and continues until book 3, line 715. In book 3 (294–355), Aeneas describes his chance encounter with Andromache, which took place when he had entered Chaonia's harbour near the city of Buthrotum in Epirus. As we have seen, Euripides depicts Andromache as a captive of war, far from home, whose childhood and marital homes have been destroyed by Achilles and Neoptolemus, Achilles' son, respectively. That she then bears children to Neoptolemus puts her in an unthinkable situation, but while grieving her dead husband, she also protects the son she bore to Neoptolemus. Virgil essentially continues from where Euripides left off at the end of *Andromache*, in that Andromache is now married to Helenus. In line with Thetis' prophecy, Helenus has become king of a Greek city, and the two may now begin their own dynasty. However, Virgil's version clearly has its own motivations. He isn't interested in the descendants of Andromache with either Hector or Neoptolemus but in those of Aeneas, who will eventually found the city of Rome. There are no detailed accounts of the future of Andromache's children. Poignantly, Andromache does inquire after Aeneas' child, Ascanius, and in a roundabout way of his mother Creusa, who was lost while Aeneas fled from the burning city of Troy.

Interestingly, two travel writers, Strabo (64/63 BCE–24 CE) and Pausanias (110 CE–180 CE), mention Andromache in their surveys of the Greek world. The geographer Strabo (13.1.27) records Molossus, son of Andromache and Neoptolemus, as having been the first king of the Molossians, and it appears that this may have been based on an earlier traditional myth, which would have been available to Virgil.[12] Likewise, the geographer/travel writer Pausanias claims (1.4.4) that Andromache had three children by Neoptolemus. Pausanias also mentions the death of Neoptolemus (Pyrrhus), when writing about Delphi. The geographer adds that Andromache left Epirus and travelled east with her son Pergamus, who founded the eponymous city Pergamon, where she dies in her old age. According to Pausanias, Hermione has a son Tisamenus, with Orestes, but again, Virgil is only interested in Aeneas.

In considering the permutations in the relationships among Andromache, Hermione, Orestes, and Neoptolemus (in this case now called Pyrrhus), who have been discussed as a romantic tetrad,[13] Virgil leaves his readers in no doubt as to what his Andromache's feelings had been for Pyrrhus:

> But we, when they'd burned up our homeland, were split up and
>   shipped off
> Far away over the seas. I bore the conceit of Achilles'
> Offshoot, arrogant youth, bore the pains of birth as his slave-girl.
> He, then, went chasing Hermione, Leda's grandchild, a decent

Lacedaemonian wedding! – signed over the rights to his housemaid,
Me, to a house-slave, Helenus.

(*Aeneid* 3.325–29, Ahl)

Andromache has lost her childhood home, her marital home, her husband
and her child, and then suffered rape at the hands of her captor. It is no
wonder that Virgil describes her as almost fainting at the sight of Aeneas
(*Aeneid* 3.306–9). However, she collects herself enough to ask about Ascanius
(3.337–41).

Interestingly, Virgil clearly states that Pyrrhus had handed Andromache
over to Helenus, who was also his bondman, as soon as he wed Hermione.
This would have taken away all cause for Hermione's jealousy of Andromache,
a lynchpin in the plot of *Andromache*. The only person described as having
experienced a jealous rage in this version is Orestes, who killed Pyrrhus.
Again, Virgil sets out clearly who had prior claim to Hermione. Orestes had
been betrothed to Hermione, but she had later on been given to Pyrrhus:[14]

now enter Orestes
Blazing with passionate love for the girl (who's the wife he's been robbed
of).
Maddened by ghosts of his crimes he catches his rival [Pyrrhus] when off
guard,
Butchering him at his father's shrine.

(3.330–32, Ahl)

We may bear in mind that Aeneas, a fellow Trojan, is reporting what
Andromache told him, so it would not have been fitting for Andromache to
have expressed herself in any other way with regard to Pyrrhus or Orestes. As
Aeneas had expected to find Andromache with Pyrrhus, he must have heard
that she had been taken to be the concubine of Achilles' son, but has not
heard anything about what took place afterward. The version of events as told
by Andromache to Aeneas thus departs from that of Euripides, in that
Pyrrhus now actively pursues Hermione and the supposed benefits of a
marriage alliance with Sparta. On gaining his Spartan bride, he hands
Andromache over to Helenus, Hector's younger brother. So, in this version,
Pyrrhus steals Hermione from Orestes, much as Paris stole Helen from
Menelaus. Virgil does not exhibit great sympathy for either Greek, but
emphasizes the nobility of the Trojans, Rome's assumed ancestors. The Greek
Orestes is, if anything, an even greater villain here than in any other version.
In fury, Orestes himself arrived at the altar to Achilles and slew Pyrrhus in
revenge. Part of Pyrrhus' kingdom passed to Helenus, but without the

intercession of Thetis. Achilles' and Pyrrhus' ancestors are of no interest to Virgil, who concentrates on the divine ancestry of Aeneas. The Trojan Helenus is also characterized in a favourable light in the *Aeneid* (3.356–471).

Around the time of Virgil, Hyginus (64 BCE–17 CE) wrote his *Fabulae*, which take the form of a series of short notes dealing with mythological characters from the beginning of time. Hyginus was made superintendent of the Palatine library, where he would have been able to access Greek and Latin manuscripts.[15] Hyginus is thought to have based some of the brief records of his characters' exploits on the scholia of Apollodorus (180–120 BCE), a Homeric scholar who became the head librarian at Alexandria, before fleeing to Athens around 146 BCE.

Hyginus briefly mentions that Orestes marries Hermione after Neoptolemus was slain. Section 123 records that Neoptolemus had a son, Amphialus, with Andromache, but this is the only mention of Andromache in the *Fabulae*. In this version Hermione was actually betrothed to Neoptolemus before Menelaus promised her to Orestes. After Neoptolemus demands Hermione from Menelaus, she is taken away from Orestes and given to Neoptolemus. Orestes kills Neoptolemus out of jealousy and fury. None of the other characters' feelings are made clear. Readers are not informed whether Hermione loves Neoptolemus or Orestes or how Andromache felt about losing her child's father.

The *Bibliotheca*, a compendium of Greek myths and heroic legends, generally dated to the second century CE and attributed to Apollodorus, records that Andromache's son Astyanax was thrown from the battlements of Troy (*Epitome* 5.23) and then mentions that Andromache was given to Neoptolemus. Various explanations for Neoptolemus handing Andromache over to Helenus are offered. Helenus apparently warned Neoptolemus to return home by land, so saving him from the storm which shipwrecked many Greek leaders.[16] Helenus also had revealed to the Greeks the way in which they could defeat Troy (Apollodorus, *Epitome* 5.10).

Ovid created a refreshingly different account, with one of the fifteen letters forming the *Heroides* addressed to Orestes from Hermione. As such, this account concentrates entirely on Hermione's experience and emotions. There are different versions of Hermione's childhood once her mother, Helen, left with Paris for Troy. Some say she was left with her aunt Clytemnestra, while others suggest that it was her grandfather, Tyndareus, who brought her up. In either case, she would not have known her cousin Orestes while they were both young, as according to Aeschylus, Sophocles, and Euripides, Orestes was sent away to his uncle Strophius in Phocis when he was an infant and stayed there until his return some time after Agamemnon was murdered. In *Heroides* Letter 8, Hermione writes to Orestes that although she was betrothed to

Orestes by Tyndareus her grandfather, she was promised to Pyrrhus by her father who was fighting at Troy and had not known of this arrangement. However, she claims: 'yet my grandsire, as being first in order, has rank above my father' (8.34). This matches Hyginus' *Fabulae*, and is interesting in light of the scene in Euripides' *Orestes*, in which it is Tyndareus who attempts to seal his grandson's fate, after he murdered Clytemnestra. In the Ovidian version it appears to have been Tyndareus who brought up Hermione, not Clytemnestra. Furthermore, according to Ovid, Hermione was passionately fond of Orestes and had not wanted to marry Pyrrhus. In his unique fictional love letters written from Heroines to Heroes, all are caught in fraught or tragic circumstances: Hermione writes to Orestes urging him to rescue her from marrying Pyrrhus. In great contrast to her Euripidean predecessor, Hermione complains to Orestes that Pyrrhus is holding her captive. She bewails her fate as being worse than that of Andromache, who lost everything when Troy was burned. She begs Orestes to act like Menelaus, and to come and reclaim his wife. Like Euripides' Hermione, she makes light of Pyrrhus and of his father Achilles, glorifying instead the accomplishments of Menelaus and Agamemnon. Ovid's Hermione also flatters Orestes, paying him devoted compliments. She is, if possible, even more emotionally unbalanced than Euripides' anti-heroine. She writes of her cheeks and heart glowing with rage. Perhaps, however, Ovid, more than any other author, captures the source of the young woman's trauma. He has Hermione describe herself after her mother left for Troy, mournfully saying: 'Mother, will you go away, will you go away without me?' (*Heroides* 8.80), for her father was gone as well. She continues:

> In my childhood I had no mother; my father was ever in the wars – though the two were not dead, I was reft of both. You were not near in my first years, O my mother, to receive the caressing prattle from the tripping tongue of the little girl; I never clasped about your neck the little arms that would not reach, and never sat, a burden sweet, upon your lap. I was not reared and cared for by your hand; and when I was promised in wedlock I had no mother to make ready the new chamber for my coming. I went out to meet you when you came back home – what I shall say is truth – and the face of my mother was unknown to me! That you were Helen I none the less knew, because you were most beautiful; But you – you had to ask who your daughter was!
>
> (*Heroides* 8.89–100, Showerman, revised by Goold)

There are no references to Hermione being barren, or to Andromache poisoning her womb. The letter focuses only on Hermione's longing for

Orestes to come to her rescue and her hatred for Pyrrhus. As we shall see, the situation is reversed in versions to come. As discussed by Alden Smith,[17] the unique nature of Ovid's letters draws the reader into the romanticized fantasy of the poet's texts, creating a newly imagined nature for the heroines, who retell the myths from their own perspective. It would have been interesting to see what he would have written in a letter from Andromache, though the only possible recipient would have been Hector, and Homer and Euripides had already explored that relationship.

It is only in Seneca and his tragedy, *Trojan Women*, that Andromache comes vividly back to life, showing intelligence and fortitude in the face of disaster, when she is embroiled in a life and death battle of wits with Ulysses over the fate of her son, Astyanax. Seneca's play appears to condemn war in general, emphasizing both the pity and futility of war and the horrendous human suffering resulting from it. Although his plot is set immediately after the defeat of Troy, and as such follows Euripides' *Trojan Women* more than his *Andromache*, it is his heroic characterization of Andromache that eventually reappears in Racine's *Andromaque*. Seneca, like other Roman authors, glorifies the Trojans while depicting the Greeks (particularly Ulysses) as cunning, heartless victors in war, who cannot be trusted. The Romans saw themselves as the descendants of the Trojans, the people who ultimately conquer the Greeks, with Rome being the new Troy. As we will see, in Racine's play Astyanax is still alive years after the Trojan War has concluded, though in Euripides' *Trojan Women*, Astyanax was to be hurled from the ramparts of Troy to his death.

Seneca's *Trojan Women* is considered by many to be Seneca's most powerful tragedy, his crafting of Andromache particularly outstanding. Her line: 'It is utterly wretched to fear when you have no hope' (425) epitomizes the helpless terror of war's victims. Furthermore, Seneca takes divine intervention out of the drama, emphasizing instead the devastating depths to which human behaviour descends in times of war. Seneca's Andromache uses powerful rhetoric, displaying her inventive intelligence as she fights to save Astyanax. Although in *Trojan Women* she eventually fails, years later in Racine's *Andromaque* she will win that fight, allowing a direct bloodline from Hector through Astyanax to the French nobility, an idea reintroduced from medieval manuscripts by Ronsard over a century before Racine. Seneca made Hector's tomb the hiding place for Astyanax. He dies proudly by leaping to his death (although according to Racine he was actually saved by Andromache and another boy died in his place). The pitiless wiles of Ulysses as he wears down Andromache's resistance, until she reveals clues to where Astyanax, still alive, is hidden, are devastating to behold. Astyanax speaks only two words: *Miserere, mater*, 'Pity (me), mother' (792). Seneca's

Andromache has been described as resembling a typical Roman *matrona*, who had to head the family when the men were away at battle or had been killed. Although in Seneca's play she is defeated by Ulysses, it is Seneca's strong presentation of Andromache that actually prevails.

Receptions in the Middle Ages

Before proceeding to the most famous adaptation of *Andromache*, Racine's *Andromaque*, we need to stop off at a few more stations en-route. As strange as it may seem today, the works of Homer and the Greek tragedians did not circulate in the Latin Middle Ages, being largely replaced by Virgil's *Aeneid*. However, during this time two other Latin texts, best known by the names of their supposed authors *Dictys* and *Dares*, were the most popular versions of the Trojan War and its aftermath, although these are now treated as literary forgeries or *pseudepigraphia*.[18] As in later versions, the gods do not appear in these texts, making them readily adaptable for later authors. The first text is supposedly by *Dictys Cretensis* or Dictys of Cnossos in Crete, who purported to be a Greek soldier, who claimed to give an eyewitness account of the Trojan War. It was supposed to have been written in Phoenician and later translated into Greek during the first century CE. Around the fourth century CE, one Septimius translated it into Latin with the title *Ephemeris belli Trojani* or the *Journal of the Trojan War*. In Book 6, Dictys records that after the War Orestes took control of Mycenae. Menelaus sought to have Orestes punished for matricide, but it was decided he should go to Athens and stand trial at the court of the Areopagus, where he was acquitted. The text then describes Neoptolemus setting sail through a rough sea to the Sepiades in search of his grandfather Peleus, who had been driven out of his kingdom by Acastus, and was now in hiding. Neoptolemus found Peleus, killed Acastus' two sons, and started planning how to trap and kill Acastus. After hearing of Peleus' difficulties, Thetis arrived and prevented Neoptolemus from killing Acastus, who handed over control of his kingdom to Neoptolemus.

The Dictys text then follows the events as described in Euripides' *Andromache* fairly closely, even though the amazing claim is made by Dictys that he heard of these events from Neoptolemus himself, when he was a guest at Neoptolemus' wedding to Hermione. However, in this version one of Andromache's sons by Hector, called Laodamas, has survived. After consummating his marriage to Hermione, Neoptolemus went to Delphi to give thanks to Apollo that Alexander (Paris), who had murdered his father, had paid for his crime. Hermione, who was left at home with Andromache, was tortured by the thought that she had a rival for her husband's affections.

She called for her father to come and kill Andromache and her son. The people of the kingdom took pity on Andromache and helped her to escape. Orestes, who hated Neoptolemus for having married Hermione, who had been promised to him, heard of these events, and planned to kill Neoptolemus at Delphi. Menelaus in turn heard of Orestes' plans and returned to Sparta, wanting no part in the planned murder. Orestes returned to Mycenae, taking Hermione with him. Peleus and Thetis arrived to find out what had happened to their grandson. At this time Andromache was pregnant by Neoptolemus. On hearing of Neoptolemus' death, they sent Andromache to the Molossians, to protect her and her baby from Hermione and Orestes. Neoptolemus' son would become king of the country where he would be born.

The fanciful work of Dictys and the similar but pro-Trojan account by Dares the Phrygian were major sources for medieval works related to the Trojan War. The text known as *History of the Fall of Troy* was supposedly written by Dares, a Trojan priest, eyewitness to the War, and as such offers an opposing viewpoint to that contained in Dictys' account. It was believed to have been translated into Latin in the late fifth or early sixth century CE.[19] Dares himself is mentioned in one line each of the *Iliad* and *Aeneid*, as a priest of Hephaestus and a companion of Aeneas. Most of the prose text focuses on events before the defeat of Troy, but ends with Helenus' voyage away from Troy after the Greek victory, instead of with the voyage of Ulysses or Aeneas, and in this way converses with the *Iliad* and the *Aeneid*, but in brief, summarized form. In this version, the Trojans assemble a fleet of ships to attack Greece. Menelaus sails past the fleet. In the meantime, Helen has gone to sacrifice on Cythera, and Alexander abducts her from there, although since they were both struck by each other's great beauty, Helen was not unwilling to accompany Alexander. The vast majority of the text describes the fighting in the War, and discussions between the combatants. At the end of the fighting, Neoptolemus cuts Polyxena's throat over his father's tomb. Helenus is recorded to have sailed to the Chersonese, accompanied by Cassandra, his sister, and by Andromache, the wife of his dead brother Hector, and by his mother Hecuba. In this way, Dares' text ends with Helenus and Andromache sailing off together, but none of the plot of Euripides' *Andromache* is actually included. The importance of this text is that it convinced Medieval writers that the Trojan War was a historic event, with a factual background, making it a popular topic.

From the fifth century until the twelfth century, with few exceptions there was little interest in Greek literature in western Europe, beyond religious texts. Anicius Manlius Severinus Boethius (born *c.* 480 CE), a prominent translator of Greek texts to Latin, was aware of the importance of such translations due to the dwindling knowledge of the Greek language. Boethius only directly quoted two lines of Greek tragedy in his works: lines 319–20 of *Andromache* (*Consolatio philosophiae* 3,6,1). In this case, his purpose for quoting Andromache's attack on Menelaus was to demonstrate that having a reputation did not necessarily make someone a good or worthy man. However, he did make a second allusion to Andromache (3,7,1), this time lines 418–20, but he twisted the meaning to suit his purpose: 'All mankind, it seems, find that children are their very souls. Whoever finds fault with this through inexperience, [420] although he has less pain, has a sorry happiness.' As will be further discussed later in this chapter, the prominence of the theme of children and legacy in *Andromache*, as discussed in this book in the chapter on the Unity of *Andromache*, is identified in many receptions of the work.

By the early twelfth century, the revival of education that had begun shortly after the millennium was in full swing. Beginning in the mid-eleventh century, individual scholars would occasionally set up a 'school' of their own and gather students around them, with the Universities of Bologna, Paris, Oxford, and Cambridge becoming more permanent centres of learning, divided into 'faculties', including arts, law, medicine, and theology. University scholars rediscovered Aristotle's texts and shortly afterwards the Athenian tragedies. The arts faculty was for the basic training of students, before they proceeded to one of the 'higher' faculties. It was John Lydgate's *Troy Book*, completed in 1420, based on Benoît de Sainte-Maure's Old French *Roman de Troie* (*c.* 1160) and Guido delle Colonne's *Historia destructionis Troiae* (1287) that brought the Troy narrative as told by Dictys to the attention of the English-speaking world, eventually giving rise to *The Recuyell of the Historyes of Troye* by William Caxton, translated from Raoul Lefévre's *Recoeil des Histoires de Troie*.[20] In 1474 or 1475, Caxton printed his book, the first book in English to appear in print. As noted by Edwards, citing Schirmer, tales of Troy were regarded as historical, but also included moral and political lessons.[21] This, as we will see, was later continued by Racine in seventeenth-century France. It is also significant that in the *Troy Book*, lessons 'apply on one level to kingship and statecraft and on another to the individual within an aristocratic, chivalric world ... The principle lesson that Lydgate's Troy story offers its royal, aristocratic, and noble readers is the virtue of prudence.'[22]

After the introduction of printing presses, printed copies of Sophocles and Euripides in Greek became available in Renaissance Europe from about 1500. Yet from the end of the western Roman Empire until the sixteenth century, while Euripides' Greek texts (and texts of Homer, Aeschylus, and Sophocles) were not widely accessible in local western European languages, texts in Latin (such as the translations of Dictys and Dares) served as 'gatekeepers' and 'messengers' of Greek literature and myth.[23] Dictys' idea to have Andromache's son by Hector survive (albeit with various different names) continued through several other versions, with the French works *Franciade* and *Andromaque* promoting the idea that the French aristocracy was directly descended from Trojan nobility.

Receptions in Early Modern France and England

Fast forward to seventeenth-century France, and the importance of the intermediate Latin texts becomes obvious. The inspiration for Jean Racine's masterpiece *Andromaque* was indeed Euripides' text, but he was influenced by others as well. Among other important works was the unfinished epic poem, *Franciade*, conceived of by Pierre de Ronsard during the 1540s and finally published in 1572. The poem carries on from Vergil's *Aeneid* in that it starts in Epirus, where its hero Francus is an indolent young man, living with his mother, Andromache, and his uncle Helenus. This Francus is in fact none other than Astyanax, son of the great Trojan hero, Hector, renamed to serve Ronsard's purposes, with the epic connecting the French monarchy to the noblest of all Trojan royalty.

A twenty-first-century translation of the *Franciade* into English by Phillip John Usher has been well received. It begins:

> Muse atop the summits of Parnassus,
> Steer my speech and sing for me that race
> Of French kings descended from Francion,
> Hector's son and of Trojan stock,
> Who in his tender childhood was called
> Astyanax or by the name Scamandrius.
> Tell me of this Trojan's misfortunes,
> Of the wars he fought, of his mission,
> And tell me how many times on the seas
> (Despite Neptune and Juno) he overcame Fortune
> And how many times on solid ground he escaped
> From danger, before going on to build the walls of Paris.

Jupiter saved Astyanax (Francus) and Ronsard did the same, by making him the hero of his epic. Francus starts his project by building ships, and the rest of his journey was planned out by Ronsard, although it was never completed. It tellingly appeared on canvasses painted at the time of the entry of Charles IX into Paris in 1571 in celebration of the king's marriage to Elisabeth of Austria. There were noticeable parallels between Francus and Charles IX.

Francus apparently was to found the city of Sicambria in Germany, and then marry a German woman, before founding the city of Paris on the banks of the Seine, naming the city in honour of his uncle, the Trojan Prince, Paris. Pharamond, the legendary first truly French king, appeared in the paintings with Francus. Ronsard originally planned to write the poem for King Henry II, but it was eventually dedicated to Charles IX, with only four books out of a planned twenty-four actually finished when Charles IX died. This leaves Francus stranded on the island of Crete, and readers never know how his other adventures continued. As it stands, in the *Franciade*, Francus has survived all attempts to kill him, by Ulysses, Hermione, Menelaus, and possibly Orestes, and is described as living without much purpose, which is interesting because he is also considered the ancestor of the French royal family. Francus eventually sets off on his own odyssey, predictably meeting his own fair share of troubles on the way. The ship is wrecked, perhaps fortuitously, off the coast of Crete, and it is there that Francus meets Prince Dicée. Francus saves the prince's son from a giant, and the prince's two daughters fall in love with him. One of the sisters prophesizes that after his travels, Francus will eventually found France. The importance given by Ronsard to the survival of Astyanax (Francus) was obviously influential for Racine and must have shaped the plot of his play. The popularity of the poem did not survive beyond the eighteenth century, but when first published, it was enthusiastically received.

All of these works finally bring us to the most famous seventeenth-century reception of *Andromache* written in French. The playwright, Jean Racine, born in 1639, was orphaned at an early age, and in 1646 his grandmother took him to a convent near Paris where he studied Latin and Greek literature. Racine's *Andromaque* finally returns some of *Andromache*'s original characters to a situation in some ways parallel to that the audience encountered in Euripides' play. In Seneca's *Trojan Women*, readers saw Andromache trying to outwit Ulysses in order to save her son, Astyanax; they got to know Hermione through her imaginary letter in Ovid's *Heroides*; and they heard of Andromache's surviving sons ready to start their own dynasties in Virgil's *Aeneid* and Ronsard's *Franciade,* but none of these works show Andromache facing off with Hermione. In his introduction, Racine explains that the material for his play is found in Virgil's *Aeneid* Book 3 and in Euripides' *Andromache.* The connection of Troy's descendants to France seemed entrancing to French writers, who associated Alexander, or Paris, with the capital of France.

However, Racine is also writing for the audience of his own time, so Neoptolemus (Pyrrhus) becomes to some extent a knight of the Romance courts, based on Celadon, a character in Honoré d'Urfé's novel, *L'Astrée,* written during the first years of the seventeenth century.[24] This massive work (5,399 pages or 900,000 words long!) was popular in the European royal courts of the time.[25] Celadon states at one point that his duty is that of a lover and not of a man, and indeed all of the characters seem primarily motivated by a desperate, unrequited, romantic love. Matching these ideals of courtly love, Pyrrhus defers his contracted and long-awaited (by her) marriage to Hermione because he is desperately in love with Andromache.

While the Euripidean Neoptolemus may have had feelings for Andromache, we are never informed of this. Having fathered one or more children by her did not necessarily indicate a romantic attachment between master and concubine, either in ancient myth or in Euripides' own time. Andromache's heart is still too crushed from the loss of Hector to think beyond him. In Racine's *Andromaque*, her response to Pyrrhus' repeated offers of the life of a queen is to wish to take her own life, once she has assured the survival of Astyanax. Orestes is besotted with Hermione, and does everything possible to win her back from Pyrrhus, eventually planning his murder, though he himself is not the one to put an end to his rival's life. Hermione, for her part, is driven to insanity by her unrequited passion for Pyrrhus. In Euripides' *Andromache*, her episode of suicidal madness is brought on by fear of Neoptolemus discovering what she and her father have tried to do to his son and his son's mother. Racine brilliantly turns this upside down. In *Andromaque*, Hermione is reduced to a fit of frenzied hysteria when she hears that, once again, Pyrrhus has rejected her. Having hoped against hope for so long that Pyrrhus would finally fulfil his promise to marry her, she was almost deliriously happy when it appeared that the longed-for day had finally arrived. But Hermione is shattered when she hears that she has once more been rejected in favour of Andromache. In a fit of jealous rage Hermione instructs Orestes to kill Pyrrhus. In Racine's play Menelaus is absent, being superfluous to a plot based mainly on the trials and tribulations of romantic love. However consumed by passion she may be, Hermione remains astute enough to castigate Orestes for not having realized that her instructions to him were nothing but a jealous lover's fleeting aberration. Hermione ends her life beside the corpse of her beloved.

The English scholar Ambrose Philips adapted *The Distrest Mother* from his translation of Racine's *Andromaque* in 1712. Philips was a politician as well as a fellow of Cambridge University and in *The Distrest Mother* he follows Racine closely, with a few exceptions. Though a translation from the French, this is also a play perfused with the English spirit.[26] At times, it almost seems to anticipate Churchill's clarion call to raise the nation's morale in facing an impossible task, only here it is the characters 'girding their loins' to follow whatever task they have set themselves. Fittingly, therefore, the prologue for a Drury Lane performance in the Theatre Royal, written by a Mr. Steele, and spoken by a Mr. Wilks, mentions Shakespeare many times, saying that out of modesty, and being in no way comparable to Shakespeare, the poet preserves the rules of time and space in his play, whereas Shakespeare took his audiences on flights of fancy to distant shores, travelling at whatever speed suited the bard's purpose.

The 'English' spirit of the characters is seen in short additions, mainly as scenes added on to the end of Acts I, IV, and V. At the end of Act I in a brief added scene, Andromache declares to Cephisa she will die together with her son. In *Andromaque*, Cephisa and Andromache are together in this way only in the very brief Act III scene 5, with Cephisa seemingly silent at the end of Act I. In Philip's Act II scene 2, Hermione is happy to flee with Orestes, and Orestes is overjoyed at what he thinks is Hermione's profession of love. In Act II scene 4 in both plays, fortunes are told as Pyrrhus decides to marry Andromache – even if we know that decision will not last long. Philips' version has an additional scene 5: here Pyrrhus is thinking out loud, addressing his thoughts to Phoenix. It becomes quite obvious that he will not go through with the proposed marriage to Hermione.

Act IV scene 3 is much shorter in Philips' version. Hermione's long, furious speeches, depicting her loss of balance, are chiselled down to the bare bones. However, at the end of Act IV extra scenes are added. In scene 7, Phoenix appears alone, having already warned Pyrrhus, but now he speaks of his fears for Pyrrhus out loud. He announces the arrival of Andromache, who now is to be queen, decked out in royal finery. Phoenix wants to guard her son from danger, but perhaps is not careful enough of Pyrrhus' life. In scene 8, Cephisa enjoys seeing Andromache returned to her former splendour, but Andromache is still buried under her grief and shares her own dark thoughts. She wants Pyrrhus to care for Astyanax but she herself has no intention of continuing to live. Cephisa describes how tenderly Pyrrhus is dressing Astyanax for the wedding. This is one of the longest scenes of the play. As matches the title, the grief of the mother is the focus of attention, far more here than in Racine, where Andromache disappears after Act IV scene I. While Hermione has moved further to the background in Philips' play, Andromache is mainly concerned with preparing Cephisa to convince Pyrrhus to take care of Astyanax.

In the final act (Act V), Hermione learns of the murder of Pyrrhus, and while the first scenes closely follow *Andromaque*, once again, after scene 5 further scenes are added. Phoenix believes Orestes is to blame for Pyrrhus' murder, but thinks he has escaped. In scene 7, Phoenix, Andromache, Cephisa, and their attendants gather together. To avoid marrying Pyrrhus, Andromache was determined to die, but following her suitor's death she realizes that she can live to bring up her son herself. Relieved of all conflicts of loyalty between the two princes, Hector and Pyrrhus, Andromache finally grieves for Pyrrhus, and acknowledges his bravery, which she failed to do in his lifetime, saying her tears will never cease. In scene 8, Andromache suddenly expresses real joy as she is about to greet her son, who now is a prince and will inherit Pyrrhus' throne. Interestingly, this ending returns Andromache closer to her character in Euripides, in that the survival of Andromache's child becomes the crucial message of the play, and in this knowledge the surviving characters are finally content.

In the nineteenth century, Baudelaire addressed his long poem *Le Cygne* (*The Swan*) to Victor Hugo (a symbol of exile in his time).[27] Though written in a particular time and place, during Hausmann's renovation of Paris, it brings *Andromache* a new timelessness, in that she becomes all widows, all refugees who have lost their childhood home and families. The main themes are exile and compassion.[28] While the poet's thoughts began with the changes occurring in his beloved city of Paris, the themes are universal.[29] Baudelaire, struggling with a sense of anonymity, feeling a stranger in this newly modernized town, takes the reader on a sweeping flight from ancient Greece, as symbolized by Andromache, to his memory of seeing a swan escape from a cage at a market, in search of water, its safe home environment. Baudelaire includes fleeting images of Andromache, first when newly widowed, weeping by the banks of the Simois on the Trojan plain, then forced into the arms of Pyrrhus, and finally as Helenus' wife when she is encountered by Aeneas. He likens the swan to Ovid's version of the myth of Cycnus, who jumps off a cliff but transforms into a swan, flying away. Both the swan and Andromache symbolize all displaced persons. Baudelaire's mention of orphans suckled by a she-wolf appears to be an allusion to Romulus and Remus, the mythological founders of Rome, descendants of a Trojan hero, thus casting Rome, and later Paris, as a rebuilt Troy. In the last stanza, Baudelaire moves from the particular to the universal. His mind passes through forests and seas to all the captives, the vanquished . . . and the dispossessed. With Baudelaire Andromache has come full circle, from her beginnings in ancient Greek epic and tragedy, through literature belonging to a particular time and place, and now transcending these as a universal message to mankind, urging compassion for all, without noting their race or creed.

Although Baudelaire's message may indeed be a universal call for compassion, like the other texts discussed throughout this chapter, it too is influenced by the style of the time when it was written. We have seen how from Lydgate's *Troy Book* through Ronsard's *Franciade*, to Racine's *Andromaque* and Philips' *The Distrest Mother*, the ideas of chivalry and courtly love brought about stylistic changes to the plot themes. A parallel may be drawn here with the development of the Arthurian myths. The earliest stories rendering these myths set after the Roman withdrawal from Britain speak of a local warlord, possibly of Welsh origins, leading British tribes defending their lands from invading Angles and Saxons. A ninth-century monk, Nennius, first used the name Arthur in his *Historia Brittonum* describing twelve battles led by a Christian king, culminating in a period of peace.

Geoffrey of Monmouth started the first book of his *History of the Kings of Britain* (*c.* 1136) with an account of the early settlement of Britain by Brutus of Troy, great-grandson of Aeneas. The last five books deal with Arthur, from his birth in Tintagel, Cornwall, to his victories over the Saxons, which gave peace to the land until after Arthur's death. In thirteenth-century France, these stories gained an element of romance and chivalry found also in the poems and novels of Chrétien de Troyes, among others, who invented the characters Lancelot and Percival and introduced the ideas of 'Camelot' and the 'Holy Grail' in the Vulgate and Post-Vulgate cycles. The romantic elements involving the Knights of the Round Table and the Lady of the Lake were further developed in Thomas Malory's 1485 *Le Morte d'Arthur*. The ancient British warlord has transmuted into a full-blooded, chivalrous English knight, much in the same way as Neoptolemus and Orestes gained the romantic manners of the French medieval courts.

Throughout the development of the Arthurian legends, the topics of heritage and legacy are as important as in *Andromache*. Monmouth's Arthur becomes king because he is the son of King Uther, and thus able to release the sword Excalibur from the stone where it was set, and it is Arthur's own son Mordred who eventually brings about Arthur's death. However, an additional twist to the interpretation of the Holy Grail also highlights the importance of children and legacy in the Arthurian legend. Early Arthurian stories describe a bowl familiar from Celtic legends producing sufficient soup to feed an entire army. Later authors turned the bowl into a cup, which in thirteenth-century France became the 'Holy Grail', the cup which Jesus drank from in his last supper, and which Joseph of Arimathea, having used it to collect drops of Jesus' blood, later brought to England. In the 2003 novel by Dan Brown, the 'Grail' actually represents the bloodline of Jesus, as in children descended from Jesus and Mary Magdalene.

While the offspring of Andromache with either Hector or Neoptolemus/ Pyrrhus are not given this metaphorical significance, their crucial involvement in the motivation of many of the later authors discussed in this chapter certainly gives them a unique status, connecting the reception of Euripides' play with the themes of lineage analysed in Chapter 3, where children and legacy are identified as the unifying theme of the play. As noted throughout this chapter, in the texts under discussion Andromache's surviving child is given different names and is variously fathered by Hector or Neoptolemus/ Pyrrhus. However, as mentioned earlier in reference to Virgil's *Aeneid*, Ronsard's *Franciade*, and Racine's *Andromaque*, one of the playwrights' motives behind shaping the story in the particular way they chose is to emphasize the connection of these children to the latter-day royal families in their home countries.

Opera and Visual Arts

Apart from literature, the story of Euripides' *Andromache* had a broad reception in the worlds of art and opera. The seventeenth, eighteenth, and nineteenth centuries saw numerous operatic performances based on the ancient play in Italy, Germany, Austria, France, and England.[30] Chong-Gossard, who gives brief plot summaries of the numerous libretti for these performances, states:

> Over time as Euripides' characters were thrown into increasingly complex scenarios, they became more and more like 'stock' roles. Andromache was always the faithful woman, either Hector's widow, or Pyrrhus' rejected lover/wife; Hermione was the woman fought over by two men (much like her mother, Helen); Orestes was the aggressor, sometimes envisioning himself as the rescuer; and Pyrrhus was the king who wants to have two women, but can't. Throughout all these stories runs a dramatic assumption that men and women should be 'paired off' in the end, and in most cases Andromache is united (or re-united) with Pyrrhus.[31]

One example of the bizarre directions that operatic libretti may take is found in one of the operas by Aurelio Aureli, performed in Venice in 1662, where Orestes, Hermione, Andromache, and Pyrrhus are shipwrecked on an enchanted island. As with many other libretti, it has very little to do with Euripides. Antonio Salvi's *Astianatte* (Astyanax) performed in Florence in 1710 is one operatic adaption of Racine's *Andromaque* that does retain the touching scene in which Andromache pleads with Pyrrhus to spare Astyanax, although he reshaped the ending into a happy one. A further variation of the themes, involving many sources of the myth but distancing itself from them, is found in Apostolo Zeno's *Andromaca*, first performed in Vienna in 1724, with music composed by Antonio Caldara. The deviations from well-known myths are mind boggling. Andromache is raising not only her son Astyanax, but also Ulysses' son Telemachus, and all three of them are hiding in Hector's tomb. Although Pyrrhus is in love with Andromache, he does eventually marry Hermione, with both Andromache and Astyanax being set free.

In visual arts, most depictions of Andromache choose the context of her marriage to Hector, or her suffering during the sack of Troy and her grief after the deaths of Hector and Astyanax, rather than her later life with Neoptolemus. Some fine art paintings do however refer to the plot of Racine's *Andromaque*. Perhaps the best known is *Andromaque et Pyrrhus*, by the Paris-born Pierre-Narcisse Guérin, first exhibited in the Louvre in 1810. It is a large canvas of 3.42 metres by 4.57 metres, showing Pyrrhus on a throne, staring at a man holding a staff, most probably Orestes, who is delivering his message demanding the death of Astyanax.[32] However, Pyrrhus' hands are held out to Andromache, who is kneeling in the foreground, wrapping her arms protectively around Astyanax, while Hermione appears to be hurrying out of the room. The high drama of *Andromaque* is thus captured in one frozen moment in the facial expressions and gestures of the four main characters.

Conclusion

Two studies by Timothy Reiss offer some important clues as to the importance of Andromache's children in the reception of the play. His 1999 essay 'Between Sovereignty and Tyranny: *Britannicus*' highlights Racine's political and social interests, using his plays as a 'serious plea for rational, internal political and legal order',[33] while his 2002 chapter '*Andromaque* and the Search for Unique Sovereignty' explores how sovereignty is established.[34] Reiss goes on to explain that Racine changed the preface to his second edition of the play by emphasizing his reliance on the passage he quotes from the third book of the *Aeneid* about Andromache, instead of on Euripides' *Andromache*.[35] He notes that in the *Aeneid*, Astyanax has remained alive, and as the child of Andromache's first husband he is the sole object of her concern. Racine was concentrating on making Hector's heir the ancestor of French royalty (as Francus had been for Ronsard). The political implications of *Andromaque* are thus related to Astyanax as the ancestor of French monarchy; furthermore, Racine was 'making a point about the bond between rational and legitimate political order and right control of the passions'.[36] When discussing the unifying themes of the play, it is these two ideas which ultimately come to the fore. In the preface to his adaptation of Racine's play, Ambrose Philips explains that the name of Hector could not have been more terrible to the Greeks than that of the Duke of Marlborough to the French.

He relates the play to the lines from Virgil and to Euripides' *Andromache*. He discusses how in Euripides' play, Andromache was most concerned for the son she bore to Pyrrhus. However, Philips decided to conform to more recent interpretations, and make her only the widow of Hector, and the mother only of Astyanax, Hector's son. There was a dramatic consideration, in that it was thought she would be far more convincing and raise more compassion in having concerns for Hector's son. Sufficient time had passed to allow the myth to be altered. Euripides might have had more difficulty with this. Ambrose Philips is not concerned with Astyanax founding France or Molossus founding the Molossian tribe of Epirus, so he just quietly apologizes for prolonging the life of Astyanax a little!

Notes

Chapter 1

1 Skouroumouni Stavrinou 2014.
2 For the various conundrums and ambiguities that the play presents in terms of the relationship between the various characters as *philoi* (relatives/friends) and/or enemies, see the excellent treatment of Belfiore 2000: 81–100.
3 There are various versions about Achilles' death. In *Iliad* 21.276–78 Achilles states that his mother told him that Apollo himself will be his killer. Hector, on the other hand, in *Iliad* 22.359 forewarns Achilles that it would be Apollo together with Paris who would shoot the fateful arrow.
4 The ten are: *Hecuba, Orestes, Phoenician Women, Medea, Hippolytus, Andromache, Alcestis, Rhesus, Trojan Women* and *Bacchae*.
5 The remaining extant eight plays by Euripides came to light purely by chance when a codex containing the play *Hecuba* (which belongs to the selected ten) and eight other plays, which were probably part of a completed edition and arranged alphabetically, came around 250 CE into the possession of a Byzantine scholar who copied these eight plays, together with the selected ten, all of which have reached us. These eight are known as the 'Alphabetical Plays' because their titles begin with the Greek letters epsilon, eta, iota, and kappa: *Helen, Electra, Heraclidae, Heracles, Suppliants (Hiketides), Ion, Iphigenia among the Taurians, Iphigenia at Aulis,* and the satyr play *Cyclops*.
6 Netz 2011.
7 For a production in Athens, see Wilamowitz-Moellendorff 1963 [1875]: 148; Allan 2000: 149–60; Lamari 2017: 54–6. Others, such as Nauck 1900: xvii, n. 21, Page 1936: 223–8, and Lesky 1983 [1972]: 462, n. 90, suggest Sicyon; Csapo and Slater 1995: 15 maintain that the premiere was in Argos. Goossens 1962: 376–7 and Taplin 1999: 45 suggest some place in Thessaly; Stewart 2017: 139–44 and Butrica 2001 Molossia; Cairns 2012 claims it was either Molossia or Thessaly.
8 See Harder 1985: 126, n. 4. Furthermore, although there remains no record for an *Andromache* by Euripides in the *Didaskaliai*, a play of the same name was performed in Athens, and attributed to an unknown poet given the name Democrates. Verrall (1905: 23–4) suggested that the statement by Callimachus (310–240 BCE), the prolific Hellenistic librarian responsible for cataloguing many books held in the library at Alexandria, that the play was 'superscribed' to Democrates, may have indicated that the said poet might have added a prefixed prologue to some editions, and his name could have been added mistakenly to the whole play, which in fact was composed by

Euripides. Most importantly, the text was eventually handed down as part of the Euripidean canon.

9   For further discussion, see Aldrich 1961: preface, and chapter II, n. 44; Stevens 1971: 15–18.

10 Stevens 1971: 17.

11 A case in point is the former assumption that Euripides' *Trojan Women* was a political play offering biting criticism of the Athenians' behaviour after their victory over Melos in 415 BCE, when they killed the men, enslaved the women and children, and burned the towns of the island. Van Erp Taalman Kip (1987) proved in a meticulously argued article – asking such questions as how much time it took Euripides to compose a play; how much time it took to train a chorus, etc. – that the play could not have been written after the Melian events and still be produced in 415. The process of writing and then producing a play simply took too much time for its performance to concur with an event that had just happened.

12 Stevens 1971: 19; Allan 2000: 149 with n. 3.

13 For general information on Greek tragedy, see Sommerstein 2002.

14 His *Vita* (1) mentions only Magnesia and Macedonia as places to which he travelled.

15 *Pace* Stewart 2017: 141–4, who maintains that the play 'could have appealed to multiple audiences, and specifically a Panhellenic One'. The reason for this general appeal, the scholar asserts, is principally that *Andromache* is 'a play about travel'. It is true that while the play can be characterized as a frustrated *nostos*, return of Neoptolemus home, and the further future migration of Andromache, it does not have a greater breadth of foreign descriptive travel than other extant plays – e.g. Sophocles' *Women of Trachis, Oedipus at Colonus*; Euripides' *Helen, Hippolytus*, which would render the play Panhellenic. Menelaus and Andromache have returned long ago. There is no travel here but that of Orestes.

16 For further information on the Dionysia, see Csapo and Slater 1995: 103–21, 287.

17 For general information on satyr plays, see Sutton 1980; Griffith 2015.

18 See Stevens 1971: 27–8.

19 For a detailed study of the institution of the *choregoi*, see Wilson 2000.

20 See Griffin 1999 on the relation between historical events and democratic ideology of fifth-century Athens and tragic drama.

21 See Bers 2014; Kovacs 2014; Meineck 2012: 3; Csapo 2014: 53–4.

22 See also Csapo and Slater 1995: 289–90.

23 On the question of women's presence in the audience, see Csapo and Slater 1995: 286–7, 290–3; Taplin 1996: 193–4.

24 For the problematics of the lottery and the decision procedure, see Csapo and Slater 1995: 158–60.

25 Pickard-Cambridge 1973: 38.

26 His first win at the City Dionysia occurred in 441 BCE, but it is not known which plays were entered. The set in which the extant *Hippolytus* was

performed in 428 BCE also won first prize, as did posthumously *Iphigenia at Aulis, Alcmaeon in Corinth, and Bacchae*. In 431 BCE, *Philoctetes, Dictys, Medea*, and *Harvesters* came second.

27 Wiles 1997: 44–52 maintains the *orchēstra* was circular; others that it was rectangular or trapezoidal. On the interpretations of the various archaeological remains of theatres, see Moretti 1999–2000.

28 See Bosher 2014.

29 See Levett 2014.

30 *Pace* Mastronarde 1990: 269: 64, I take τῶν ἱπποβότων Φθίας πεδίων (*tōn hippobotōn Phtias pediōn, Andr.* 1229–30) literally 'on the ground of horse-pasturing Phthia' not 'land of Phthia'. The periphrasis of 'land of Phthia' would fail to explain Thetis' direct address to Peleus, and diminish the closeness between them.

31 Specifically violence exhibited in the act of killing humans or animals, or striking a person. For an analysis of the presentation of violence in ancient Greek drama, see Sommerstein 2010: 30–46, who also notes that the impaling of Prometheus ([Aesch.] *Prom.* 55–62) is an exception to the rule that no figure strikes another figure in Greek tragedy.

32 Cf. Hall 2002 on the function of the voice. Also Pavlovskis 1977: 113; Owen 1936: 148–54; Damen 1989: 318, who offers a para-dramatic treatment of the actors and the roles they play.

33 See Hall 2002: 9–10.

34 For further discussion, see Taplin 1978: 16–19, 179.

35 Kovacs (1995), before lines 879–80, introduces him as wearing a 'travelling costume', but if so, why don't the Phthian women define the garment as such?

Chapter 2

1 For discussion, see also Alaux 2011: 142–3.

2 Burgess 2004: 1–4; Nagy 1990: 70–9.

3 Burgess 2004: 1–16.

4 Burgess 1996: 78, n. 8.

5 Burgess 2001: 1.

6 Winnington-Ingram, Gould, Easterling, and Knox 1989: 259 remark, 'One could say that the stories came to the tragedians rough-shaped for drama by epic and lyric poets.'

7 See discussion by Roisman 2021: 167–76 and forthcoming.

8 The *Little Iliad* describes Neoptolemus killing Astyanax by throwing him from the walls of Troy (frags. 18, 29, 30 West). *Iliou Persis* (*Sack of Troy*) attributes the killing of Astyanax to Odysseus; cf. *Trojan Women* 721–25.

9 Sommerstein 2006: 14–22 identifies Sophocles' *Hermione* with his play *Women of Phthia* (*Phthiotides*) giving a possible summary of the play and comparing it with Euripides' *Andromache*.

10 There are scholars, however, who are confident that Sophocles' *Hermione* preceded Euripides' *Andromache*. See Sommerstein 2006: 20; Allan 2000: 16, n. 51.
11 In fact, Allan 2000: 25–8 maintains that 'the most radical reworking of myth in *Andromache* is the transformation of Neoptolemus'. Indeed, based on Neoptolemus' other portrayals, Most 1985: 160 refers to him as 'the first great war criminal of Greek cultural history'.
12 Cf. Sommerstein 2006: 20.
13 Foley 2001: 89–90.
14 In some ways, this arrangement parallels the motif of Neoptolemus' cohabitation with two women.
15 Quoted in Sommerstein 2006: 4.
16 The story appears in Apollodorus *Epit.* 6.14; Servius, on Virgil, *Aen.* 3.330, where Pyrrhus (i.e. Neoptolemus) is said to have acted 'trusting in the support of Menelaus'; and probably Ovid, *Heroides* 8.81–82, which seems to envisage Hermione, already married to Orestes, being seized during her husband's absence by Neoptolemus, the suitor approved by Menelaus (8.33).
17 Sommerstein 2006: 4.
18 Sommerstein 2006: 4–5.
19 Sandys 1930.
20 For translation by Kovacs, see Kovacs 1995.
21 For discussion see Roisman 1997 and 2005: 88–105.
22 For Menelaus in the Homeric epics, see Roisman 2011.
23 Ambühl 2010: 116.
24 Ambühl 2010: 120.
25 Ambühl 2010: 121.

Chapter 3

1 Others divide it into lines 1–801 and 802–1288, and still others divide it into three distinct parts: 1–801, 802–1046, 1047–1288. For Verrall 1905: 8, the play 'presents three incidents, (1) the visit of Menelaus to Phthia, (2) the visit of Orestes, (3) the murder of Neoptolemus at Delphi, not one of which is connected as cause or effect with another'. The latter is also stated by Phillippo 1995: 355, a harsh judgement and not entirely correct. When Orestes appears, he knows Neoptolemus will not be returning from the deadly trap set by Orestes himself. Peleus' arrival is utterly ignored. For a summary of the different views about the play's structure, divided into those who see the contrasts of love, jealousy, and the ensuing conflicts as the unifying element, see Aldrich 1961: 13–15. For those who see the play as an anti-Spartan political pamphlet (15–18), and the various questions that the 'rationalists pose' (18–19), see as well Verrall's and Grube's views (19–22).

For an excellent explanation of problematic structure of the play, see Aldrich 1961: 60–79.

2 Erbse 1966.

3 Hartung 1844: 108–25, developed by Friedländer 1926 followed by Mossman 1996.

4 Kitto 1966: 230–6.

5 Stevens 1971: 13; Aldrich 1961: 69–80.

6 Cf. Brooks and Wimsatt 1957: 33–4; cf. also Papadimitropoulos 2006, who maintains that the motifs of marriage and strife, although they do not unify the play as a whole, are dominant in the play and may be considered elements that ensure the thematic unity of the drama. Allan 2000: 43–8 gives a full account of the many views suggested about the unifying element of the play. His suggestion that we should also consider the ability of the poet 'to keep the audience hooked' (43) is a unifying theme worthy of consideration.

7 See Aldrich 1961: 19.

8 Allan 2000: 268.

9 As suggested by Stevens 1971 and Aldrich 1961.

10 Storey 1989.

11 See *Cypria* for the connection between the Judgement of Paris and the intervention of Eris at the wedding of Thetis and Peleus, as a result of Zeus and Themis planning to bring about the Trojan War.

12 For translation by Lloyd, see Lloyd 2005.

13 Storey 1989.

14 'You heavy with wine, you with the front of a dog but heart of a deer, never have you had the courage to arm yourself for battle with your people, or go forth to an ambush with chiefs of the Achaeans . . ' (*Iliad* 1.225–27).

15 For example, Aldrich 1961; Kitto 1966; Stevens 1971.

16 For a brief account of childlessness in Greek tragedy and the quest for achieving legacy through generational continuity, see Tzanetou 2014.

17 Papadimitropoulos 2006.

18 The Messenger gives a graphic description of the weapons that the enemies hurled at Neoptolemus: stones, arrows, javelins, darts, pikes, double-pointed ox-piercing spits (1117–34).

19 Skouroumouni Stavrinou 2016.

20 The theme of deceit/betrayal in this play is woven with that of supplication (*Andr.* 115–116, 528–29), which links the play to other plays around the motif of supplication; see Alaux 2011: 146.

21 Papadimitropoulos 2006: 153.

22 For such comments cast 'at the departing back', which are likely not to be heard by the departing figure, usually including insults, as here, threats and taunts, see Taplin 1977: 221–2.

23 Papadimitropoulos 2006.

24 For a discussion, see also Aldrich 1961: 67–9.

25 Although the myth offered such a possibility for Euripides, see Chapter 2, p. 25.

26 Cf. Papadimitropoulos 2006: 151.

27 Llewellyn-Jones 2012: 28–33.

28 Roisman 1999: *passim*. For messages to different audiences, see Verrall 1967 [1895]: 82–9; Vellacott 1975: 19; Parry 1963; Lyne 1995.

29 Norwood 1921: 35.

30 See Papadodima 2014. For presenting the barbarian Andromache as expressing Greek views, see also Chapter 3, p. 50, Chapter 4, pp. 63–6.

31 Poole 1994: 10 maintains that Hermione's attack on her sex 'goes beyond the needs of the dramatic situation and the requirements of anti-Spartan propaganda'. However, the dramatic scene is so full of extreme behaviour on Hermione's part that this attack on her own sex is a rather well integrated segment of the whole.

32 See, for example, Dover 1974: 98–102; Walcot 1996: 91–102; Lefkowitz 1986: 61–79; Buxton 1994: 122–7 on representations of deceptive mythic heroines and their 'feminine' crafts, especially weaving, for which see also Jenkins 1985: 112–20; for Homer see, for example, Katz 1991: 24–119, 128–30; for tragedy, see, for example, Zeitlin 1996: *passim*; Rabinowitz 1993: 132–41, 166–9.

33 For fuller discussion of deceit and femininity, see Roisman 2021: 3–7.

34 Allan 2000: 182.

35 For this statement of Andromache, see Chapter 4, n. 5.

36 For *nostos* as dramatic motif in extant Greek tragedy, see Alaux 2011: 145–6.

37 The first references to Apollo's role in Achilles death is to be found in *Iliad* 19.408–17 and 22.356–60.

38 See Chapter 2, n. 8.

39 *Pace* Mossman 1996.

40 See, for example, Aldrich 1961: 15–18.

41 Cf. Aldrich 1961: 58–60, and pp. 4–5, 9–10, 31, 34, 40, 46, 49 of the present text.

42 Vester 2009: 302. In her article Vester discusses Andromache's civic identity in terms of the Greek views of *physis* and *nomos*. Although due to her *physis* she is a non-Greek, she behaves according to what is considered *nomos*.

43 Poole 1994: 11 discards the idea that the city in question could be either Argos or Mantinea because their treaty with Athens in 420 BCE was too late to influence the play. Pool suggests that probably Euripides did not have a specific city in mind; he just provided an example of a principle which Sparta usually followed.

44 Poole 1994: 11.

45 In terms of the Athenian spectators' perception of legitimacy of children, it should be noted that Pericles' law of citizenship (451 BCE) according to which citizenship would be conferred only on children both of whose parents were Athenians, cannot be sweepingly applied to heroic Phthia. In fact, even if Hermione had conceived, her children would have not been

considered 'citizens' according to the principle of this law because Hermione is a Spartan, not a Phthian. However, the issue must have been in the minds of the spectators once the theme of bastardy came up as explicitly as it did. Eventually, in 413 BCE, Pericles' citizenship law was relaxed to allow Athenian men to beget legitimate children from two Athenian women, although only one of these could be a legitimate wife. While *Andromache* was performed years prior to this new permission, we cannot preclude the possibility that the drama's presentation of a bigamous household and its dire consequences represented what was on the audience's mind and anticipated the legal response.

46 Following Phillippo 1995, I use the word 'patronymic' rather broadly, not necessarily as appearing in the special Greek form ending in -ιδης, but as any phrase denoting kinship. Thus Andromache is usually referred as 'a wife of Hector' in a variety of phrases in 4, 656, 908, 960. Her relationship to Hector brings to mind that she is also the mother of Astyanax, who has been cruelly executed by Neoptolemus, and thus echoes the theme of parenthood. By name she is referred in 5, 806, 1243. Hermione is referred to as 'the child of Zeus' daughter' in 145, as 'daughter of Menelaus' in 40, 486–87, 897, 1049; by name in 29, 86, 114, 122, 519, 804, 889, 1192. Neoptolemus: patronymics used in 21, 25, 125, 268, 881–82, 971, 993–94, 1069, 1119, 1149–50, 1163, 1169–70, 1239; by name in 14. Orestes: patronymics used in 884, 892, 1034, 1061, 1090, 1115; by name in 885, 1109, 1242. Achilles is referred to only as 'the son of Thetis' in 108.

47 Phillippo 1995 explores the use of patronymics in the play as a vehicle for discussing family relationships as well 'as the volatile relationship between kinship ties and individuality of certain characters and their circumstances' (360). She does not consider the theme of parents and children that is inherent in the use of patronymics as a unifying theme.

48 There is obviously no textual support for Verrall's claim (1905: 20–1) that Menelaus was in cahoots with Orestes and left only seeming to give ground to Peleus, in order to make it possible for his nephew to take Hermione away, but see the degree to which this suggestion would illuminate Orestes' character in Chapter 4, n. 32.

Chapter 4

1 Signore 2007: 1, 37 states that the two share 'cross-gender similes' (Foley 1978) in the description of their grief: Achilles for Patroclus and Andromache for Hector.

2 Cf. the Chorus speaking of double marriage in 123–25, 465; Hermione's claiming that it is not right for one man to hold the reins of two women (177–80); and Orestes referring to Hermione's circumstances as those of one man having two women (907–9).

3 *Pace* Papadimitropoulos 2006: 150.

4 Vester 2009: 296.

5 Cf. Andromache's claim in *Trojan Women* 655–56: 'I knew where I ought to be the winner over my husband and where I should yield the victory to him.' For the expectation of submissiveness of the wife in Athenian culture, see Just 1989: 277 and *passim*.

6 Hall 1989: 188 refers to lines 168–78 as 'the most flamboyant passage of anti-barbarian rhetoric in extant tragedy'.

7 As Grube 1961: 201 notes: 'One notes that all the crimes of which she accuses barbarians are common in Greek legend', and as Verrall (1905: 29) well puts it: 'one wonders, not without a shudder, whether the wife of Orestes [her cousin] remembered these words of nights'.

8 For a discussion of internalized misogyny, see Chong-Gossard and Ng 2018.

9 For full discussion of the sentence, see Roisman 2021: 113.

10 Hermione speaks fifty-six lines to Andromache's sixty-seven. Hermione: 147–80, 234–35, 237, 237, 239, 241, 243, 245, 247, 249, 251, 253, 255, 257, 259, 261–68; Andromache: 183–231, 236, 238, 240, 242, 244, 246, 248, 250, 252, 254, 256, 258, 260, 269–73.

11 For parallels, see Lloyd 2005 on 184–91.

12 Lloyd 2005 on 192–204.

13 See Chong-Gossard and Ng 2018: 77, 88.

14 Compare Helen's similar needling of Paris, according to Hecuba. Whenever word came that Menelaus had the upper hand, Helen would praise Menelaus to vex Paris, but if the Trojans were fortunate, she regarded Menelaus as nothing (*Trojan Women* 1002–7).

15 For a discussion of the scholarly uneasiness over the tone of Andromache's comment in lines 222–27, see Gregory 1999–2000: 67–9, in which she shows how these lines accord with the characterization of Andromache elsewhere in the play.

16 Cf. Lesky 1983 [1972]: 256.

17 For discussion, see Roisman 2021: 124–5.

18 Stevens 1971: on 565 ff.

19 See, for example, Dover 1974: 98–102; Walcot 1996: 91–102; Lefkowitz 1986: 61–79; Buxton 1994: 122–7 on representations of deceptive mythic heroines and their 'feminine' crafts, especially weaving, for which see also Jenkins 1985: 112–20; for Homer see, for example, Katz 1991: 24–119, 128–30; for tragedy, for example, Zeitlin 1996: *passim*; Rabinowitz 1993: 132–41, 166–9.

20 For deception as one of the themes characterizing tragic heroines, see Roisman 2021: 4–5.

21 Lefkowitz 1981: 7.

22 Lloyd 1992: 6; Allan 2000: 125–48.

23 Roisman 2021: 167–9.

24 See discussion by Llewellyn-Jones 2012: esp. 28–32.

25 For discussion of Hermione's costume, see Skouroumouni Stavrinou 2016.

26 For the idea of inner beauty, see Socrates' prayer, Plato, *Phaedrus* 279 B: 'O beloved Pan and all you other gods in this place, grant me that I become beautiful within, and that my external possessions be akin with those within me.'

27 Apollodorus 2.8.3, where Tisamenus is mentioned as Orestes' son, Hermione is not mentioned; Strabo 8.7.1.

28 For this terminology used for *Women of Trachis*, see Winnington-Ingram 1980: 75, 86, 90, 240). For a full discussion of Deianeira, see Roisman 2021: 193–207.

29 Roisman 2021: 5.

30 Achelous is the largest river of Greece. It does not travel through Phthia, or Thessaly for that matter, but flows through Aetolia, that is to say to the west of the country, and into the Ionic sea. Why Euripides is allowing Hermione to make such a blunder is unclear. Either he wants to show this young ferocious woman as utterly ignorant of geography, in which case the spectators will know better, or it is used as metonymy alluding to river water in general, as is suggested by Eur. *Bacchae* 625; Aristoph., *Lysistrata* 382.

31 Euripides has Andromache in *Trojan Women* 651–52 claim when she praises her own good name: 'I did not admit within my walls women with their clever talk' (Kovacs).

32 For this view, see Aldrich 1961: 46–7: 'Thus she ties two strings to her bow. On the one hand she works on Orestes, her immediate chance of escape; on the other hand, she plans for an eventual meeting with Neoptolemus.'

33 For a discussion, see Roisman 2021: 80–1. For a similar change in spirit, Iphigenia's change of mind, see Roisman 2021: 109–17.

34 Grube 1961: 213.

35 The play does not mention Megapenthes, his son with a servant woman (*Odyssey* 4.11–12).

36 See Roisman 1988, 2011: 506–7; Stelow 2020: 29–115.

37 Cf. Odysseus' unemotional and legalistic reply to Hecuba's plea that he save Polyxena in Euripides' *Hecuba* 299–331. For discussion, see Roisman 2021: 171–3.

38 For Euripides' rejecting the unabated quest for revenge, see Roisman 2014a.

39 Cf. Grube 1961: 206–7.

40 Grube 1961: 213.

41 Grube 1961: 207.

42 Peleus' passing over Andromache speaks against the suggestion that he might be coming back accompanied by both Andromache and the boy. For the difficult question whether Andromache is brought back as a silent character or not, see especially the discussion by Stevens 1971: 10–11 on 1047–1288, who reluctantly accepts the possibility of Andromache's re-entry with Peleus. Allan 2000: 74–6, 226–8 is confident that she is present.

43 For other cases of indifference to chronological probability, see Grube 1961: 211, n. 2; for discussion and explanation of the time sequence, see Aldrich 1961: 53–4; Allan 2000: 76–7.

44 For a similar sentiment, see 612–13, 714, 1207, 1216.

45 Line 1242 is surely metaphorical.

46 If we could trust Orestes, there were letters sent to him by Hermione allegedly telling him not to come (964). However, there has been no other mention of any letter from Hermione to him. Is it a lie on Orestes' part in hope to cast a more positive light on Hermione as a faithful wife prohibiting him from coming for her? After all, he intends to marry her, and a more positive image would be welcome. It is a possibility, but nowhere does Euripides suggest this scenario. Orestes is clearly not portrayed as a truthful character, but unlike his other lies the text does not disprove him in this regard. For potential lies of characters, see Erp Taalman Kip 1996. Lloyd 2005 on 964 states that such '*ad hoc* invention would have the function of stressing Orestes' initiative'. However, such an 'initiative' on his part would counter his traditional portrayal of lacking initiative and relying solely on Electra and Pylades. Diggle 1984 in the *apparatus criticus* for *Andromache* 964 suggests that the line is 'perhaps corrupt' (*fort. corruptus*), but lets it stand. Sommerstein 2006: 21, who assumes that Sophocles' *Hermione* preceded Euripides' *Andromache*, suggests that Euripides answers in 964 Sophocles' lost play *Hermione/ Women of Phthia*, in which Sophocles' Hermione had sent messages to Orestes begging him to rescue her from Neoptolemus. According to this claim, 'Euripides is emphasizing to his audience that in his treatment this is *not* the explanation of Orestes' opportune arrival.'

47 Although there is no evidence for Verrall's 1905: 20–2 assertion that there was a preceding play to which our *Andromache* is a sequel, which was familiar to the audience and in which Orestes and Neoptolemus have contrived the situation in which Menelaus would leave Hermione and Orestes would come and rescue her, including the murder of Neoptolemus in Delphi, one must admit that the scenario is not altogether unlikely and would explain Orestes' surprising arrival just in time and Menelaus' reckless 'abandonment' of his daughter. It would also explain Orestes' thorough knowledge of Hermione's affairs at home. This would also accord with the typical portrayal of Orestes, who shows nowhere else any initiative of his own.

48 It is important to contextualize what might sound as if Orestes is proud of killing his mother, as Allan 2000: 23 suggests: 'The myth of the matricide, Orestes' defining experience, is mentioned almost proudly by the killer himself (999–1001).' Orestes is 'answering' Neoptolemus here, following the latter's taunts about him being a matricide. He is pointing out to the son of Achilles that even though he is a matricide, he can still topple him.

49 Conacher 1967: 169–70.

50 Grube 1961: 213.

51 For example, Calame 2017; Ley 2007; Esposito 1996; Gould 1996; Mastronarde 1999, 2010: 88–152; Swift 2013.

52 Easterling 1997a: 164.

53 Cf. Easterling 1997a: 156–8, 163–5. For discussion of the Chorus as representing the alternative voice of the 'other', opposed to the heroic voice of the main character(s), and the nature and complexity of this 'otherness', see Gould 1996: 221–35.

54 Swift 2013; Calame 1999.

55 There are plays in which the chorus is split into sub-groups or in which individual choreuts debate what action they are supposed to take, e.g. Aeschylus, *Agamemnon* 1346–71, but there is no evidence in *Andromache* for such a split or internal debate within the chorus.

56 For example, Mastronarde 1999.

57 Calame 2013: 38–41, 54–8.

58 See Mastronarde 2010: 91.

59 Gagné and Hopman 2013. For a good summary of the development of the Chorus, see Ley 2014.

60 Ley 2007: 150–73 and *passim*.

61 For example, Aeschylus, *Agamemnon* 1343–71.

62 For discussion of the judgement of Paris in this ode, see Stinton 1965: 13–22.

63 Lloyd 2005: 274–308.

64 Stevens 1971: 127 claims that the ode has no direct relevance to the dramatic situation. For an opposite view, see Allan 2000: 205.

65 The first stasimon enjoys praise even from scholars who are rather ambivalent about the play as a whole, e.g. Stinton 1990: 34: 'it is among the finest of Euripides' lyrics, a welcome oasis in an indifferent play'.

66 Swift 2013.

67 Verrall 1905: 20–2.

68 See also n. 32 above.

69 See Mastronarde 1999.

70 Aldrich 1961: 42.

71 For seeing 'you alone' in line 1041 as referring to Andromache, and as some suggest possibly having her present with Peleus, see p. 135 n.42. For discussion and bibliography, see Allan 2000: 74–6.

72 For example, Lloyd 2005 on 642–4 and 727–78.

73 See also Mastronarde 1999: 103–4.

74 For further discussion, see Allan 2000: 196–232.

Chapter 5

1 For a comprehensive account of Euripides' reception and bibliography, see Chong-Gossard 2015.

2 Brouzas 1951; Dooley 2018: 1; Battezatto 2016: 4; Tyrrell 2020: 19.

3 Dooley 2018: *passim*.

4 Ambühl 2010: 100–1.

5 Tsagalis 2008: 14–15.

6 For example, *Little Iliad* frag. 14 West; cf. Muich 2010: 4; Burgess 2001: 64–5.
7 Ley 2014: *passim*; Gagné and Hopman 2013.
8 Wilson 2005.
9 Cf. Pavlovskis 1977.
10 Hill 2000.
11 See Suárez de la Torre 1997.
12 Strabo, *Geography* 7.7.8 mentions that the Molossians became subject to Pyrrhus, the son of Neoptolemus and his descendants, who were Thessalians. Also see below. Hyginus' *Fabulae* 123 names the child of Neoptolemus and Andromache as Amphialus. In Apollodorus' *Bibliotheca Epit.* 6:12–13, a different version is given, with Neoptolemus and Helenus having defeated the Molossians in battle, after which Neoptolemus eventually fathered Molossus with Andromache. Helenus founded a city in Molossia.
13 Chong-Gossard 2015: 143.
14 This matches Apollodorus' *Bibliotheca Epit.* 6:14, which states that when Orestes went mad, Neoptolemus carried off his wife, Hermione, who had previously been betrothed to him in Troy, and for that reason Orestes killed Neoptolemus at Delphi.
15 The manuscripts of Euripides' original plays were not lost at this time, as they were stored in a large number of libraries (Kovacs 2005). The librarians copied the texts of plays they received, possibly introducing changes to the manuscript either through human error or because of artistic and societal influences of the time and place where they lived. The librarians of Alexandria in the second and third centuries BCE were described as receiving manuscripts of the fifth-century tragedies, including *Andromache*, copying them, and then returning the original copies to the original owners. Comments added to these manuscripts, by scribes or scholars, have become an integral part of the legacy of the plays, collectively termed scholia.
16 Servius on Vergil, *Aeneid* 2.166, 3.297.
17 Smith 1994.
18 Yavuz 2015: 30; Goldwyn 2015: 16; Champlin 1981: 194. For a more recent account, see also Gainsford 2012.
19 Galli 2013: the understanding was that Cornelius Nepos translated the original manuscript from a Trojan dialect of Greek into Latin.
20 Goldwyn 2015: 6–9, 16–20.
21 Edwards 1998; Schirmer 1961.
22 Edwards 1998.
23 Goldwyn 2015: 1.
24 Published between 1607 and 1627.
25 See Wine 2000: 32–3, who discusses how Racine cites d'Urfé in his first preface as representing the opposition between epic and romance, yet the behaviour of his characters and their amorous speeches seem to be directly influenced by him.
26 For discussion, see Sebastià-Sáez 2019.

27 Babuts 1993.
28 See Verdicchio 2015.
29 Babuts 1993.
30 See also Ograjensek 2010.
31 Chong-Gossard 2015: 158–9.
32 There is also a small pencil sketch by Guérin of *Andromaque et Pyrrhus* exhibited in the Louvre.
33 Reiss 1999: 73.
34 Reiss 2002: 25.
35 Reiss 2002: 27.
36 Reiss 1999: 74.

Bibliography

Ahl, F. 2007. *Virgil: Aeneid.* Oxford: Oxford University Press.

Ahl, F. and H. M. Roisman. 1996. *The* Odyssey *Re-formed.* Ithaca, NY: Cornell University Press.

Alaux, J. 2011. 'Acting Myth: Athenian Drama.' In *A Companion to Greek Mythology,* eds K. Dowden and N. Livingstone. Chichester: Wiley-Blackwell: 141–56.

Aldrich, K. M. 1961. 'The *Andromache* of Euripides.' *University of Nebraska Studies,* n.s. 25.

Alexander, P. S., A. Lange, and R. J. Pillinger, eds. 2010. *In the Second Degree: Paratextual Literature in Ancient Near Eastern and Ancient Mediterranean Cultures and Its Reflections in Medieval Literature.* Leiden: Brill.

Allan, W. 2000. *The* Andromache *and Euripidean Tragedy.* Oxford: Oxford University Press.

Ambühl, A. 2010. 'Trojan Palimpsests: The Relation of Greek Tragedy to the Homeric Epics.' In *In the Second Degree: Paratextual Literature in Ancient Near Eastern and Ancient Mediterranean Cultures and Its Reflections in Medieval Literature,* eds P. S. Alexander, A. Lange, and R. J. Pillinger. Leiden: Brill: 99–121.

Babuts, N. 1993. 'Baudelaire in the Circle of Exiles: A Study of "Le Cygne".' *Nineteenth Century French Studies* 22 (1/2): 123–38.

Bailey, C., E. A. Barber, C. M. Bowra, J. D. Denniston, and D. L. Page, eds. 1936. *Greek Poetry and Life: Essays Presented to Gilbert Murray on His Seventieth Birthday.* Oxford: Clarendon Press.

Battezzato, L. 2016. 'Euripides the Antiquarian.' In *Wisdom and Folly in Euripides,* eds P. Kyriakou and A. Rengakos. Berlin: Walter de Gruyter: 3–19.

Beck, F. A. G. 1964. *Greek Education, 450–350 B.C.* London: Methuen.

Belfiore, E. S. 2000. *Murder Among Friends: Violation of Philia in Greek Tragedy.* New York: Oxford University Press.

Bers, V. 2014. 'Audiences in the Greek Tragic Plays.' In *Encyclopedia of Greek Tragedy,* vol. I, ed. H. M. Roisman. Chichester: Wiley-Blackwell: 173–8.

Birberic, A. L. and R. Ganim, eds. 2002. *The Shape of Change: Essays in Modern Literature and La Fontaine in Honor of David Lee Rubin.* Amsterdam: Rodopi.

Bosher, K., ed. 2012. *Theater Outside Athens: Drama in Greek Sicily and South Italy.* Cambridge: Cambridge University Press.

Bosher, K. 2014. 'Ancient Greek Theaters.' In *Encyclopedia of Greek Tragedy,* vol. I, ed. H. M. Roisman. Chichester: Wiley-Blackwell: 101–9.

Bradford, A. S. 1994. 'The Duplicitous Spartan.' In *The Shadow of Sparta,* eds A. Powell and S. Hodkinson. London: Routledge: 59–85.

Brooks, C. and W. K. Wimsatt, Jr. 1957. *Literary Criticism: A Short History*. New York: Knopf.

Brouzas, C. G. 1951. 'Libraries in Ancient Athens: A Condensation of a Paper.' *The Classical Outlook* 29: 13–15.

Brown, P. and S. Ograjensek. 2010. *Ancient Drama in Music for the Modern Stage*. Oxford: Oxford University Press.

Burgess, J. S. 1996. 'The Non-Homeric *Cypria*.' *Transactions and Proceedings of the American Philological Association* 126: 77–99.

Burgess, J. S. 2001. *The Tradition of the Trojan War in Homer and the Epic Cycle*. Baltimore, MD: Johns Hopkins University Press.

Burgess, J. S. 2004. 'Performance and the Epic Cycle.' *The Classical Journal* 100: 1–23.

Butrica, J. L. 2001. 'Democrates and Euripides' *Andromache* (Σ andr. 445 = Callimachus Fr. 451 Pfeiffer).' *Hermes* 129: 188–97.

Buxton, R. G. A. 1994. *Imaginary Greece: The Contexts of Mythology*. Cambridge: Cambridge University Press.

Cairns, F. 2012. 'Pyrrhic Dancing and Politics in Euripides' *Andromache*.' *Quaderni Urbinati di Cultura Classica* n.s. 100.1: 31–47.

Calame, C. 1999. 'Performative Aspects of the Choral Voice in Greek Tragedy: Civic Identity in Performance.' In *Performance Culture and Athenian Democracy*, eds S. Goldhill and R. Osborne. Cambridge: Cambridge University Press: 125–53.

Calame, C. 2013. 'Choral Polyphony and the Ritual Functions of Tragic Songs.' In *Choral Mediations in Greek Tragedy*, eds R. Gagné and M. G. Hopman. New York: Cambridge University Press: 35–57.

Calame, C. 2017. *La tragédie chorale: poésie qrecque et rituel musical*. Paris: Les Belles Lettres.

Calame, C. 2020. 'The Chorus in Euripides.' In *Brill's Companion to Euripides*, vol. II, ed. A. Markanatonatos. Leiden: Brill: 775–96.

Cameron, A. 1968. *The Identity of Oedipus the King*. New York: New York University Press.

Champlin, E. 1981. 'Serenus Sammonicus.' *Harvard Studies in Classical Philology* 85: 189–212.

Chong-Gossard, J. H. K. O. 2015. 'Andromache.' In *Brill's Companion to the Reception of Euripides*, eds R. Lauriola and K. N. Demetriou. Leiden: Brill: 143–73.

Chong-Gossard, J. H. K. O and Lin Li Ng. 2018. 'Euripidean Women and Internalized Misogyny: Agones in *Troades*, *Electra*, and *Andromache*.' In *Engaging Classical Texts in the Contemporary World: From Narratology to Reception*, eds L. Pratt and C. M. Sampson. Ann Arbor, MI: University of Michigan Press: 71–90.

Collard, C. and J. Morwood. 2017. *Euripides. Iphigenia at Aulis, vol. I: Introduction, Text, and Translation*. Liverpool: Liverpool University Press.

Conacher, D. J. 1967. *Euripidean Drama: Myth, Theme and Structure*. Toronto: University of Toronto Press.

Cousland, J. R. C. and J. R. Hume, eds. 2009. *The Play of Texts and Fragments: Essays in Honour of Martin Cropp*. Leiden: Brill.

Cropp, M., K. H. Lee, and D. Sansone, eds. 1999–2000. *Euripides and Tragic Theatre in the Late Fifth Century*. Illinois Classical Studies, vol. XXIV–XXV. Champaign, IL: Stipes Publishing.

Csapo, E. 2007. 'The Men Who Built the Theatres: *Theatropolai, Theatronai*, and *Arkhitektones*.' In *The Greek Theatre and Festivals*, ed. P. Wilson. Oxford: Oxford University Press: 87–115.

Csapo, E. 2014. 'Performing Comedy in the Fifth through Early Third Centuries.' In *The Oxford Handbook of Greek and Roman Comedy*, eds M. Fontaine and A. C. Scafuro. Oxford: Oxford University Press: 51–69.

Csapo, E. and W. J. Slater. 1995. *The Context of Ancient Drama*. Ann Arbor, MI: University of Michigan Press.

Damen, M. 1989. 'Actor and Character in Greek Tragedy.' *Theatre Journal* 41: 316–40.

Diggle, J. 1984. *Euripidis Fabulae*, vol. 1. Oxford: Oxford University Press.

Dooley, D. C. 2018. *Greek Tragedy and the Epic Cycle: Narrative Tradition, Texts, Fragments*. Dissertation. Baltimore, MD: John Hopkins University. https://jscholarship.library.jhu.edu/handle/1774.2/59132

Dover, K. J. 1974. *Greek Popular Morality in the Time of Plato and Aristotle*. Oxford: Blackwell.

Dowden, K. and N. Livingstone, eds. 2011. *A Companion to Greek Mythology*. Chichester: Wiley-Blackwell.

Easterling, P. E. 1997a. 'Form and Performance.' In *The Cambridge Companion to Greek Tragedy*, ed. P. E. Easterling. Cambridge: Cambridge University Press: 151–77.

Easterling, P. E., ed. 1997b. *The Cambridge Companion to Greek Tragedy*. Cambridge: Cambridge University Press.

Easterling, P. E. 2014. 'Hypotheseis.' In *Encyclopedia of Greek Tragedy*, vol. II, ed. H. M. Roisman. Chichester: Wiley-Blackwell: 706–10.

Easterling, P. E. and B. M. W. Knox, eds. 1989. *The Cambridge History of Classical Literature, vol. 1: Greek Literature, part 2: Greek Drama*. Cambridge: Cambridge University Press.

Easterling, P. E. and E. Hall, eds. 2002. *Greek and Roman Actors: Aspects of an Ancient Profession*. Cambridge: Cambridge University Press.

Edwards, R. R. 1998. 'Introduction.' In *Troy Book: Selections*, by J. Lydgate, ed. R. R. Edwards. https://d.lib.rochester.edu/teams/text/edwards-lydgate-troy-book-introduction.

Erbse, H. 1966. 'Euripides' *Andromache*.' *Hermes* 94: 276–97.

Erp Taalman Kip, A. M. van. 1987. 'Euripides and Melos.' *Mnemosyne* 40: 414–19.

Erp Taalman Kip, A. M. van. 1996. 'Truth in Tragedy: When are We Entitled to Doubt a Character's Words?' *American Journal of Philology* 117: 517–36.

Esposito, S. 1996. 'The Changing Roles of the Sophoclean Chorus.' *Arion*, 3rd ser., 4.1: 85–114.

Finkelberg, M., ed. 2011. *The Homer Encyclopedia*, 3 vols. Chichester: Wiley-Blackwell.

Foley, H. P. 1978. '"Reverse Similes" and Sex Roles in the Odyssey.' *Arethusa* 11: 7–26.

Foley, H. P. 2001. *Female Acts in Greek Tragedy*. Princeton, NJ: Princeton University Press.

Fontaine, M. and A. C. Scafuro, eds. 2014. *The Oxford Handbook of Greek and Roman Comedy*. Oxford: Oxford University Press.

Friedländer, P. 1926. 'Die griechische Tragödie und das Tragische.' *Die Antike* 2: 79–112.

Gagné, R. and M. G. Hopman. 2013. 'Introduction: The Chorus in the Middle.' In *Choral Mediations in Greek Tragedy*, eds R. Gagné and M. G. Hopman. New York: Cambridge University Press: 1–34.

Gagné, R. and M. G. Hopman, eds. 2013. *Choral Mediations in Greek Tragedy*. New York: Cambridge University Press.

Gainsford, P. 2012. 'Diktys of Crete.' *Cambridge Classical Journal* 58: 58–87.

Galli, D. 2013. '*De Excidio Troiae* by Dares Phrygius and Valerius Flaccus.' *Mnemosyne* 66: 800–8.

Goldhill, S. and R. Osborne, eds. 1999. *Performance Culture and Athenian Democracy*. Cambridge: Cambridge University Press.

Goldwyn, A. J., ed. 2015. *The Trojan Wars and the Making of the Modern World*. Uppsala: Uppsala University Library.

Goossens, R. 1962. *Euripide et Athènes*. Bruxelles: Palais des Académies.

Gould, J. 1996. 'Tragedy and Collective Experience.' In *Tragedy and the Tragic: Greek Theatre and Beyond*, ed. M. S. Silk. Oxford: Clarendon Press: 217–43.

Gregory, J. 1999–2000. 'Comic Elements in Euripides.' In *Euripides and Tragic Theatre in the Late Fifth Century*, eds M. Cropp, K. H. Lee, and D. Sansone. Illinois Classical Studies, vol. XXIV–XXV. Champaign, IL: Stipes Publishing: 59–74.

Gregory, J. 2005a. 'Euripidean Tragedy.' In *Companion to Greek Tragedy*, ed. J. A. Gregory. Malden, MA: Blackwell: 251–70.

Gregory, J., ed. 2005b. *Companion to Greek Tragedy*. Malden, MA: Blackwell.

Griffin, J. 1999. 'Sophocles and the Democratic City.' In *Sophocles Revisited: Essays Presented to Sir Hugh Lloyd-Jones*, ed. J. Griffin. Oxford: Oxford University Press: 73–94.

Griffin. J. ed. 1999. *Sophocles Revisited: Essays Presented to Sir Hugh Lloyd-Jones*. Oxford: Oxford University Press.

Griffith, M. 2015. *Greek Satyr Play: Five Studies*. Berkeley, CA: University of California Press.

Grube, G. M. A. 1961. *The Drama of Euripides*, 2nd edn. London: Methuen.

Hall, E. 1989. *Inventing the Barbarian: Greek Self-Definition through Tragedy*. Oxford: Oxford University Press.

Hall, E. 1999. 'Actor's Song in Tragedy.' In *Performance Culture and Athenian Democracy*, eds S. Goldhill and R. Osborne. Cambridge: Cambridge University Press: 96–122.

Hall, E. 2002. 'The Singing Actors of Antiquity.' In *Greek and Roman Actors*, eds
P. Easterling and E. Hall. Cambridge: Cambridge University Press: 3–38.

Hammond, N. G. L. 1967. *Epirus: The Geography, the Ancient Remains, the
History and the Topography of Epirus and Adjacent Areas*. Oxford: Clarendon
Press.

Harder A., ed. 1985. *Euripides' Kresphontes and Archelaos: Introduction, Text,
and Commentary*. Leiden: Brill.

Harlow, M., ed. 2012. *Dress and Identity*. Oxford: Archaeopress.

Hartung, J. A. 1844. *Euripides Restitutus, sive Scriptorum Euripidis Ingeniique
Censura*, Vol. II. Hamburg: F. Perthes.

Hill, D. E. 2000. 'Seneca's Use of Choruses.' *Mnemosyne* 53: 561–687.

Hopman, M. G. 2013. 'Chorus, Conflict and Closure in Aeschylus' *Persians*.' In
Choral Mediations in Greek Tragedy, eds R. Gagné and M. G. Hopman. New
York: Cambridge University: 58–77.

Jacoby, F. 1957–1969. *Die Fragmente der griechischen Historiker (FGH)*, 3 vols.
Leiden: Brill.

Jenkins, I. D. 1985. 'The Ambiguity of Greek Textiles.' *Arethusa* 18: 109–32.

Just, R. 1989. *Women in Athenian Law and Life*. London: Routledge.

Katz, M. A. 1991. *Penelope's Renown: Meaning and Indeterminacy in the
Odyssey*. Princeton, NJ: Princeton University Press.

Kitto, H. D. F. 1966. *Greek Tragedy*. London: Methuen.

Kovacs, D., ed. and trans. 1995. *Euripides: Children of Heracles, Hippolytus,
Andromache, Hecuba*. Cambridge, MA: Harvard University Press.

Kovacs, D. 2005. 'Text and Transmission.' In *Companion to Greek Tragedy*, ed.
J. A. Gregory. Oxford: Blackwell: 379–93.

Kovacs, G. 2014. 'Performance.' In *Encyclopedia of Greek Tragedy*, vol. II, ed.
H. M. Roisman. Chichester: Wiley-Blackwell: 952–8.

Kullmann, W. 1960. *Die Quellen des* Ilias: *Troischer Sagenkreis*. Hermes
Einzelschriften, Heft 14. Wiesbaden: Steiner.

Kullmann, W. 1968. 'Vergangenheit und Zukunft in der *Ilias*.' *Poetica* 2: 15–37.

Kyriakou, P. 1997. 'All in the Family: Present and Past in Euripides' *Andromache*.'
Mnemosyne 50: 7–26.

Kyriakou, P. and A. Rengakos, eds. 2016. *Wisdom and Folly in Euripides*. Berlin:
de Gruyter.

Lamari, A. A. 2017. *Reperforming Greek Tragedy: Theater, Politics, and Cultural
Mobility in the Fifth and Fourth Centuries*, BC. Berlin: de Gruyter.

Lauriola, R. and K. N. Demetriou, eds. 2015. *Brill's Companion to the Reception
of Euripides*. Leiden: Brill.

Lefkowitz, M. R. 1981. *Heroines and Hysterics*. London: Duckworth.

Lefkowitz, M. R. 1986. *Women in Greek Myth*. Baltimore, MD: Johns Hopkins
University Press.

Lesky, A. 1983 [1972]. *Greek Tragic Poetry*, trans. M. Dillon. New Haven, CT:
Yale University Press

Levett, B. 2014. 'Deus ex Machina.' In *Encyclopedia of Greek Tragedy*, vol. I, ed.
H. M. Roisman. Chichester: Wiley-Blackwell: 277–9.

Ley, G. 2007. *The Theatricality of Greek Tragedy: Playing Space and Chorus.* Chicago, IL: University of Chicago Press.

Ley, G. 2014. 'Chorus.' In *Encyclopedia of Greek Tragedy*, vol. I, ed. H. M. Roisman. Chichester: Wiley-Blackwell: 220–4.

Llewellyn-Jones, L., ed. 2002. *Women's Dress in the Ancient Greek World.* London: Duckworth/Swansea: Classical Press of Wales.

Llewellyn-Jones, L. 2012. 'Veiling the Spartan Woman.' In *Dress and Identity*, ed. M. Harlow. Oxford: Archaeopress: 17–35.

Lloyd, M. 1992. *The Agon in Euripides.* Oxford: Oxford University Press.

Lloyd, M. 2005. *Euripides: Andromache*, 2nd edn. Warminster: Aris & Phillips.

López Pérez, J. A. 2019. 'Myths and Mythical Names in Euripides' *Andromache.' Mouseion*, ser. iii, vol. 16, suppl. 3: 337–50.

Lydgate, John. 1998. *Troy Book: Selections*, ed. and introduction by R. R. Edwards. https://d.lib.rochester.edu/teams/text/edwards-lydgate-troy-book-selections.

Lyne, R. O. A. M. 1995. *Horace: Behind the Public Poetry.* New Haven, CT: Yale University Press.

Markantonatos, A., ed. 2020. *Brill's Companion to Euripides*, 2 vols. Leiden: Brill.

Marrou, H. I. 1982 [1956]. *A History of Education in Antiquity.* Madison, WI: University of Wisconsin Press.

Mastronarde, D. J. 1990. 'Actors on High: The Skene Roof, the Crane, and the Gods of Attic Drama.' *Classical Antiquity* 9: 247–94.

Mastronarde, D. J. 1999. 'Knowledge and Authority in the Choral Voice of Euripidean Tragedy.' *Syllecta Classica* 10: 87–104.

Mastronarde, D. J. 2010. *The Art of Euripides: Dramatic Technique and Social Context.* Cambridge: Cambridge University Press.

McAuslan, I. and P. Walcot, eds. 1996. *Women in Antiquity.* Oxford: Oxford University Press.

Meineck, P. 2012. 'The Embodied Space: Performance and Visual Cognition at the Fifth Century Athenian Theatre.' *New England Classical Journal* 39: 3–46.

Méridier, L., trans. 1927. *Euripide: Hippolyte, Andromaque, Hecube*, vol. II. Paris: Les Belles Lettres.

Michelini, A. N. 2014. 'Euripides: Dramatic Innovations.' In *Encyclopedia of Greek Tragedy*, vol. I, ed. H. M. Roisman. Chichester: Wiley-Blackwell: 375–8.

Moretti, J.-C. 1999–2000. 'The Theater of the Sanctuary of Dionysus Eleuthereus in Late Fifth-Century Athens.' In *Euripides and Tragic Theatre in the Late Fifth Century*, eds M. Cropp, K. H. Lee, and D. Sansone. Illinois Classical Studies, vol. XXIV–XXV. Champaign, IL: Stipes Publishing: 377–98.

Mossman, J. 1995. *Wild Justice: A Study of Euripides'* Hecuba. Oxford: Oxford University Press.

Mossman, J. 1996. 'Waiting for Neoptolemus: The Unity of Euripides' *Andromache.' Greece & Rome* 43.2: 143–56.

Most, G. W. 1985. *The Measure of Praise: Structure and Fiction in Pindar's Second Pythian and Seventh Nemean Odes.* Göttingen: Vandenhoeck & Ruprecht.

Muich, R. M. 2010. *Pouring Out Tears: Andromache in Homer and Euripides.*
Dissertation. Urbana, IL: University of Illinois at Urbana-Champaign. http://
hdl.handle.net/2142/16755

Murray, G. 1902. *Euripidis Fabulae*, vol. I. Oxford: Clarendon Press.

Nagy, G. 1990. *Greek Mythology and Poetics.* Ithaca, NY: Cornell University Press.

Nauck, A. 1900. *Euripidis Tragoediae*, 3rd edn., 3 vols. Leipzig: Teubner.

Netz, R. 2011. 'The Bibliosphere of Ancient Science (Outside of Alexandria):
A Preliminary Survey.' *NTM Zeitschrift für Geschichte der Wissenschaften,
Technik, und Medizin* 19.3: 239–69. https://link.springer.com/content/
pdf/10.1007/s00048-011-0057-2.pdf

Norwood, G. 1921. *Euripides and Shaw, with Other Essays.* London: Methuen.

Norwood, G. 1954. *Essays on Euripidean Drama.* Berkeley, CA: University of
California Press.

Ograjensek, S. 2010. 'The Rise and Fall of Andromache on the Operatic Stage,
1660s–1820s.' In *Ancient Drama in Music for the Modern Stage*, eds P. Brown
and S. Ograjensek. Oxford: Oxford University Press: 112–38.

Owen, A. S. 1936. 'The Date of Sophocles' *Electra*.' In *Greek Poetry and Life:
Essays Presented to Gilbert Murray on His Seventieth Birthday*, eds C. Bailey,
E. A. Barber, C. M. Bowra, J. D. Denniston, and D. L. Page. Oxford:
Clarendon Press: 145–57.

Page, D. L. 1936. 'The Elegiacs in Euripides' *Andromache*.' In *Greek Poetry and
Life: Essays Presented to Gilbert Murray on His Seventieth Birthday*, eds
C. Bailey, E. A. Barber, C. M. Bowra, J. D. Denniston, and D. L. Page. Oxford:
Clarendon Press: 206–30.

Papadimitropoulos, L. 2006. 'Marriage and Strife in Euripides' *Andromache*.'
Greek, Roman, and Byzantine Studies 46: 147–58.

Papadodima, E. 2014. 'Euripides and Subversiveness.' In *Encyclopedia of Greek
Tragedy*, vol. I, ed. H. M. Roisman. Chichester: Wiley-Blackwell: 483–5.

Papenfuss, D. and V. M. Strocka, eds. 2001. *Gab es das Griechische Wunder?
Griechenland zwischen dem Ende des 6. und der Mitte des 5. Jahrhunderts v.
Chr.* Mainz: Philipp von Zabern.

Parry, A. 1963. 'The Two Voices of Virgil's *Aeneid*.' *Arion* 2: 66–80.

Pavlovskis, Z. 1977. 'The Voice of the Actor in Greek Tragedy.' *Classical World*
71: 113–23.

Phillippo, S. 1995. 'Family Ties: Significant Patronymics in Euripides'
Andromache.' *Classical Quarterly* 45.2: 355–71.

Pickard-Cambridge, A. 1973. *The Dramatic Festivals of Athens.* 2nd edn., revised
by J. Gould and D. M. Lewis. Oxford: Clarendon Press.

Poole, W. 1994. 'Euripides and Sparta.' In *The Shadow of Sparta*, eds A. Powell
and S. Hodkinson. London: Routledge for the Classical Press of Wales: 1–33.

Powell, A. and S. Hodkinson, eds. 1994. *The Shadow of Sparta.* London:
Routledge for the Classical Press of Wales.

Pratt, L. and C. M. Sampson, eds. 2018. *Engaging Classical Texts in the
Contemporary World: From Narratology to Reception.* Ann Arbor, MI:
University of Michigan Press.

Rabinowitz, N. S. 1993. *Anxiety Veiled: Euripides and the Traffic in Women.* Ithaca, NY: Cornell University Press.

Radt, S., ed. 1999 [1977]. *Tragicorum Graecorum Fragmenta (TrGF). Sophocles,* vol. 4. Göttingen: Vandenhoeck & Ruprecht.

Redfield, J. 1975. *Nature and Culture in the* Iliad: *The Tragedy of Hector.* Chicago, IL: University of Chicago Press

Reiss, T. 1999. 'Between Sovereignty and Tyranny: *Britannicus.' Dalhousie French Studies* 49: 73–89.

Reiss, T. 2002. '*Andromaque* and the Search for Unique Sovereignty.' In *The Shape of Change: Essays in Modern Literature and La Fontaine in Honor of David Lee Rubin,* eds A. L. Birberic and R. Ganim. Amsterdam: Rodopi: 23–51.

Roisman, H. M. 1988. 'Nestor's Advice and Antilochus' Tactics.' *Phoenix* 42: 114–20.

Roisman, H. M. 1997. 'The Appropriation of a Son: Sophocles' *Philoctetes.' Greek, Roman, and Byzantine Studies* 38: 127–71.

Roisman, H. M. 1999. *Nothing Is As It Seems: the Tragedy of the Implicit in Euripides'* Hippolytus. Lanham, MD: Rowman & Littlefield.

Roisman, H. M. 2005. *Sophocles:* Philoctetes. London: Duckworth.

Roisman, H. M. 2011. 'Menelaos.' In *The Homer Encyclopedia,* vol. II, ed. M. Finkelberg. Chichester: Wiley-Blackwell: 506–7.

Roisman, H. M. 2014a. 'Medea's Vengeance.' In *Looking at* Medea, ed. D. Stuttard. London: Bloomsbury: 111–22.

Roisman, H. M., ed. 2014b. *Encyclopedia of Greek Tragedy,* 3 vols. Chichester: Wiley-Blackwell.

Roisman, H. M. 2021. *Tragic Heroines in Ancient Greek Drama.* London: Bloomsbury Academic.

Roisman, H. M. forthcoming. 'The Human Cost of Conflict: Greek Tragedy and the Trojan War.' *Giornale Italiano di Filologia.*

Ronsard, Pierre de. 2010. *The Franciad* (1572), trans. P. J. Usher. New York: AMS Press.

Sandys, J. 1930. *The Odes of Pindar, including the Principal Fragments.* London: Heinemann/New York: G.P. Putnam.

Schirmer, W. F. 1961. *John Lydgate: A Study in the Culture of the XVth Century,* trans. A. E. Keep (from *John Lydgate: Ein Kulturbild aus dem 15. Jahrhundert,* Max Niemeyer, 1952). London: Methuen/Berkeley, CA: University of California Press.

Schwartz, E. 1887–91. *Scholia in Euripidem.* Berlin: G. Reimer.

Scodel, R. 2001. 'The Poet's Career, the Rise of Tragedy, and Athenian Cultural Hegemony.' In *Gab es das Griechische Wunder? Griechenland zwischen dem Ende des 6.und der Mitte des 5. Jahrhunderts v. Chr.,* eds D. Papenfuss and V. M. Strocka. Mainz: Philipp von Zabern: 215–26.

Sebastià-Sáez, M. 2019. 'Ambrose Philips' *The Distrest Mother*: The Myth of Andromache in English (Neo)classicism.' *Beyond Philology* 16.2: 109–24.

Sebesta, J. L. 2002. 'Visions of Gleaming Textiles and a Clay Core: Textiles, Greek Women, and Pandora.' In *Women's Dress in the Ancient Greek World,* ed. L. Llewellyn-Jones. London: Duckworth/Swansea: The Classical Press of Wales: 125–42.

Showerman, G. 1977. *Ovid: Heroides and Amores*, 2nd edn., revised by G. P. Goold. Cambridge, MA: Harvard University Press/London: Heinemann.

Signore, S. N. 2007. *Achilles and Andromache: Gender Ambiguity in Motif, Narrative, and Formula*. Athens, GA: University of Georgia, Theses and Dissertations. http://getd.libs.uga.edu/pdfs/signore_sean_n_200708_ma.pdf

Silk, M. S., ed. 1996. *Tragedy and the Tragic: Greek Theatre and Beyond*. Oxford: Clarendon Press.

Skouroumouni Stavrinou, A. 2014. 'Inside and Out: The Dynamics of Domestic Space in Euripides' *Andromache.' Hermes* 142: 385–403.

Skouroumouni Stavrinou, A. 2016. 'Hermione's Spartan Costume: The Tragic *skeue* in Euripides' *Andromache.' Illinois Classical Studies* 41: 1–20.

Smith, R. A. 1994. 'Fantasy, Myth, and Love Letters: Text and Tale in Ovid's *Heroides.' Arethusa* 27: 247–73.

Snell, B., ed. 1986. *Tragicorum Graecorum Fragmenta* (*TrGF*), vol. 1. Göttingen: Vandenhoeck & Ruprecht.

Sommerstein, A. H. 2002. *Greek Drama and Dramatists*. London: Routledge.

Sommerstein, A. H. 2010. *The Tangled Ways of Zeus: And Other Studies In and Around Greek Tragedy*. Oxford: Oxford University Press.

Sommerstein, A. H. 2006. 'Hermione or the Women of Phthia.' In *Sophocles: Selected Fragmentary Plays*, vol. I, eds A. H. Sommerstein, D. Fitzpatrick, and Th. Talboy. Oxford: Oxbow Books: 1–40.

Sommerstein, A. H., D. Fitzpatrick, and Th. Talboy, eds. 2006. *Sophocles: Selected Fragmentary Plays*, vol. I. Oxford: Oxbow Books.

Sorum, C. E. 1995. 'Euripides' Judgment: Literary Creation in *Andromache.' American Journal of Philology* 116: 371–88.

Stelow, A. R. 2020. *Menelaus in the Archaic Period. Not Quite the Best of Achaians*. Oxford: Oxford University Press.

Stevens, P. T. 1971. *Euripides:* Andromache. Oxford: Oxford University Press.

Stewart, E. 2017. *Greek Tragedy on the Move: The Birth of a Panhellenic Art Form c. 500–300 BC*. Oxford: Oxford University Press.

Stinton, T. C. W. 1965. *Euripides and the Judgement of Paris*. London: Society for the Promotion of Hellenic Studies.

Stinton, T. C. W. 1990. *Collected Papers on Greek Tragedy*. Oxford: Oxford University Press.

Storey, I. C. 1989. 'Domestic Disharmony in Euripides' *Andromache.' Greece & Rome* 36.1: 16–27.

Stuttard, D., ed. 2014. *Looking at* Medea. London: Bloomsbury Academic.

Suárez de la Torre, E. 1997. 'Neoptolemus at Delphi.' *Kernos* 10: 153–76.

Sutton, D. F. 1980. *The Greek Satyr Play*. Meisenheim am Glan: Hain.

Swift, L. 2013. 'Conflicting Identities in the Euripidean Chorus.' In *Choral Mediations in Greek Tragedy*, eds R. Gagné and M. G. Hopman. New York: Cambridge University Press: 130–54.

Taplin, O. 1977. *The Stagecraft of Aeschylus: The Dramatic Use of Exits and Entrances in Greek Tragedy.* Oxford: Clarendon Press.

Taplin, O. 1978. *Greek Tragedy in Action.* Berkeley, CA: University of California Press.

Taplin, O. 1996. 'Comedy and the Tragic.' In *Tragedy and the Tragic: Greek Theatre and Beyond*, ed. M. S. Silk. Oxford: Clarendon Press: 188–202.

Taplin, O. 1999. 'Spreading the Word through Performance.' In *Performance Culture and Athenian Democracy*, eds S. Goldhill and R. Osborne. Cambridge: Cambridge University Press: 33–57.

Taplin, O. 2012. 'How was Athenian Tragedy Played in the Greek West?' In *Theater Outside Athens: Drama in Greek Sicily and South Italy*, ed. K. Bosher. Cambridge: Cambridge University Press: 226–50.

Tsagalis, C. 2008. *The Oral Palimpsest: Exploring Intertextuality in the Homeric Epics.* Hellenic Studies Series 29. Washington, DC: Center for Hellenic Studies.

Tyrrell, W. B. 2020. 'Life of Euripides.' In *Brill's Companion to Euripides*, vol. I, ed. A. Markantonatos. Leiden: Brill: 11–28.

Tzanetou, A. 2014. 'Childlessness.' In *Encyclopedia of Greek Tragedy*, vol. I, ed. H. M. Roisman. Chichester: 217–18.

Vellacott, P. 1975. *Ironic Drama: A Study of Euripides' Method and Meaning.* New York: Cambridge University Press.

Verdicchio, M. 2015. 'Rereading Baudelaire's "Le Cygne".' *MLN* 130.4: 879–97.

Verrall, A. W. 1967 [1895]. *Euripides the Rationalist: A Study in the History of Art and Religion.* New York: Russell & Russell.

Verrall, A. W. 1905. *Essays on Four Plays of Euripides:* Andromache, Helen, Heracles, Orestes. Cambridge: Cambridge University Press.

Vester, C. 2009. 'Bigamy and Bastardy, Wives and Concubines: Civic Identity in Andromache.' In *The Play of Texts and Fragments: Essays in Honour of Martin Cropp*, eds J. R. C. Cousland and J. R. Hume. Leiden: Brill: 293–305.

Walcot, P. 1996. 'Greek Attitudes Towards Women: The Mythological Evidence.' In *Women in Antiquity*, eds I. McAuslan and P. Walcot. Oxford: Oxford University Press: 91–102.

West, M. L. 2003. *Greek Epic Fragments: From the Seventh to the Fifth Centuries BC.* Cambridge, MA: Harvard University Press.

Wilamowitz-Moellendorff, U. von. 1963 [1875]. *Analecta Euripidea.* Hildesheim: G. Olms.

Wiles, D. 1997. *Tragedy in Athens: Performance Space and Theatrical Meaning.* Cambridge: Cambridge University Press.

Wilson, P. 2000. *The Athenian Institution of the* Khoregia: *the Chorus, the City, and the Stage.* Cambridge: Cambridge University Press.

Wilson, P. 2005. 'Music.' In *Companion to Greek Tragedy*, ed. J. A. Gregory. Malden, MA: Blackwell: 183–93.

Wilson, P., ed. 2007. *The Greek Theatre and Festivals: Documentary Studies.* Oxford: Oxford University Press.

Wine, K. 2000. *Forgotten Virgo: Humanism and Absolutism in Honoré d'Urfé's*
    L'Astrée. Geneva: Droz.
Winnington-Ingram, R. P. 1980. *Sophocles: An Interpretation*. Cambridge:
    Cambridge University Press.
Winnington-Ingram, R. P., J. Gould, P. E. Easterling, and B. M. W. Knox. 1989.
    'Tragedy.' In *The Cambridge History of Classical Literature, vol. 1: Greek*
    Literature, part 2: Greek Drama, eds P. E. Easterling and B. M. W. Knox.
    Cambridge: Cambridge University Press: 258–345.
Yavuz, N. K. 2015. *Transmission and Adaptation of the Trojan Narrative in*
    Frankish History between the Sixth and Tenth Centuries. PhD Thesis,
    University of Leeds. uk.bl.ethos.684522
Zeitlin, F. I. 1996. *Playing the Other: Gender and Society in Classical Greek*
    Literature. Chicago, IL: University of Chicago Press.

Glossary

Achilles Peleus' son and Neoptolemus' father
Aeacus Peleus' father
Agamemnon brother of Menelaus; father of Iphigenia
agōn formal debate, a pair of set speeches
Andromache wife of Hector and Helenus; mother of Astyanax and Molossus; concubine of Neoptolemus
antistrophe *see* 'strophe' below
Astyanax son of Hector and Andromache
Atreus father of Agamemnon and Menelaus
Clytemnestra sister of Helen; wife of Agamemnon; mother of Orestes and Electra
Delphi home to the temple of Apollo
deus/a ex machina 'god/goddess from the machine'
Didaskaliai performance records
eisodoi/parodoi side paths which served as entrances for the chorus and characters
episode any act of the play between the choral odes and after the prologue
epode a closing strophe/stanza with no corresponding antistrophe
exodos final part of the play following a choral ode
Hector son of Hecuba and Priam; husband of Andromache; father of Astyanax
Helen wife of Menelaus and Paris; Hermione's mother; sister of Clytemnestra
Helenus son of Hecuba and Priam; younger brother of Hector; future husband of Andromache
Hermione daughter of Helen and Menelaus; wife of Neoptolemus; future wife of Orestes
hypothesis preface
kommos lyric dialogue between the chorus and a key character
mēchanē 'flying machine'
Menelaus husband of Helen; father of Hermione; brother of Agamemnon; king of Sparta
Molossus son of Neoptolemus and Andromache, whose name is not mentioned in the play
Neoptolemus son of Achilles; husband of Hermione; father of Molossus; master of Andromache
Nereus Thetis' father
orchēstra circular dancing space of the chorus in a Greek theatre, in front of the stage-building
Orestes son of Clytemnestra and Agamemnon; a matricide, future husband of Hermione

parodos technical term for the ode the chorus sing as they enter; one of the two aisles on either side of the *orchēstra* running up to the stage-building

Paris son of Priam and Hecuba; husband of Helen; judge of the beauty contest between Aphrodite, Hera and Athena

Peleus son of Aeacus; husband of Thetis; father of Achilles; grandfather of Neoptolemus; king of Phthia

Phthia kingdom of Peleus

Pharsalus city in Phthia where Peleus resides

prologue first portion of the play before the entrance of the chorus

scholia annotations

Scyros Neoptolemus' birthplace

skēnē stage building at the back of the *orchēstra*, in *Andromache* it represents the palace of Neoptolemus

Sparta Menelaus' kingdom, Hermione's birthplace

stasimon antiphonal choral song after the entry song, during which the chorus also dance

stichomythia rapid exchange of single lines between two parties

strophe a stanza in a choral song, which has a metrically corresponding stanza called antistrophe

Thetis daughter of Nereus; wife of Peleus; mother of Achilles

Thetideion town in Phthia where Neoptolemus resides

Index